The Trademark Guide

The Trademark Guide

A Friendly Handbook
To Protecting and Profiting
From Trademarks

LEE WILSON

Second Edition

ALLWORTH PRESS
NEW YORK

Published by Allworth Press
An imprint of Allworth Communications
10 East 23rd Street, New York, NY 10010

Cover and interior design by Derek Bacchus
Typography by Integra Software Services

ISBN: 1-58115-390-2

LIBRARY OF CONGRESS CATALOGING-IN-PUBLICATION DATA
Wilson, Lee, 1951-
  The trademark guide: a friendly handbook to protecting and profiting from trademarks/ Lee Wilson.-- 2nd ed.
    p. cm.
Includes index
1.   Trademarks--Law and Legislation--United States--Popular works. I. Title.
2.
  KF3180.Z9W55 2004
  346.7304'88--dc22   2004018489

Printed in Canada

DEDICATION

This book is dedicated
to my old friend and
business partner Bill King,
my favorite serial capitalist,
whose accomplishments in the
business world are proof that good
ideas and hard work are rewarded
in a free enterprise society.

Contents

Appendixes

Introduction

As more and more of the wealth of our country becomes embodied in intellectual property, it becomes increasingly important for businesspeople to grasp the basics of intellectual property law. Almost everyone has a hard time remembering the difference between the three major sorts of intellectual property: trademarks, copyrights, and patents. Trademarks are the subject of this book. Before you can completely understand trademarks, however, you need a passing knowledge of copyrights and patents. After we briefly distinguish trademarks from copyrights and patents, we'll consider trademarks in detail.

Although all three protect products of the human imagination, trademarks, copyrights, and patents are distinct but complementary types of intellectual property. Each is governed by a different federal law. The copyright and patent statutes both originate in Article I, Section 8, Clause 8 of the Constitution, which empowers Congress "to Promote the Progress of Science and useful Arts, by securing, for limited Times to Authors and Inventors, the exclusive Right to their respective Writings and Discoveries." Our federal trademark statute originates in the "commerce clause" of the Constitution, which gives Congress the power to regulate interstate commerce. Only our federal government regulates copyrights; copyright registrations are granted by the Copyright Office, which is a department of the Library of Congress. Similarly, only the federal government can grant a patent. However, although the federal government grants trademark registrations, so do all fifty states. And for complicated reasons, the U.S. Patent Office and the U.S. Trademark Office are two halves of the same division of the Department of Commerce, called the United States Patent and Trademark Office.

Confused? It gets easier. In fact, the best way to understand copyrights, patents, and trademarks is to consider them together, in relation to each other.

Copyrights

A copyright is a set of rights that the copyright statute gives to the creators of artistic, literary, musical, dramatic, and audiovisual works. Only the person who created the copyrighted work is legally permitted to reproduce, perform, or display it, distribute copies of it, or create variations of it; any unauthorized exercise of any of these rights is called "copyright infringement" and is actionable in federal court.

Since January 1, 1978, in the United States, a copyright is created whenever a creator "fixes" in tangible form a work for which copyright protection is available. Under most circumstances, a copyright will endure until seventy years after the death of the creator of the copyrighted work; after copyright protection expires, a work is said to have fallen into the "public domain" and anyone is free to use it. Registration of a copyright enhances the rights that a copyright owner gains automatically by the act of creation, but is not necessary for copyright protection. The chief limitation on the rights of copyright owners is that copyright protects only particular expressions of ideas rather than the ideas themselves. This means that several people can create copyrightable works based on the same idea; in fact, there is no infringement no matter how similar one work is to another unless one creator copied another's work.

(For more information about copyrights, see my book *The Copyright Guide*, published by Allworth Press.)

Patents

The word "patent" is used ordinarily to designate the rights granted by the federal government to the originator of a physical invention or industrial or technical process (a "utility patent") or an ornamental design for an "article of manufacture" (a "design patent"). A patent holder earns the exclusive right to make, use, and sell the invention, process, or design for which the patent was granted. Utility patents last seventeen years; design patents last fourteen years. Any unauthorized manufacture, use, or sale of the patented invention, process, or design within this country during the term of the patent is infringement.

(For more information about patents, see *The Patent Guide* by Carl Battle, also published by Allworth Press.)

Trademarks

Trademarks are words or designs that identify products or services to consumers. Unlike copyrights, in which their creators have protectable rights from the inception of the copyrighted work, rights in a trademark accrue only by use of the trademark in commerce and then belong to the company that applies the mark to its products rather than to the person who comes up with the name or designs the logo that becomes the trademark. Roughly speaking, a company gains rights in a trademark in proportion to the geographic scope and duration of its use of the mark; ordinarily, the company that uses a mark first gains rights in that mark superior to any other company that later uses it for the same product or services. Unauthorized use of a trademark is trademark infringement.

Trademark infringement is a commercial sin. It is one of the more common forms of a large and not-very-well-defined area of the law called "unfair competition." Basically, the law of unfair competition has, over the years and in numerous cases, labeled certain efforts at commercial competition "unfair"—even fraudulent—because they are too aggressive or less than honest. Unfair competition is, generally speaking, competition by dirty tricks, although several forms of unfair competition can result from otherwise innocent blunders. By declaring certain actions "unfair" in commerce, the courts seek to promote both free competition *and* fair competition. Among the types of trademark-related commercial conduct that have been held to constitute unfair competition are:

- Trademark infringement
- Trademark dilution
- Use of confusingly similar business names
- Use of confusingly similar literary titles

x

- The unauthorized use of a distinctive literary or performing style
- Copying a product's trade dress and configuration
- Infringement of the right of publicity

Not every action that has been or could be labeled unfair competition is codified, that is, enumerated and written down, in a statute. Judges may add to the list of unfair business tactics as new situations are presented that seem to them to entail overreaching by a marketer.

As is the case with copyrights, registration enhances rights in trademarks but does not create them. It is generally easy to register a mark within a state, but federal trademark registration, which confers much greater benefits, is more difficult to obtain. Trademark rights last indefinitely; as long as a mark is used in commerce, its owners have protectable rights in it.

A trademark represents the commercial reputation of a product or service as embodied in, usually, a word or design. Trademark law prohibits certain trade practices that are considered unfair, such as the imitation of another's trademark in order to profit from consumers' mistaken belief that the imitation trademark and the product it names are the real thing; this is trademark infringement. Trademark law also exists to protect consumers. It ensures, for instance, that when you buy a pair of running shoes marked with the NIKE® name, they are of the high quality you have come to expect in NIKE products because they are, indeed, manufactured by NIKE. (Lawyers use capital letters to indicate the precise verbal content of trademarks; we'll do the same with all trademarks and with all titles, slogans, and names used like trademarks.)

The two things anyone who markets a product needs to know about trademarks are how to choose them and how to use them.

Choosing a new product name is not a simple undertaking, or should not be. Certain kinds of names are not registrable as trademarks with the U.S. Patent and Trademark Office; the knowledgeable businessperson who christens a new product will take these restrictions into account, since federal registration is, or should be, the goal of every trademark owner. The other major consideration in choosing a trademark is picking one that no one else is using. This process is called "trademark clearance." You ignore it at your peril, since adopting and using someone's established trademark, even innocently, is trademark infringement, and trademark infringement can result in lawsuits that are expensive to settle and hopelessly expensive to defend.

In the United States, trademark ownership accrues by use of the trademark in commerce. Unless a trademark is used in the market-place, there is no trademark, because there is no commercial reputation that can be symbolized by the word or design. Roughly speaking, trademark owners earn the right to prevent others from using the same design or word to represent or name a product or service similar to theirs in direct proportion to the extent of their use of that name or design, geographically and otherwise.

The owner of the four MISS MIRIAM'S ladies' clothing stores in northeast Idaho can probably keep other retailers from calling new clothing stores of any kind by the MISS MIRIAM'S name or any name that is confusingly similar to MISS MIRIAM'S only within the same general area—that is, within the geographic area where the commercial reputation of the stores has spread.

The long-standing fame of BLOOMINGDALE'S®, however, allows the company to stop the use of that or any confusingly similar name for a department or specialty clothing store anywhere in the United States, even in areas geographically remote from the famous New York store. Although the BLOOMINGDALE'S stores are physically located in and around New York City (and more recently Beverly Hills and Miami), their reputation has spread across the United States and U.S. trademark law prohibits competitors anywhere in the country from competing with them unfairly by appropriating their famous name.

Once a trademark is "cleared for takeoff" and is in use, *how* the mark is used is very important. If a trademark is used as a noun rather than as an adjective ("WINKLES" rather than "WINKLES toy trucks"), it can lose its status as a trademark. That's what happened to "aspirin," "cellophane," and "escalator," all of which once named particular brands of the products for which they are now the generic names.

If the ® symbol is not used properly in conjunction with a federally registered trademark, the trademark owner's right to collect money damages in a lawsuit against a trademark infringer may be diminished.

In the abstract, these may seem like niggling considerations; in actuality, proper trademark usage can be crucial to the overall health of the company that owns the mark, since the company trademark may represent the most valuable asset of the company, its goodwill. The Xerox Company thinks so, at least. Otherwise it would not run thousands of dollars worth of ads every year pointing out that photo-copiers are not "xerox machines" and that its machines are "XEROX® brand photocopiers."

Xerox doesn't want to end up like the Otis Elevator Company, whose famous ESCALATOR ironically lost its uniqueness because of that very fame, thanks to the popularity and success of the moving stairways marketed under the ESCALATOR name. When the name ESCALATOR became a generic term applicable to all moving stair-ways, the ESCALATOR moving stairway was demoted to "escalator" and faded into the woodwork, so to speak, becoming so famous it became anonymous.

The chapters that follow contain the rest of the story. I hope I have told it well, because trademarks and the law and their interaction have consumed almost half my working life. Like many English majors, after graduation from college I looked for areas of commerce where my love of language could be useful. I tried most of the usual ones: I have been a newspaper reporter; I wrote and produced advertising for several years; and I supported myself—badly—during law school by working as a freelance writer. But I had missed one interesting area of the law that is especially suitable to anyone who cares about the effects of language (and symbols) on human behavior—trademark law. Then, during my second and third years of law school, I clerked for a crusty but kind intellectual-property lawyer named Edwin Luedeka, who one day pointedly told me "trademark law is a good field for a woman." And for English majors, I found.

Trademark law is more like linguistics than any other area of the law. Once you grasp the real nature of trademarks, the intricacies of trademark law seem logical. And the importance of trademarks is hard to overstate, because nearly every dollar spent in our capitalistic society is directed into one corporate pocket rather than another because of the reputation of the product or service purchased, which is represented by its trademark.

This book is designed to be a primer for anyone who creates or uses trademarks, which is just about everyone employed in any management position in American business, whether that business is a one-person, headquarters-at-home, cottage industry or a giant corporation that employs thousands of people. Since I have nibbled several of the edges of American business and have practiced trademark law for more than twenty years, I believe I am well suited to talk about the issues, concerns, and problems of both trademark owners and of those who encounter trademarks in their business life and must know how to choose, handle, and protect them.

My twenty-five-year tutor in matters of business, especially start-up businesses, is my friend and former business partner Bill King, to whom this book is dedicated. I am also indebted to another friend and lawyer, Larry Woods, for some of the ideas and insights in chapter 6; his years of experience helped me expand my own observations beyond the one-person-one-viewpoint barrier that faces anyone who writes on topics as broad as the legal profession.

xiv   I enjoy trademarks, although they sometimes make *my* head hurt. Trademarks are one variety of intangible creations of the human imagination that have a very tangible, dollars-and-cents effect on both our commercial and personal lives. I hope you find my fascination with trademarks informative and useful. If you live in America, chances are that you will play several innings in capitalism, a game even more characteristic of this country than either baseball or basketball. This book can help you avoid some of the pitfalls that can take out even talented players too early in the game.

Thanks, Mr. Luedeka.

Chapter 1
Understanding Trademarks

This is a short chapter because, beyond knowing what a trademark is (as you must already know if you live in the United States) and how trademark ownership arises (which is not a very long story) the main thing you need to know about trademarks is how not to infringe them. We'll get to that just as soon as you really do understand trademarks.

The Lanham Act, which is a federal statute governing unfair competition and trademarks, defines a trademark as "any word, name, symbol, or device or any combination thereof adopted and used by a manufacturer or merchant to identify his goods and distinguish them from those manufactured or sold by others." The statute defines a service mark as "a mark used in the sale or advertising of services to identify the services of one person and distinguish them from the services of others." A word or symbol qualifies as a trademark when it is both actually used in commerce to identify the goods or services of a manufacturer or merchant or provider of services and when it functions to identify and distinguish the goods or services from those of other manufacturers, merchants, or providers of services. More than one trademark may identify a product—think of the various logos and versions of the name used to market COCA-COLA® soft drinks.

In a free enterprise society, trademarks are everywhere. Trademarks are the guideposts of commerce; they embody the commercial reputations of products or services in the marketplace. Manufacturers use trademarks to communicate to consumers the origin of the products they market. Consumers use trademarks to help them find the particular products and services they want. Economists have declared that trademarks perform at least two market functions: 1) they encourage the production of quality products and 2) they make shopping easier by facilitating purchasing decisions. It seems clear that as long as you can't thump a television set like a watermelon to decide whether to buy it, but must rely instead on what you know about the television manufacturer, trademarks will remain an important part of life in America.

We all rely on trademarks every day. Almost everything you use, from the coffee you drink to the mattress you sleep on, was bought by brand name, which is another way of saying "trademark." Nobody shows up with a checkbook at the nearest auto dealer and asks, simply, to buy "a car"; you drive a Toyota or an Infiniti or a Volvo, and you bought your car by name because of the reputation, for economy or prestige or reliability, that attaches to that car by its name. We avoid products we dislike, by name, and we seek out the ones we want, by name. These names come to mean something to the consumer; when you ask for CHANEL NO. 5® cologne at the perfume counter of a department store, you won't be satisfied by WHITE SHOULDERS® or OBSESSION®, and when you ask for a DIET COKE® at a fast-food drive-in window, you don't want DIET PEPSI®.

In the United States, a trademark owner gains rights in a particular name or logo for a product or service by using the name or the logo in the marketplace. ("Logos," short for "logotypes," are simply design trademarks, as opposed to names, which are verbal trademarks.) Trademarks can also be combinations of names or words and designs or logos. Service marks are the variety of trademarks that name services. (For simplicity's sake, the general term "trademark" or simply "mark," will be used hereafter to refer to both the names or symbols for services and those for products.)

It is very important to understand that in this country trademark rights are gained by use of a mark, not by registration of it. State or federal registration of a trademark enhances the rights of the owner of the trademark and serves as notice to others of ownership of the mark, but a business that uses a trademark in the marketplace owns the right to use that mark *because* of that use—unless some other business has a better claim to it through longer and/or wider use—whether or not the mark is ever registered. Trademark ownership is also determined by *priority* of use: to own a trademark, you must do more than simply use it in the marketplace; you must also be the *first* to use the mark. In other words, a person or company acquires rights in a trademark roughly commensurate with the length of use, the geographic scope of use, and the variety of commercial uses it makes of the mark. So, for example, a large company that has long marketed a variety of products across the U.S. under its trademark has a much stronger claim to its mark and is much better able to halt anyone else's use of any similar mark for any similar products than does a recently established mom-and-pop company that sells its products only in the city where it is located.

Nor can registration perpetuate the existence of a moribund trademark. If a trademark owner ceases for too long to use a trademark in the marketplace, that owner can lose all ownership rights in the mark, regardless of whether the mark has been registered. Without *use* of a name to market a product or service, there *is* no trademark—the name has ceased to embody a current reputation for the product or service to which it was applied. Think of it this way: a person's reputation dies with him or her—that is, the reputation that remains after someone's death is only the memory of that person's actions in life. Because a person's activities cease at death, his or her reputation does not continue to accrue in the present. The same is true of trademarks, which are simply the reputations of products and services. If there is no use of a trademark in the channels of commerce, the reputation of the product or service formerly marketed under that trademark becomes defunct.

Anyone involved in the marketing process knows what enormous effort and expense go into developing and publicizing new products. Trademark law allows companies that spend time and money developing their market shares to reap the benefits of that effort. Trademark law lets you enjoy the benefits of your own commercial reputation and prohibits anyone else from taking a free ride on your commercial coattails. It also protects consumers by allowing them to spend their money on the products and services they have grown to trust. This is the heart of the concept of "branding" that has garnered so much ink in the U.S. business press in the past few years.

When marketers today speak of branding, they are talking about marketing efforts aimed at creating a relationship between their products and their customers. This relationship is a combination of old-fashioned brand loyalty combined with the newer concept of creating a mystique for the product. When such a relation can be established, it is a very powerful connection. During the early decades of the twentieth century, when American advertising was just beginning to assume the incredible power and ubiquity it has today, people bought products almost solely for their utility. That is, the ability of soap to clean and the durability of work clothes were of prime importance to the buyer of those products. Now, although the utility of many products is still important, the buying decision may be more influenced by the *feeling* the product gives the customer—whether that feeling is confidence that GERBER® baby food is safe and healthy or the self-assurance that an ARMANI® suit creates. The baby food is evaluated on a different basis than the suit—GERBER® baby food is recognized as healthy and nutritious for infants, but ARMANI® suits are valued as much for their cachet as their style and structure. Every brand that survives has its own personality, a halo of residual goodwill that attaches to it and surrounds any product it names. And in a world where almost all products are sold by brand—by trademark—and practically nothing is sold *without* a brand name, brands and the personalities they exemplify are the keys to the survival of a product in the marketplace.

Almost anything can be a trademark so long as it is used on a product or in advertising a service in such a manner as to indicate the origin of the product or service. In other words, trademarks answer two questions: *who made the product* and *who renders the service.* All the following can and do serve as trademarks because consumers have come to associate them with the products and services they are used to market:

- **Words**—ACE® bandages; PLEDGE® furniture polish; AERON® desk chairs; KODAK® film and cameras
- **Names**—WATERMAN® fountain pens; HARTMANN® luggage; DELL® computers; HEINZ® sauces; TOM'S OF MAINE® for personal care products; JIMMY DEAN® sausage

4

- **Designs**—the embroidered JORDACHE® jeans hip pocket design; the Coca-Cola "dynamic ribbon device"; the NIKE® "swoosh" design; the Ralston-Purina checkerboard design symbol
- **Slogans**—"WHEN IT RAINS, IT POURS®" (for Morton salt); "SOMETIMES YOU FEEL LIKE A NUT, SOMETIMES YOU DON'T®" (for Peter Paul Mounds/Almond Joy candy bars); and "TASTES SO GOOD CATS ASK FOR IT BY NAME®" (for Meow Mix cat food)
- **Drawings**—Prudential's Rock of Gibraltar logo for insurance; the GERBER® baby for baby foods and products
- **Likenesses of fictitious people or characters**—BETTY CROCKER® for cake mixes; RONALD MCDONALD® for hamburgers; the QUAKER OATS® Quaker man for oatmeal; the Energizer Bunny for ENERGIZER® batteries
- **Likenesses and/or names of living people**—Paul Newman's image used as a logo for NEWMAN'S OWN® salad dressing and spaghetti sauce; Wally Amos's likeness used on packaging for his FAMOUS AMOS® cookies
- **Likenesses and/or names of deceased people** — Colonel Harlan Sanders's image on KENTUCKY FRIED CHICKEN® containers; a depiction of the SMITH BROTHERS® on Smith Brothers Cough Drop packaging; L. L. BEAN® for clothing and sporting goods
- **Characters**—the main characters in the STAR WARS® movies are trademarks for a variety of goods; so are the characters from the PEANUTS® comic strip; RONALD MCDONALD® and his buddies for restaurant services; the PILLSBURY® Dough Boy for ready-to-bake food
- **Abbreviations and nicknames**—BUD® for BUDWEISER® beer; VW® for VOLKSWAGEN® automobiles; HOG® for large HARLEY-DAVIDSON® motorcycles
- **Initials**—IBM®; CBS®; A&W®
- **Radio and television station call letters and radio broadcast frequency designations**—WSM® radio; WTBS® television; WGBH® television; RADIO 1430

- **Telephone numbers**—DIAL-A-MATTRESS® for home mattress delivery; 800-SEND-FTD® for florists
- **Numbers**—A.1.® steak sauce; V8® vegetable juice; FORMULA 409® household cleaner
- **Music or songs**—the SESAME STREET® television show theme song; the MR. RODGERS® television show theme song; the NBC® chimes; the roar of the MGM® lion
- **Package designs**—the well-known CHANEL NO. 5® perfume bottle shape; the familiar shape of the classic bottle for COKE® soft drinks
- **Architectural features of businesses**—the MCDONALD'S® hamburger restaurants' golden arches; the characteristic HOWARD JOHNSON® hotels' orange roofs; the design of WHITE CASTLE® hamburger restaurants
- **Characteristics of products**—Ivory Soap is "99 44/100 PERCENT PURE®"; Bon Ami cleanser "HASN'T SCRATCHED YET!®"; Morton Salt—"WHEN IT RAINS, IT POURS®"; the shape of LIFESAVERS® candies
- **Internet domain names**—AMAZON.COM® for online bookselling; REDENVELOPE.COM® for online sales of gifts; GODIVA.COM® for online sales of chocolate products

6

Is It a Trademark?

As you can see from the list of established trademarks above, almost anything can serve as a trademark. However, this does not mean that *every* element of a product or of the presentation of services can or does serve as a trademark. Marketers familiar with the variety of offbeat sorts of marks are often surprised to learn that some characteristic of their product that they consider to be unique is not considered by the Trademark Office to meet the minimum requirement for registration; that is, it does not serve as "an indicator of source" for the product. Serving as a source indicator is the most basic function of a trademark and unless a name or other sort of mark does serve as a source indicator, it's not a trademark, no matter how clever or attractive it is. Almost any product element can fail to serve as a trademark, depending on the way it is used in the marketing of the product, but there are three reasons that are commonly cited. They are:

1. **The mark is "merely decorative"**—This is an objection that commonly has to be overcome for design marks, especially those that are design elements of the product (think of the NIKE® "swoosh" device, the POLO® polo player design, the COCA-COLA® "dynamic ribbon device"). The application to register a design as a trademark may be rejected if the trademark examiner feels that a design is used more to decorate the product than to serve as an indicator of the product's origin. This is because the federal trademark statute denies registration to any "device . . . that does not primarily serve to distinguish and identify the goods." The "merely decorative" ground for rejection of a trademark registration application is often raised with applications to register clothing marks, especially those that are printed or embroidered directly onto the clothing, but it can also occur with other products.

    Obviously, there are many famous design marks that are both decorative *and* registered. Remember that the objection that a design does not serve as a trademark is that the design is *"merely decorative"*—so long as a design mark also serves to indicate the source of the product to which it is applied, it is a trademark, no matter how decorative it may be. Sometimes the question can be resolved by repositioning the mark on the product—moving the depiction of the sunflower for SUNFLOWER ladies' tops from the front of the T-shirt, where it is the predominant decorative element, to the label sewn inside the T-shirt and to the hangtag for the T-shirt. Or, such a design may appear both as a decorative element on the front of a shirt *and* on the label and hangtag. The Trademark Office just wants to make sure that consumers look for the sunflower design *as a trademark* in addition to whatever ornamental use is made of it on the clothing it helps to sell.

    And sometimes marks that were originally "merely decorative" come, over a period of time, to signify a source for the products to which they are applied because consumers get used to looking for them, even on the front of a shirt. Think of the various forms in

7

which the name "Tommy Hilfiger" appears, in whole or in part, on TOMMY HILFIGER® clothing. There is no question that these marks serve *as* marks; there is also no question that they are to some extent decorative. There are numerous examples of decorative marks that did not function as trademarks until they had acquired "secondary meaning," which means that a mark used to market a product or service has become famous enough to be associated with one particular marketer. All this is true of common geometric shapes and colors, too, which are subject to the same "merely decorative" objection as designs, at least until they become famous enough as signifying a particular product of a particular manufacturer to overcome this objection to registrability.

2. **The mark is "functional"**—This is similar to the "merely decorative" scenario. A mark is "functional" when it is part of what the product or service *does*, rather than being merely an indicator of the source of the product or service. A very good example of this is the characteristic roar of HARLEY-DAVIDSON® motorcycles, which is recognizable by motorcycle aficionados. The Harley-Davidson company applied in 1994 to register this sound as a trademark with the U.S. Trademark Office; its application said: "The mark consists of the exhaust sound of applicant's motorcycles, produced by V-twin, common crankpin motorcycle engines when the goods are in use." Harley-Davidson met with opposition from nine of its competitors who opposed registration on the ground that the sound mark was "functional" and therefore not eligible for registration. Honda said that any motor of the same sort would produce the sound that Harley-Davidson said was characteristic of its motorcycles and indicated their source. After some years of haggling over the issue, Harley-Davidson dropped its application to register its "roar."

One basis for this principle of trademark law is that the law recognizes that it cannot grant a monopoly, in the form of a trademark, to any truly functional feature of a product because doing so would deprive other marketers of the same sort of product from using that functional feature in their own products. In other words, if it is protectable by patent, it should be protected by a patent rather than a trademark; there is no "backdoor" protection for a functional element of a product through trademark law.

3. **The mark does not** *yet* **serve as a trademark**—This objection is perhaps only applicable to the names of certain sorts of series of products, such as series of books, movies, magazines, etc. The Trademark Office will deny registration of a series name if there is not yet a series. That is, if only one title of a planned series has been published, there is no series yet and there is no series trademark—yet. Before a name is applied to two or more of the series installments, it is viewed as merely a literary title rather than a trademark that indicates the source of the series. For example, the name of the extremely popular HARRY POTTER® series of books would not have qualified for trademark registration in the U.S. Trademark Office prior to the publication of the second book in the series. Trademark owners who want to protect the names of series of books, etc. can get around this restriction to some extent by filing what is called an "intent-to-use" federal trademark registration application just after the publication of the first book in the series. This sort of application gives the applicant three years to begin to actually use the mark in interstate commerce— enough time to publish the second series title and qualify for trademark registration.

For more, and more detailed, information about the inherent characteristics of trademarks and how they affect the registrability of trademarks, see chapter 4.

Naming the Baby

Businesspeople often encounter trademarks in what is perhaps the most critical period of their existence—their birth. When this happens, they are being asked to "incubate" brand-new trademarks. Designing a new corporate logo or design trademark is one of the most important business functions you will undertake. Naming a product well is nearly as challenging as naming a new baby. And it's also risky, perhaps more so than any other creative activity undertaken for a business purpose. That's because we are running out of trademarks. That is, we have more trademarks than ever before bombarding us, seeking to attract our attention in magazine and television and billboard ads. What we are running out of is material for new trademarks—the number of applications for new registrations that the U.S. Trademark Office receives annually has mushroomed in recent years. In 1983, only 51,000 new applications for trademark registration were filed; in 2000 this number had increased nearly 75 percent, to more than 375,000. Since 2000, applications to register new marks have leveled off somewhat—in 2003 just over 267,000 applications were filed—but the Trademark Office, despite its best efforts, is still overwhelmed. To some extent, so is the marketplace. Each annual crop of new marks adds to the nearly one million currently registered United States trademarks that already crowd the media. With such a deluge of new trademarks annually joining the existing vast reservoir of active marks, it is easy to see why it has become very difficult to avoid infringing an existing trademark when you design a new logo or name a new product. It can be done, however, and the next chapter will tell you how.

U.S. Trademark Office FAQs

What is a trademark?

A trademark includes any word, name, symbol, or device, or any combination, used, or intended to be used, in commerce to identify and distinguish the goods of one manufacturer or seller from goods manufactured or sold by others, and to indicate the source of the goods. In short, a trademark is a brand name.

What is a service mark?

A service mark is any word, name, symbol, device, or any combination, used, or intended to be used, in commerce, to identify and distinguish the services of one provider from services provided by others, and to indicate the source of the services.

What is a certification mark?

A certification mark is any word, name, symbol, device, or any combination, used, or intended to be used, in commerce with the owner's permission by someone other than its owner, to certify regional or other geographic origin, material, mode of manufacture, quality, accuracy, or other characteristics of someone's goods or services, or that the work or labor on the goods or services was performed by members of a union or other organization.

What is a collective mark?

A collective mark is a trademark or service mark used, or intended to be used, in commerce, by the members of a cooperative, an association, or other collective group or organization, including a mark that indicates membership in a union, an association, or other organization.

Where can I get basic trademark information?
The U.S. Patent and Trademark Office Web site at *www.uspto.gov/main/trademarks.htm* provides a wide variety of information about trademarks and offers electronic filing of trademark applications and other trademark documents. The Trademark Electronic Business Center contains all the information needed for the entire registration process. You can search the trademark database for conflicting marks using the Trademark Electronic Search System (TESS), at *http://tess2.uspto.gov/bin/gate.exe?f= login&p_lang=english&p_d=trmk*, file applications and other trademark documents online using the Trademark Electronic Application System (TEAS), at *www.uspto.gov/teas/index.html*, and check the status of applications and registrations through the Trademark Applications and Registrations Retrieval (TARR) database at *http://tarr.uspto.gov*.

For information about applying for a trademark, see the Trademark Office pamphlet, *Basic Facts about Trademarks*, [reprinted as appendix C]. If you need answers to specific trademark questions, contact the Trademark Assistance Center at 1–800–786–9199 or (703) 308–9000 if you live in Northern Virginia.

Where can I ask a question about trademarks?
If you need answers to specific trademark questions or want to know more about trademarks in general, please contact the Trademark Assistance Center at 1–800–786–9199 or (703) 308–9000 if you live in Northern Virginia.

What official publications and information are available concerning trademarks?
The following publications are available:
Basic Facts about Trademarks can be accessed and downloaded free of charge from *www.uspto.gov/web/offices/tac/doc/basic*
Trademark Manual of Examining Procedure (TMEP), (3rd ed. May 2003), can be accessed and downloaded free of charge from *www.uspto.gov/web/offices/tac/tmep*, and is also available on a subscription basis from: Superintendent of Documents,

U.S. Government Printing Office, Box 371954, Pittsburgh, PA, 15250–7954, (202) 512–2250 (*http://bookstore.gpo.gov*).

Trademark Trial and Appeal Board Manual of Procedure (TBMP) (2nd ed. June 11, 2003) can be accessed and downloaded free of charge from *www.uspto.gov/web/offices/dcom/ttab/tbmp*

Official Gazette of the U.S. Patent and Trademark Office, can be accessed and downloaded free of charge from *www.uspto.gov/web/trademarks/tmog*. It is also available on a subscription basis from Superintendent of Documents, U.S. Government Printing Office, Box 371954, Pittsburgh, PA, 15250–7954, (202) 512–2250 (*http://bookstore.gpo.gov*).

Trademark Acceptable Identification of Goods and Services Manual can be accessed and downloaded free of charge from *www.uspto.gov/web/offices/tac/doc/gsmanual*.

Design Search Code Manual can be accessed and downloaded free of charge from *www.uspto.gov/tmdb/dscm/index.html*.

What is a PTDL (Patent and Trademark Depository Library)?
A Patent and Trademark Depository Library (PTDL) is a library designated by the U.S. Patent and Trademark Office (USPTO) to receive and house copies of U.S. patents and patent and trademark materials, to make them available to the public, and to disseminate both patent and trademark information. To be designated, a library must meet specific requirements and promise to fulfill certain obligations.

Patents and trademarks (word marks only) may be searched at the PTDL. Please note that the Patent and Trademark Depository Librarians cannot give any legal advice nor can they perform the searches for you. They will, however, provide you with the information you need to get started.

How do I register to practice before the Patent and Trademark Office?
It is not necessary to register to practice before the Patent and Trademark Office (PTO) in trademark matters. Any attorney admitted in a U.S. state or territory can practice before the trademark side of the PTO. Nonlawyers can practice only in the limited circumstances set forth in Rule 10.14 (b).

Is the name of a band a trademark?

It depends on how it is used. A band name may function as a service mark for entertainment services in the nature of performances by a musical group if it is used to identify and distinguish the service of providing live performances (see TMEP §1301.02 (b), or as a trademark for a series of musical recordings, see TMEP §1202.09 (a)).

Can a minor file a trademark application?

This depends upon state law. If the person can validly enter into binding legal obligations in the state, then that person may sign a trademark application. Otherwise, a parent or legal guardian must sign the application, clearly setting forth their status as a parent or legal guardian of the applicant.

Can the ownership of a trademark be assigned or transferred from one person to another?

Yes. A registered mark, or a mark for which an application to register has been filed is assignable. Written assignments may be recorded in the U.S. Patent and Trademark Office for a fee. Specific inquiries should be referred to the Assignment Division at (703) 308–9723.

My spouse owned a trademark registration and has since died. Do I own it now?

Perhaps. Because this depends on state law, the U.S. Patent and Trademark Office cannot provide a definite answer for all factual situations. You should consider contacting an attorney, preferably one specializing in trademark law. Local bar associations and the yellow pages usually have attorney listings broken down by specialties.

Chapter 2
Trademark Infringement

A trademark represents the commercial reputation of a product or service in the marketplace. Trademark owners often expend enormous amounts of money in establishing and promoting their trademarks. Once established, a trademark may be one of the most valuable assets owned by a company. (Think of the Coca-Cola Company; its various COCA-COLA® and COKE® trademarks are worth far more than the physical assets of the company.) Consequently, trademark owners act quickly against anyone who encroaches upon their trademarks. Adopting the wrong trademark can land you in a lawsuit for trademark infringement, even if you had no knowledge when you chose your trademark that it might infringe another trademark. This means that care in choosing a name for a new product or service is very important. Unfortunately, trademark selection in this country is, for the uninformed, a little like Russian roulette.

Imagine this scenario: After you've made three separate presentations and long after you've given up hope of landing the account, someone from the marketing department of the Omega Corporation calls to say that they have chosen your ad agency to handle all their U.S. advertising. Seems they were impressed with your proposals and have decided to give their business to an agency in your city, where they have their home office. They are happy with their decision. You are happy with their decision. You and your partners hire two more artists and a new copywriter and get to work on your first big Omega assignment, developing an ad campaign to break their new product, a universal television/VCR remote control that will work with all Omega Electronics products and with those of most other manufacturers as well.

But before you can advertise the new remote, you have to name it, so you and your three best creative people retire to your conference room late one afternoon to think of the perfect name. After several loud arguments, two six-packs, and more than three hours of intense brainstorming, you reach a consensus.

You and your staff like the name UNI-TROL. So do the Omega marketing people, when you present the name to them. They give you the go-ahead on the whole project and, simultaneously, a tight deadline. They want to have their product in the stores before the beginning of the new fall television season and they authorize you to do whatever is necessary to complete on time all the packaging and advertising materials they need. You roll up your shirtsleeves, work a lot of late nights, and meet their deadlines.

The new product is a hit. There is no other product like it that is as inexpensive or as simple to operate. Sales are through the roof. You start thinking of buying a new car. Then, out of the blue, you get an outraged call from the head of the Omega marketing department. He's just learned that the Omega Corporation has been sued in federal court for trademark infringement by a big New York law firm representing a German corporation that owns U.S. and Canadian trademark registrations it says are infringed by the name you created.

It seems that the German corporation, Unicorp, markets various sorts of electronic equipment around the world under various trademarks, all of which begin with UNI-. They are asking the court for an award of money damages and the profits from Omega's marketing of the UNI-TROL remote, plus an injunction that would force Omega to recall all its remotes previously distributed under the UNI-TROL name, to destroy all packaging and advertising materials that use or bear the offending name, and to cease using, immediately and forever, the trademark by which the public knows the new product, UNI-TROL. There is no joy in Mudville.

The only people who are not unhappy about the trademark infringement lawsuit are the lawyers hired by the Omega Corporation to defend it. They know that some of the money you thought Omega would spend with your agency is now going to be consumed by their legal fees.

The saddest news of all is hearing that Omega's lawyers have said that Omega's use of the UNI-TROL mark does infringe the Unicorp marks and that, under the circumstances, the best thing for Omega to do is to cut its losses and immediately pull all the UNI-TROL television and print ads and stop distributing the remotes completely until a new name and new packaging and promotional materials can be developed. Which, of course, means that what Omega's dealers will remember about Omega's innovative remote control product is that 1) somebody goofed in naming it and 2) that goof destroyed the momentum the product initially gained in the market, cutting their profits. And what Omega will remember, regrettably, is that you proposed the name that is causing all the trouble.

None of this had to happen. In almost every case, trademark infringement problems can be avoided by the proper attention at the right time to a few simple considerations.

Had you been better informed, you would have made some effort to check on the availability of the UNI-TROL mark when you proposed it to Omega, by recommending to Omega that it have a trademark search conducted or by commissioning one yourself, on behalf of Omega.

A "full" trademark search, that is, a search of United States federal and state registrations as well as of data regarding valid but unregistered marks, would have turned up the "family" of UNI- marks owned by Unicorp and registered in the United States for various electronic products. The lawyer interpreting the trademark search report would have picked up the phone and called you and recommended that you go back to the drawing board for the new Omega mark. The whole process would have taken no more than ten business days and cost under a thousand dollars, lawyer's fees included; an expedited search could have been performed, for an increased fee, in as little as twenty-four hours.

You could have chosen another good name for the remote. Omega could have liked it. The lawsuit might still be in the back pocket of the Unicorp lawyers. And all those carefully produced UNI-TROL ads and materials could be winning you awards instead of gathering dust in an Omega warehouse somewhere.

But perfect hindsight is poor consolation. What you really need is to know enough about trademark infringement to avoid it. Lots of trademark disputes arise because trademarks are chosen solely on the basis of artistic merit and the image they will create in the advertising media. Those are, of course, important considerations; coming up with a name that fits the new product and will attract consumers is a hard thing to do. However, the other hard part of naming a new product or service is finding a name that doesn't infringe an established mark. That part of the process can make you wish you'd gone to dental school.

Trademark infringement usually results because someone has chosen a name for a new product or service that is the same as or is very similar to a mark that has been used longer for the same or a similar or related product or service. In the United States, trademark ownership is created by use of a mark; generally speaking, the first company to begin using a mark owns it. Once a company has established ownership of a mark, anyone else who uses the mark for a similar product or service is said to be "infringing" the rights of the trademark owner. This means that any proposed trademark must be evaluated to determine whether it will infringe an established mark.

The test courts apply in determining infringing similarity between marks is "likelihood of confusion"; that is, are consumers likely to confuse the new name with the older, established trademark because of the similarity of the marks? The similarity between marks is gauged by what is called the "sight, sound, and meaning test." This means that you want to avoid choosing for a new mark any word and/or design that looks or sounds so much like and has a meaning so like an established trademark that represents a similar product that consumers will mistake the new mark for the established mark. The degree of resemblance between conflicting marks is analyzed by a comparison of the following characteristics of the marks:

1. The overall impressions created by the marks
2. The pronunciations of the marks
3. The translations of foreign words that are elements of the marks
4. The verbal translations of visual elements of the marks
5. The suggestions, connotations, or meanings of the marks

The new mark infringes the older mark if there are enough similarities between the marks that it is probable that the average buyer will 1) confuse the products or services the marks represent, or 2) believe that the new product or service is somehow related to the owner of the older mark. Confusing similarity does not exist when it is *merely possible* that consumers will confuse the similar marks, but rather, when such confusion is *probable.*

Generally, infringement occurs only when similar or identical marks name similar or related products or services. However, this is not always true in the case of "strong" trademarks. Strong marks, because they have achieved broad reputations, enjoy broad protection from upstart imitators who try to capitalize on their fame and distinctiveness by associating themselves with the famous marks. KODAK®, COCA-COLA®, and LEVI'S® are examples of strong verbal marks; the "woolmark" design logo of the International Wool Secretariat, the "Morton Salt girl" character trademark, and the Shell Oil Company logo are examples of strong trademarks that consist largely or only of design or visual elements. It is a very good idea to give famous trademarks a wide berth when naming any product or service, even if the new product or service is very different from those named by the famous marks, since most owners of widely advertised and well-known marks protect their trademarks vigorously.

All this sounds a lot harder than it usually is. Since "confusing similarity" is evaluated as if through the eyes and/or ears of an average consumer, you can function as your own first line of defense against choosing a trademark that infringes another trademark. In other words, if you think your new mark might infringe an older mark, you're probably right.

Keep in mind that it is not necessary that a new mark be identical to an established mark in order to infringe it. In fact, the degree of similarity necessary to constitute infringement varies depending on the similarity between the two products or services named by the marks. When the products or services are directly competitive, less similarity will constitute infringement; when they are not directly competitive and/or are sold in different channels of trade, more similarity is necessary to constitute infringement. A few examples will give you a feel for the degree of similarity between trademarks that constitutes "confusing similarity."

BEARCAT® for trucks will infringe BEARCAT® for boats or tires or travel trailers, but not for, say, bicycles or hunting boots or police scanner radios.

TWINKLE TOYS for a child's building block set will infringe the famous TINKER TOYS® trademark. Call your new block set TWIN-KLE BLOCKS, though, and you're probably safe.

ZESTA® for saltines does not infringe SHASTA® for soft drinks. Calling any food item the same name as any other food item, however, is asking for a lawsuit, no matter how different the two varieties of food. The reasoning behind this rule is that consumers can reasonably assume that a manufacturer of one food item has begun marketing another under the same trademark.

This sort of association confusion as to the origin of a product is a variety of trademark infringement. For example, the manufacturer of GOLD MEDAL® flour might not like having its commercial reputa- tion confused by being mistakenly believed to be the maker of GOLD MEDAL ice cream, even if the ice cream is very good ice cream.

Bear in mind that the categories of products or services named by the marks are very important in making any evaluation of possible infringement. A breakfast roll named BON JOUR probably won't infringe the mark of a department store named BON JOUR, because rolls are far removed from department store services, both in their consumers and in the channels of trade in which they are offered.

However, as we have seen, strong marks transcend the boundaries between categories of products and services. BON JOUR for a brand of breakfast rolls could infringe the trademark rights of the owners of a famous restaurant named BON JOUR, for a combination of the reasons just mentioned; that is, because consumers, familiar with the reputation of the famous restaurant, might believe that breakfast rolls were a new product of the restaurant.

Generally, infringement results when the inherent similarity between two marks is "multiplied" by the degree of similarity of the products or services the marks name and the fame of the established mark. At some point, these factors reach a critical mass and ignite into a trademark infringement lawsuit.

In the case of logos or design marks that have no verbal content, the standard for judging confusing similarity is the same as that used to evaluate the similarity between word trademarks, with the exception, of course, that a mark without any words has no "sound when spoken." With logos or design marks, you must carefully compare the appearance of the proposed logo or design mark with that of all other marks that designate similar products or services, including marks that are combinations of words and design elements. You must also consider the implications of the design elements of your proposed mark; that is, will your star logo infringe an existing mark for a similar product named STAR?

Judging similarity between logos or the design elements of marks is often more difficult than judging similarity between verbal marks because the similarity between visual elements may be much more subtle.

It is hard to talk about design trademarks in print, but a few examples of confusion between design trademarks are possible.

Any white-on-red or red-on-white curve at all similar to the famous COCA-COLA® double-curve design trademark used for any soft drink will infringe Coke's famous trademark. However, a similar curve in another color combination used for, say, a brand of farm equipment, might escape challenge.

Similarly, any design of any deer or deer-like animal used for insurance services or related services, such as financial services, would probably infringe the famous hundred-plus-year-old Hartford Insurance Company standing-stag design trademark. Use your deer for ice cream, however, and you are safe.

Any clown design or character used to advertise a fast-food restaurant, whether like McDonald's RONALD MCDONALD® trademark character or not, would probably be viewed by McDonald's as infringing upon its famous clown trademark. If your clown design or character was very different from our friend Ronald (perhaps a female clown named Pandora who wears a yellow wig and dresses all in pink), you could safely use her picture and an actress dressed like her to advertise and promote children's shoes.

Employ any depiction of a tipped cup perpetually losing the "last drop" of coffee and you will run afoul of Maxwell House. You may even get into trouble by using such a depiction in signage for a chain of coffee shops, since consumers could reasonably believe that the shops serve, or otherwise have some association, with

MAXWELL HOUSE® coffee. Set your coffee cup upright on its saucer, however, and it is probably safe to use for coffee shops.

The famous Columbia Broadcasting System "eye" symbol is as effective today as it was when first designed in 1958. That means that any abstract or realistic eye design used for any product or service that is even remotely connected with broadcasting or television or film production is going to be challenged by CBS®. You can use a dissimilar, realistic depiction of the human eye as the logo for franchise optometry shops, however, without looking over your shoulder to see if CBS is watching.

Ignore these analyses at your peril. Owners of established marks are quick to send cease and desist letters to marketers of new products who tread on their marks. An example of a cease and desist letter is reproduced in appendix A. Names have been faked to protect the guilty, but appendix A is essentially the text of an actual letter sent in circumstances very similar to those mentioned. And you can read an actual cease and desist letter, sent from a big Chicago law firm to a guy who doesn't seem to care that the owners of the GODZILLA mark are angry at him for using the mark "DAVEZILLA," at *www.davezilla.com/index.php?p= 1292.*

Too Close for Comfort

The following pairs of trademarks were held by courts to be confusingly similar when used in conjunction with identical or similar products.

AMERIBANC and BANK OF AMERICA
ARISE and AWAKE
ARM & HAMMER and ARM IN ARM
ARROW and AIR-O
AVEDA and AVITA
BEAUTY-REST and BEAUTY SLEEP
BECK'S BEER and EX BIER
BEEP and VEEP
BLOCKBUSTER VIDEO and VIDEO BUSTER
BLUE NUN and BLUE ANGEL
BLUE SHIELD and RED SHIELD
BLUE THUNDER and BLUE LIGHTNING
BREW MISER and COFFEE MISER
BUST RUST and RUST BUSTER

CAESAR'S PALACE and TRUMP'S PALACE
CAT TRAC and KATRACK
CENTURY 21 and CENTURY 31
CHAT NOIR and BLACK CAT (foreign language equivalent meanings can constitute infringing similarity)
CITIBANK and CITY BANK
CITY GIRL and CITY WOMAN
COCA-COLA and CLEO COLA
COMSAT and COMCET
CRISTÓBAL COLON and CHRISTOPHER COLUMBUS
CYCLONE and TORNADO
DAN RIVER, DAN MASTER, DAN TWILL, DAN TONE, DAN and DANFRA (a new mark that is even somewhat similar to an established family of marks can infringe those related marks by being mistakenly believed to be merely a new addition to the "family")
DATSUN and DOTSON
DELL and BELL
DERNIER TOUCHE and THE FINAL TOUCH
DOWNTOWNER and UPTOWNER
DRAMAMINE and BONAMINE
EL GALLO and THE ROOSTER
EST EST EST and IT IS IT IS IT IS
FACE TO FACE and CHEEK TO CHEEK
FIRM 'N GENTLE and NICE 'N GENTLE
GASTOWN and GAS CITY
GENTLE TOUCH and KIND TOUCH
GOOD MORNING and BUENOS DÍAS
HERITAGE and HERMITAGE
HINT O'HONEY and HIDDEN HONEY
JOUJOU and JOJO
KAHLÚA and CHULA
KEY and a picture trademark in the form of a representation of a key
KNORR and NOR-KING
LISTERINE and LISTOGEN
LONDON FOG and SMOG
LORRAINE and LA TOURAINE
MANPOWER and WOMENPOWER

MEDI-ALERT and MEDIC ALERT
MENNEN and MINON
MIRACLE WHIP and SALAD WHIP
MOUNTAIN KING and ALPINE KING
NIKON and IKON
OLD FORESTER and OLD FOSTER
ORKIN and ORKO
PHILADELPHIA and PENNSYLVANIA
PIZZERIA UNO and TACO UNO
PLAY-DOH and FUN DOUGH
PLEDGE and PROMISE
PORSCHE and PORSHA
RAIN BARREL and RAIN FRESH
ROCKLAND MORTGAGE CORP. and ROCKWELL NATIONAL
    MORTGAGE
SAVINGS SHOP and THE SAVINGS SPOT
SEIKO and SEYCOS
SILVER FLASH and SUPER FLASH
SMIRNOFF and SARNOFF
SNAPPY and SNIPPY
S.O. and ESSO
SPARKLETTS and SPRINKLETS
SQUIRT and QUIRST
STEINWAY and STEINWEG
TELECHRON and TELICON
TORO ROJO and RED BULL
TOYS "R" US and KIDS "r" US
TRAK and TRAQ
ULTRA BRITE and ULTRA-DENT
ULTRA VELVET and ULTRA SUEDE
WEED EATER and LEAF EATER
YAMAHA and MAKAHA

Close, but No Cigar

Think you've got the hang of it? Maybe not. The following pairs of trademarks were held by courts not to be confusingly similar when used in conjunction with identical or similar products.

ACCUTRON and UNITRON
AFTER TAN and APRÉS SUN
BANK IN A BILLFOLD and BANK IN A WALLET
BOSTON TEA PARTY and BOSTON SEA PARTY
CAR-X and EXXON
COCA-COLA and COCO LOCO
COCA-COLA and THE UNCOLA
CREAM OF WHEAT and CREAMY WHEAT
DAWN and DAYLIGHT
DUVET and DUET
FILM FUN and MOVIE HUMOR
FRUIT OF THE LOOM and FRUIT OF THE EARTH
GREEN LEAF and BLACK LEAF (when applied to plant sprays, the marks have opposite meanings)
HELICARB and HELI COIL
HOUR AFTER HOUR and SHOWER TO SHOWER
100 YEAR NITE-LITE and CENTURY NIGHT LIGHT
L'AIR DU TEMPS and L'AIR D'OR
LONG JOHN and FRIAR JOHN
MARSHALL FIELD'S and MRS. FIELDS
MATCH and MACHO
MOTHER BESSIE'S and MOTHER'S BEST
MR. CLEAN and MASTER KLEEN
PECAN SANDIES and PECAN SHORTEES
REJUVA-NAIL and REJUVIA
SATIN QUICK and SUDDENLY SATIN
SILKY TOUCH and TOUCH O'SILK
SUBARU and SUPRA
SURF and SURGE
TIC TAC TOE and TIC TAC
T.G.I. FRIDAY'S and E.L. SATURDAY'S
TACO TOWN and TACO TIME
THUNDERBOLT and THUNDERBIRD
TORNADO and TYPHOON
VANTAGE and ADVANCE
WHEATIES and OATIES
WINTERIZER and WINTERSTAT

Is It Infringement?

1. Q. You have been famous for years among your friends and relatives for your plum preserves and decide to market them. You tell the graphic designer you hire to create the label for your preserves that you really like the red-and-white "gingham" labels for the popular MABEL'S line of jellies and jams and you want to use something similar for your own labels. You love the label he designs; it is identical to the MABEL'S labels except that instead of "Mabel's," it says "Natalie's," and there is a little sketch of a basket of ripe plums where the MABEL'S labels use drawings of various fruits on the vine. You show your design to the lawyer who is helping you meet FDA labeling requirements for your preserves. He frowns when he sees it and tells you that you need to go back to the drawing board, since he believes the Mabel's Company will have grounds for suit if you use your label as it is. You don't see why he thinks there is a problem; NATALIE's certainly doesn't sound like MABEL'S, or look like it, or have the same meaning. And you are marketing plum preserves—the Mabel's Company markets strawberry, blackberry, peach, and grape jams and jellies, but no plum preserves, and it has never used a drawing of a basket of plums on its labels. The question is: *Is it infringement?*

   A. Sorry, but your lawyer is right. Insofar as it goes, your information as to what constitutes trademark infringement is correct, but, as the saying goes, a little knowledge is a dangerous thing. In isolation, NATALIE'S for preserves does not infringe MABEL'S for jams and jellies because it doesn't sound sufficiently like MABEL'S, or look enough like it, or have a similar enough meaning, to be likely to confuse consumers. However, you are overlooking an important factor in the analysis of possible infringement—"overall commercial impression." If you think about it, you'll have to admit that the overall commercial impression created by your label design would be extremely similar to that created by the MABEL'S labels. Consumers could easily confuse your product with MABEL'S products because the small differences in their labels

25

would not be apparent to a busy shopper who reaches for a familiar red-and-white "gingham" label, especially since your product and the MABEL'S products would be shelved in the same section of grocery stores and both use a woman's given name as a trademark.

If you proceed with your plan to use the red-and-white knockoff label, MABEL'S will sue you for trade dress infringement as well as for trademark infringement, as soon as it notices your products. Trade dress infringement is related to trademark infringement. It is the unauthorized adoption of another marketer's packaging design, colors, typeface, and even container shape. It is presumed to be an effort to pass off the copycat product as the more established product by the use of the established product's characteristic commercial "costume."

Your dilemma is not quite the situation that exists when the names of two vastly different kinds of food products are similar. There is a long-established rule that a name for any food product will infringe the same or a very similar name for any other food product. As we have seen, this is because the original user of the name could easily be presumed to have expanded its line to include the new food product named by the similar name. After all, no one would be surprised if General Mills added, say, frozen prepared cakes to its line of BETTY CROCKER® cake mixes. Here, you must take into consideration more than the name of your product, since consumers recognize products by more than just their names.

Ask your designer to create a label with a solid plum-colored background—no gingham checks—and your preserves will get you into stores and keep you out of court.

2. Q. You name your fledgling messenger service FLASH MESSENGER SERVICE and embroider a gold lightning bolt on the caps and shirts your messengers wear and paint it on the sides of your delivery vans. You are very happy with your creativity until you receive a call from the owner of another local messenger service, LIGHTNING MESSENGER SERVICE. It seems that for twenty years

LIGHTNING MESSENGER SERVICE has used a lightning bolt design as its logo. The owner of the Lightning Company is very unhappy that his only competitor in town has adopted what he thinks is his sole property in what he insinuates is a transparent effort to trade on Lightning's good reputation. You tell him you will get back to him and call your cousin Megan, who is a third-year law student. You ask Megan: *Is it infringement?*

A. If Megan was in class the day her intellectual-property law professor talked about trademark infringement, she will answer, immediately and unambiguously, "Yes." One of the factors considered in comparing two marks for the possibility of conflict is the meaning of visual elements of the marks. Here, your lightning bolt logo infringes the trademark rights of the owner of LIGHTNING MESSENGER SERVICE in two ways. First, your use of the same symbol for your logo as that long used by Lightning is likely to confuse consumers. Secondly, the reasonable verbal meaning of your logo is "lightning." This will certainly add to the likelihood that consumers will confuse the two messenger services. The best course for you may be to immediately retire your lightning bolt caps and shirts and repaint your vans to eliminate the infringing symbol that is on its way to getting you named as a defendant in a trademark infringement suit you are likely to lose. You'll at least save yourself the considerable costs of defending a suit that is a losing proposition. And maybe you can pay Megan for her help by shipping her a dozen or so slightly used lightning bolt shirts. She could probably use them; law students never get around to doing laundry.

3. Q. The day after you celebrate the first anniversary of your popular coffee shop, CAFÉ AU LAIT, you get a strange call from someone trying to make dinner reservations who seems to think that you serve Spanish food. Two days later, you get another such call. You decide that the moon must be full and think no more about the calls until you notice a new restaurant that has just opened near your favorite shopping center. The restaurant is called CAFÉ OLÉ and, upon

investigation, you discover that it serves Spanish food. You are worried. If people calling information for the CAFÉ OLÉ phone number are being given your number, what is happening to your calls—and customers? You call CAFÉ OLÉ and express your concerns to the manager. He dismisses your concerns and tells you that your coffee shop and his Spanish restaurant are not in competition for customers and that, even if the names of your respective establishments sound alike when spoken, they don't look alike in print and don't have similar meanings. You are unconvinced and remain worried. You hang up and call your lawyer. You want to ask: *Is it infringement?*

A. Your lawyer will confirm your suspicions that your predicament is a case of trademark infringement. Regardless of the difference between CAFÉ AU LAIT and CAFÉ OLÉ, the fact that their pronunciations are indistinguishable to the average ear is already resulting in what is called in trademark law "actual confusion"—in this case, the misdirection by telephone information operators of consumers who want CAFÉ OLÉ to your coffee shop and, possibly, vice versa. When proven in court, this is prima facie evidence of trademark infringement; in other words, proving that the likelihood of confusion between two marks is no longer merely a likelihood, but has become a continuing reality, is sufficient to convince any judge in a trademark infringement lawsuit that the plaintiff's rights are being infringed. Lucky for you that you applied for and were granted a federal registration for CAFÉ AU LAIT since federal registration is a prerequisite for bringing a trademark infringement lawsuit in federal court and can affect the damages the judge will award you and greatly diminish the costs you will incur to press your case.

4. Q. You and your cousin talk your dad and your uncle into investing in a bakery business you call English Teatime Cookies. You bake yummy cookies made according to your English grandmother's recipes. You start with her Butterscotch Wafers, her Raspberry Jam Tarts, and her Old-Fashioned Shortbread. All three are very popular. You decide to add her delicate little

lemon cookies, your personal favorite, which she always called Cheerios. The lemon cookies are as popular as the other cookies made from your grandmother's recipes. People start buying your cookies by the bag full and it's not long until your receipts exceed your expenses. You and your cousin consider leasing a bigger bakery.

Then you get a nasty letter from some lawyers for General Mills, the conglomerate that markets the whole-oat breakfast cereal CHEERIOS®. The letter says that because you are marketing lemon cookies called Cheerios, you are infringing the trademark rights of General Mills, the owners of the federally registered CHEERIOS trademark. You think the letter must be a joke—or a mistake. What do lemon cookies have to do with breakfast cereal? And you know for a fact that your grandmother has been baking her Cheerios— and calling them that—for nearly sixty years because she told you so. Further, in spite of your success, English Teatime Cookies is just a small operation—you only sell your cookies in your hometown and in Atlanta and Chattanooga, which are the nearest large cities.

You mention the letter in passing one day to your lawyer (who is your older brother) when you and he have a working lunch to discuss the lease for the new bakery. You think he'll get a giggle out of the ridiculous claims and demands of the General Mills lawyers, but he doesn't laugh. In fact, he insists that you call your cousin immediately and have him fax the letter to his office. Then he tells you that neither he nor you will be staying for dessert, that you both have an urgent phone call to make back at his office. You don't understand, but you do what he says. You wait until the waiter brings the check for lunch to ask him: *Is it infringement?*

A. Your brother won't answer any of your questions until he has read the faxed letter from the General Mills lawyers. Then he bends your ear for nearly fifteen minutes, while he waits for a return call from the lawyer who wrote the letter, which he tells you is something called a "cease and desist letter." He says that you have no choice but to do whatever you can to keep General Mills from suing you for infringement of its famous, federally registered CHEERIOS® trademark; that you'll be lucky if General Mills doesn't exact some payment from you to settle what would almost certainly be a winning suit; that the age of your grandmother's recipe has no bearing on whether you have stepped on General Mills' corporate toes and neither does the fact that she has been calling her cookies Cheerios. What *does* matter, he says, is that you have been calling the cookies CHEERIOS in interstate commerce. He ignores your argument that your selling cookies in Chattanooga that were baked twenty minutes across the state line in Georgia is only barely interstate commerce—apparently engaging in interstate commerce is like being pregnant: a little is enough.

30

Further, he tells you that if you have any hope of staying in business long enough to repay your (and his) father's and uncle's investment, you've got to start acting like a business person, which means that you need to have him clear any new trademark for use before you use it. You ask why, since there has been absolutely no trouble with the names of your other three cookies, which continue to sell like, well, hotcakes. He tells you that if you knew anything about trademark law you'd know that this is because the names of your other three cookies (Butterscotch Wafers, Raspberry Jam Tarts, and Old-Fashioned Shortbread Cookies) are all generic marks—that is, they simply describe what they name—and that there is much less likelihood that generic marks will infringe another, similar, generic mark because no such mark is granted very much protection by the courts. However, he adds, it is possible that they could infringe another, established mark that has achieved what he calls "secondary meaning" in spite of its genericness.

All this makes your head hurt, and you're afraid that he will shoot down your last, best argument, but you raise it anyway: "What do lemon cookies have to do with breakfast cereal?" He gives you a pitying look and tells you that it is an established principle of trademark law that the name of any food item will infringe a similar or identical established mark used for food, even if it names a dissimilar food item. This is, he says, because it is very common for food companies to branch out and begin offering new items under their popular trademarks. "Think of DANNON® yogurt and bottled water. Think of NEW-MAN'S OWN® spaghetti sauce and salad dressings," he says. "General Mills might want to market cookies named CHEE-RIOS. Or it might not. The important thing is that they don't want *you* to—and have people think that your lemon cookies are somehow related to their oat breakfast cereal."

You tell him you make great cookies and that anyone would be proud to be associated with them. He tells you that the quality of your cookies isn't the issue—the hard-won, longstanding commercial reputation of CHEERIOS is. Then he tells you to keep quiet while he talks to the General Mills lawyer. You hear him promise that you will pull all your existing Cheerios cookies from distribution, that you will destroy any and all packaging with the word "Cheerios" on it, and that you will never again use any name similar to Cheerios. Then, with a happy look on his face, he hangs up the phone. He tells you that you are one lucky entrepreneur, that the other lawyer is forwarding a written settlement agreement to him for your signature and that if you sign it and do what he promised you would do, you won't have to pay a penny in settlement. You aren't happy, but your older brother is usually right, and he *is* a lawyer, so you decide to do what he says. Then you tell him that for Christmas you are giving him a year's supply of lemon wafers; they'll have the name inked out on the packaging, but you know he'll love them.

5. Q. You and another freshly minted M.B.A. take the plunge and open your own computer components business. You choose as your logo a sphere divided into stripes in the colors of the visible spectrum (violet, blue, green, yellow, orange, and red), in order. The name of your products is SPECTRUM; that name and your striped-sphere logo appear on your stationery, on every one of your products, on all packaging materials,

and in your ads. You have just ordered the production of 10,000 of your popular trackballs to fill your biggest order yet when you get a cease and desist letter from lawyers for Macintosh, who are insistent that your logo infringes the famous Macintosh striped-apple-with-a-bite-out-of-it logo. You are indignant. You think that the Macintosh lawyers are just bullies who want to put a competitor out of business. You do not believe your logo infringes the Macintosh trademark; your logo is a sphere, not an apple, and your stripes are the colors of the spectrum, in order, while the Apple logo uses those colors in another combination (green, yellow, orange, red, violet, and blue). And you know that SPECTRUM doesn't look or sound anything like MACINTOSH® or APPLE®, nor does it have a meaning similar to either mark. You put in a call to the lawyer who handles your patent filings to find out if you can simply ditch the letter from Macintosh. What you want to ask him is: *Is it infringement?*

A. Unfortunately, your lawyer is going to tell you that you can't ignore Macintosh's letter because you are, indeed, treading on their trademark. Then he will tell you why. His explanation will sound something like this: the minor differences you can point to between your striped-sphere logo and Macintosh's striped-apple logos are immaterial. In a comparison of marks for infringement, the overall commercial impression created by the marks is determinative. In a proper analysis, the marks are not dissected and their minor dissimilarities tallied and totaled; rather, the total effect they have on consumers who encounter them in their "natural habitats," i.e., in the environments where they are sold, is judged. This impression is created in a matter of seconds in most settings where consumers encounter trademarks, and it is created primarily by the dominant elements of the trademarks. Any element of a trademark can be the dominant element because dominance can be produced by almost any characteristic of any element of a trademark: the uniqueness of the element, its size relative to other elements of the mark, its color, its visual appeal, its memorability, etc. Your striped-sphere and Macintosh's striped-apple logo are more dominant than the verbal marks used with them (SPECTRUM and MACINTOSH®, respectively) because they are more colorful and more visually appealing.

Consumers are not likely to pause in electronics stores to note that the colored stripes in your logo are the colors of the visible spectrum, in order, as opposed to the same colors in different order in the Macintosh logo, which is an apple, as opposed to your sphere. They may, however, decide that since your products bear what they may mistake for the Macintosh logo, the SPECTRUM name refers merely to a new line of Macintosh products. This is, of course, infringement.

Further, products like computer components are marketed worldwide. The visual elements of a trademark are even more important in international commerce since consumers who can't understand or remember an English verbal trademark will have no such difficulty with a memorable visual mark. It is even more likely that consumers outside the U.S. will confuse your logo with the Macintosh apple.

The last thing your lawyer says is that you could have avoided this problem—and the expense of discarding and redesigning everything that bears your old logo, including your stationery, your current ad campaign, and most of a small warehouse full of packaging materials, not to mention figuring out how to stick new logos over the infringing ones on the housings for several thousand computer components—by the simple expedient of a trademark-design search to clear your logo for use. Your protestations that you did clear SPECTRUM are of no avail. In reality, the name of your products, SPECTRUM, and your logo are two separate trademarks, usually used together, but distinct and equally capable of infringing another mark. Real life business teaches harder lessons than business school.

6. Q. You and your buddies have formed what you think is the next big rock band to emerge from an American garage. You know that trademarks are important in marketing bands,

so you put some time into coming up with a name. The name you choose, KINXS (pronounced "kinks"), suits everybody but your drummer, a second-year law student who thinks he knows everything. He likes the name but says that you will be hauled into federal court by the famous band INXS® (pronounced "in excess") for trademark infringement if you use it. You don't believe him because you don't think the names are similar enough to cause a problem and, anyway, despite your delusions of rock-and-roll grandeur, you know that your band is obscure and not likely to be famous enough for some time to attract the attention of the lawyers for any other act. Should you listen to your know-it-all drummer? Or, in other words: *Is it infringement?*

A. Sorry, Charlie. KINXS and INXS® are pronounced differently, at least by those familiar with rock bands, and have very different meanings, but their appearance in print, in ads, and on album covers is very similar. INXS is an unusual name and the band that owns it is famous; it is very dangerous to get too close to unusual trademarks that name famous products or services because the "name recognition" of such marks is so high that people are more likely to mistake similar marks for the famous ones.

Further, marks that are similar to famous marks are likely to run up against the proscriptions of the Trademark Dilution Act, which will only furnish the lawyers for INXS with further ammunition. (See chapter 5 for more detailed information about the Trademark Dilution Act.) And your complacent attitude that your band is too obscure ever to come to the attention of those lawyers is only justified to a point, because obscurity will work as a shield only so long. What usually happens with any trademark accused of infringing a more famous mark is that the upstart mark will come to the attention of the owners of the famous mark at about the time it is beginning to gain some fame. This is bad news for the owners of the new mark, because it means a lawsuit that could result in the necessity to abandon the new mark at just the point when it is becoming well known

enough to result in some money. It is always better to adopt a
new trademark that you can sink your hard work into without fear that you may be compelled to abandon it.

7. Q. You turn your collection of sports memorabilia into a pricey
little shop. It seems people are willing to pay much more than
you originally paid for autographed baseballs and the jerseys
of famous athletes. But jerseys that they buy from you for
hundreds of dollars are just too expensive to wear on
Saturday errands, so you have the bright idea to manufacture
a sports clothing line that only looks like the originals. You
order baseball caps and football jerseys in the colors of the
teams in your region. When they arrive, you take them to a
local screen printer to have the team names and logos embla-
zoned on them. To your amazement, the printer tells you he
is an honest guy and he doesn't want to go to jail. The next
screen printer you approach almost throws you out of his
office. You don't understand why they are so jumpy until you
see this story in the newspaper the following day.

35

South Carolina Man Pleads Guilty to Trafficking Clothing with Counterfeit Trademarks

Columbia, South Carolina—United States Attorney
J. Strom Thurmond, Jr., stated today that, William
Haskell Farmer, age 49, of Travelers Rest, South
Carolina, entered a conditional plea of guilty today in
federal court in Columbia, South Carolina, to traffick-
ing in clothing with counterfeit Nike and Tommy
Hilfiger trademarks and two counts of money
laundering conspiracy, violations of Title 18, United
States Code, Section 2320 and 1956(h). The plea came
on the fourth day of a jury trial, and after United
States District Judge Cameron M. Currie of Columbia
ruled that Farmer could not argue his defense to the
jury. Farmer will be sentenced after the U.S. Probation
Office prepares a presentence report.

Evidence presented during the trial established
that during 1997 and 1998, Farmer obtained blank

T-shirts from mills that manufactured shirts for Nike, and then paid to have the shirts either embroidered or screen-printed with a Nike trademark. Farmer then sold the shirts to Carolina Apparel Trading, an off-price clothing jobber in Hendersonville, North Carolina. Mark Lewis, the owner of Carolina Apparel Trading, has already been sentenced to five months in prison, to be followed by three years of supervised release and five months of home confinement. Roy Steve Sutton, who managed Heritage Embroidery of Camden, has pled guilty to trafficking in counterfeit clothing and is awaiting sentencing. Joe Bolin, who owned Dixie Screen Printing of Gaffney, pled guilty to a conspiracy charge but died before he was sentenced. Farmer's defense was that he did not violate federal trademark law because the shirt on which he placed the Nike trademark had been manufactured for Nike. Judge Currie ruled that it did not matter if the shirt was manufactured for Nike, as long as Nike did not authorize the placing of the mark on the goods, the mark was counterfeit, and thus the Government had established that Farmer violated the law.

Mr. Thurmond stated the maximum penalty Farmer can receive is a fine of $3 million and/or imprisonment for 30 years. In addition, Farmer agreed to forfeit over $500,000.00 in cash and cashiers checks seized by United States Customs Service during a search of Farmer's residence on July 16, 1998, and eight vehicles, including two Mercedes Benzs, two cargo trailers, and numerous pallets of clothing. Finally, all clothing bearing counterfeit trademarks will be destroyed, pursuant to Title 18, United States Code, Section 2320(b).

This case was investigated by the United States Customs Service, and Assistant United States Attorney Eric W. Ruschky of the Columbia office handled the case.

You are jumpy yourself when you finally figure out that you could be prosecuted by the federal government for criminal trademark infringement simply for "re-creating" sports clothing. You had no idea that what you wanted to do could be illegal. Just to be sure, however, you call your lawyer. You want to ask: *Is it infringement?*

A. Your lawyer calls you "rash" and "woefully uninformed," but you think he really wants to call you worse names, especially when he reminds you that he is a civil lawyer and knows nothing about criminal law. He tells you that what you planned to do is trademark counterfeiting and that it is a crime under more than one federal statute. He also tells you that it makes no difference that you didn't realize you would be breaking the law. Then he sends you home to do homework. He tells you to go to the U.S. Justice Department Web site to read a little more about criminal trademark infringement, the crime you had no idea existed. You do what he says. Then you donate the baseball caps and football jerseys to the homeless shelter in your city. And you never again are tempted to counterfeit *anything*, being very happy to sleep each night in your own nice, soft bed.

37

(If you want to read more actual U.S. Department of Justice press releases recounting incidences of criminal trademark infringement, go to *www.usdoj.gov/criminal/ cybercrime/ipcases.htm* and click on the cases in the chart that say "Trademark" under the Violation column. These accounts should convince you that it's an excellent idea to stay strictly out of the way of your local U.S. Attorney and that trademark piracy is *not* a viable business approach. Notice that in several cases, potential for harm to the public was created by the infringing use of the names of respected products on inferior and possibly dangerous fake products.)

Chapter 3
Trademark Clearance

The first step in avoiding infringing an established trademark is to consciously avoid choosing for your new product or service a name or design that is identical or closely similar to another trademark that is already in use for a similar or related product or service.

This seems too obvious to mention, but it needs to be said. More than a few trademark infringement lawsuits have been filed because someone mistakenly thought that because a name or design worked once it could work again. This means that in developing ideas for a new trademark, you should ask anybody who proposes one where the idea came from. Ignorance of trademark law will not save you from a trademark infringement lawsuit if you step on the toes of a trademark owner determined to protect its established mark. And it doesn't matter that you came up with the proposed new trademark without the knowledge of the established mark that it infringes; if it infringes the older mark, the source of your proposed mark is irrelevant. Nor will changing a few letters or design elements in an existing mark or spelling it differently or even combining it with other words or symbols save you from a charge of infringement, unless the changes you make are so significant that they eradicate the confusing similarity between the old and new marks.

If you make a wrong choice in choosing a new trademark, or fail to jump through all the hoops in the process of clearing a proposed mark for use, you will receive a cease and desist letter. This is a nasty document that demands, under threat of being sued, that you "cease" from doing something that is claimed to violate the rights of the person or company sending the letter and thereafter "desist" from ever doing it again. It is only the start of the troubles that can befall you. (A sample of a cease and desist letter is reproduced at the end of this book as appendix A.) The next step after a cease and desist letter is a lawsuit that requests that the court order your products pulled from distribution in order to avoid confusing consumers. ("Honey, what's the name of that cereal the kids liked so well? Was it SWEET CRUNCHIES or CRISP SWEETIES?") Such suits are often settled out of court, but a settlement would involve your abandonment of your new mark and, probably, the payment of a sizable amount in lieu of damages the court could award. Neither scenario is likely to make you (or your client) happy about having adopted a new mark. That's why it's important to do whatever you can to make sure that your new mark won't land you in a lawsuit. This means a thorough trademark search.

Searching a Mark

The most important step in developing a new trademark is a trademark search, which is a two-part process. You can perform the first part of the search, the "screening search," without a lawyer. The second and more important half of the search process is called a "full search" and is too complicated for anyone but an experienced lawyer to perform successfully. However, don't doubt the value of a careful screening search. Whether you are creating the new trademark for your own business or for a client business, it's likely that you will save yourself a lot of time by early elimination of any mark that will have to be abandoned. A screening search is also a very good way to reduce the expense of developing a new mark. By eliminating an unavailable name before making it the subject of a full search, you avoid the expense of a full search for that name.

The Screening Search

A screening search is an examination of readily available data on trademarks that are already in use, whether registered or unregistered. By searching for conflicting, existing trademarks when you have narrowed your choices for your new mark to three or four names, you can eliminate names that are already registered, are the subject of pending registration applications, or are in use but unregistered. This saves the expense of conducting a full trademark search for every proposed name and speeds up the selection process by halting your further consideration of unavailable names. You probably already have access to the equipment you need for a reasonably thorough screening search—a computer, Internet access, and some reference materials. And all the sources listed for use in a screening search are free, so you can preliminarily screen the names on your list yourself without incurring any expense for your company or your client. You can spend your money later, where it will do the most good, when you hire a trademark lawyer to conduct a full trademark search.

Step One: U.S. Government Trademark Records

40

The best source for information on established U.S. trademarks is the U.S. Patent and Trademark Office Trademark Electronic Search System (TESS). Go to the U.S. Patent and Trademark Office home page at *www.uspto.gov* and click on "search" under the Trademarks heading. This will take you to TESS, which is a searchable online database of more than three million pending, registered, and dead federal trademarks. (Even trademark registrations that have expired may alert you to marks that are still in use and, therefore, still protectable, even though their registrations have expired.) TESS is intended for use by the general public and is a very good place to *start* to clear a mark.

Since using TESS is free, the best way to figure out how to use it is to wander around through the various search options to educate yourself as to the capabilities of the TESS service. TESS does not contain information on marks that are in use but never registered or on foreign marks that are not registered in the United States. However, it can quickly eliminate as potential new trademarks any U.S. trademarks that are already owned by people sophisticated enough and careful enough to seek registration for them. Owners of registered marks are typically vigilant about challenging infringers, so finding a mark in the TESS database that is very similar or identical to your proposed mark and is used for an identical or closely similar product is a clear signal that you should abandon that mark and move on to the next on your list. (A search hint: the TESS system may be less congested after business hours.)

Let's say you started with a list of four potential names for a new product. Because you found during your TESS search that one of your proposed marks is identical to a mark that is already registered for a similar product and that another one of them is the subject of a pending registration (which means that it is already in use and, therefore, someone else has gained protectable rights in it by using it), you have two names left to consider.

So far, so good, but there are several more steps in the screening search process. You should now further examine the availability of your two remaining proposed marks by looking at every other source of information about similar or identical marks that you can find.

41

Step Two: State Government Records

Many marketers ignore state trademark registrations in evaluating proposed trademarks. It is true that state trademark registration is much less valuable than federal registration in terms of the protection it offers a mark. And registration (or use) of a mark only within a state does not confer widespread rights in the mark. However, from the viewpoint of the owner of a mark registered in a state, state trademark registration is very important because it alerts other marketers to the existence of the conflicting, registered trademark.

Even if an existing mark is used only within the boundaries of one or two states and is registered only there rather than in the U.S. Patent and Trademark Office, it can cause problems for a new, similar product marketed under the identical or a similar name. Procter and Gamble would abandon a proposed name for new bath soap if it discovered that a small company in California produced and marketed soap under the same name because, of course, Procter and Gamble would want to sell its product in California and would advertise through media that would be read or viewed in California.

And even if you operate your restaurant in only two locations in your state, if its name is too close to the name of a famous restaurant, even in a distant state, you could be liable for trademark infringement. Consumers who are familiar with the reputation of the famous nearly-one-hundred-year-old Bourbon Street restaurant Galatoire's would assume that your new restaurant of the same name, although operating in New Hampshire rather than New Orleans, was simply a new location of the famous New Orleans restaurant; that's trademark infringement.

While it's a good idea to take state trademark registrations into account when you are performing a scanning search to clear a trademark, records on such registrations may be hard to locate. Some states offer online databases of the trademarks registered in those states; in other states, you have to call the trademarks division of (usually) the office of the secretary of state to ask whether the mark you are considering has already been registered for a similar product or service. You can easily access the Web site for each state's secretary of state's office—without charge—by going to the site for the National Association of Secretaries of State; the Web page there that offers options for locating offices of the secretaries of state for all fifty states is *www.nass.org/sos/sos.html.* You can choose from "State Web Links (U.S. map)" or "State Web Links (with state flags)." There is also a directory with the names, addresses, and phone numbers of all fifty state trademark offices in appendix B of this book.

If a state does not offer a database that is searchable online, call the trademark office and ask how you can find out whether a particular mark has been registered in that state. Sometimes there is a provision for submitting questions online. In any event, complete information on state trademark registrations may be hard to find or hard to interpret. Further, remember that you would have to search the trademark registrations in *every* state to make sure that no existing trademark registered in one of those states would be infringed by a proposed mark—information from one or two or even three states is really not complete enough to clear a mark for any use that is, or could become, more widespread than strictly local. However detailed your search of state trademark records, make notes of the information you gather to give to the lawyer you will later hire to conduct a full search.

You are ready to proceed to the third stage of the screening search, in which you will examine trademark registrations outside the United States.

Step Three: Foreign Government Records
If you know or even suspect that the product that will be named by your new trademark will be marketed outside the United States, whether immediately or later on, you should consider that fact at this point in your screening search. You owe it to yourself or the client or company for whom you are developing the new mark to consider the possibility that your proposed marks will infringe marks that are already in use in the country or countries where the new product will be marketed. In deciding whether it is advisable to search foreign marks in your screening search, remember that although trademark laws in other countries vary from the U.S. trademark statute, the criteria for judging infringement elsewhere are basically the same as in the United States and that all it takes to halt plans for marketing a product in another country is an injunction from a court in that country based on a claim that a mark registered there has been infringed.

Even though you may not be able to get complete information about existing marks in other countries from your own screening search, do what you can and make a careful note of any information that you even suspect may present a conflict. What you are looking for throughout your screening search is red flags; information you uncover can be used by your lawyer (he or she is just over the horizon) to help you evaluate the advisability of adopting your proposed mark. Depending on the country or countries whose trademark registrations you examine, you may be able to perform this part of your screening search online. (In addition, it may be that any searching of foreign registration records that you cannot perform online is not worth the effort or the time it would take.)

The World Intellectual Property Organization (WIPO) has established an online portal to trademark databases in countries around the world as a way of preventing domain name disputes stemming from the similarity of domain names to established trademarks. You can search records in countries from Andorra to Uzbekistan, many online, by accessing the WIPO portal at *http://ecommerce.wipo.int/databases/trademark*. For products produced in the United States and marketed primarily on this continent, existing Canadian and Mexican marks probably present the biggest potential for conflict with proposed marks. Remember that the names of many U.S. products that are not physically marketed in other countries can creep across national boundaries by means of television and print advertising and the Internet. This probably will not be the case for a new doughnut shop that will operate only in your city, but it could well be a problem for a rock band or a toothpaste or kitchen utensils, any of which could reach across borders for sales, whether by means of physical presence or in ads or catalogs or through online sales.

44

Remember too that French is spoken in Canada and Spanish is spoken in Mexico. A U.S. mark in English could infringe a Canadian or Mexican mark named by a word with the same (or a similar) meaning or sound, even though the U.S. mark varies from the foreign mark when spoken. A Canadian trademark L'ETOILE would be infringed by an identical American product named STAR, as a Mexican trademark CIELO would be infringed by an identical American product named SKY. And don't forget the earlier CAFÉ AU LAIT/CAFÉ OLÉ example of conflicting marks that are pronounced the same way even though they are spelled differently and have different meanings. Some of the sites to which the WIPO portal can direct you are presented in the language of the pertinent country; some charge for access to their information (Mexico falls into both these categories). Don't worry if you can't read the language and don't fret if you don't want to pay the access fee—you will be hiring a complete search later and at this stage your own search is just a preliminary effort to eliminate marks that would be problematic if adopted.

You are ready for the fourth stage of the screening search.

Step Four: Nongovernmental Trademark Records

If even one of the proposed marks on your list has survived to this stage, you're lucky. As we have seen, we are running out of trademarks—so many products and services are being marketed so widely by all the very effective means of modern communication that it is becoming progressively difficult to find an effective new trademark that does not infringe any existing mark. In other words, almost any new trademark will be, potentially, seen and heard all over the global village. So if you haven't been sent back to the drawing board by discovering in your screening search that *all* your proposed marks are trademark infringement lawsuits waiting to happen, you should proceed to the fourth and last stage of the trademark search that you can conduct yourself.

The fourth stage of a screening search is a search of any non-governmental records, of any sort you can locate, for evidence of trademarks that, although unregistered, are in use and protectable. This can include names that most people don't think of as trademarks. Even if there is no federal or foreign registration for the famous Mark Hopkins Hotel in San Francisco, it has been building its reputation as a four-star hotel since it opened in 1926. Naming any business that offers hotel or hospitality services "The Mark Hopkins" would have the owners of the San Francisco hotel knocking on your door pretty quickly—or saying mean things about you in a trademark infringement complaint in federal court. That's why you must take into account what are called "common law" records—that is, nongovernmental records of every sort that mention the names of businesses and services and products that, because they already exist, represent valuable property rights that are protectable in court.

Look for names that would be infringed by your remaining proposed marks in every sort of database you can lay your hands on. You should start with any trade publications or directories of products and services specific to the industry in which your proposed marks would be marketed. This includes any sort of business directory that you or your client have or know about. For example, you can search the print or online version of the national Thomas Register (*www.thomasregister.com*) for names and products of U.S. manufacturers. And don't forget the library; the reference section of your local main library or a university library, especially a business-school library, may prove to be a treasure trove of information. Whether you visit one or several libraries, ask the reference librarians for help—they're an amazing resource—tell them why you are searching and what sort of product or service your proposed mark would name. Then let them suggest directories—print or otherwise—that may have information about the names of similar products or services. Some names of this sort of reference book are *Brands and Their Companies*; *Companies and Their Brands*; the *Encyclopedia of Consumer Brands*; *Logos of America's Largest Corporations*; *Thomas Register of American Manufacturers* (mentioned above); the *Trademark Design Register*; and the *Trademark Register of the United States*. Very few libraries will have all these directories; larger libraries may have several of them. Look at as many as you can locate.

Continue your screening search on the Internet. First look at nationwide telephone Yellow Pages–type directories like SuperPages.com (or, for Canadian businesses, CdnBusiness-Directory.com). And use several search engines to turn up uses of your proposed names, including Google and several other metasearch engines. Remember to search for dominant verbal elements in your mark—for instance, in screening the proposed mark ASTROWORLD, search for uses of ASTRO and WORLD as well as for ASTROWORLD. Remember that you are looking for closely similar names for closely similar products—RELIABLE for tires would not be infringed by RELIABLE for cough drops but would be infringed by RELIABLE for car batteries. And try to keep an eye out for marks that are spelled differently from your proposed mark but would be infringed by it—DUNKIN' DONUTS® would be infringed by DUNCAN DONUTS.

If you can't decide whether an existing mark would be infringed by your proposed mark, either because your proposed mark is not identical to the established mark or because your product and that named by the established mark are different, print out information on the product named by the established mark and save it to show to your trademark lawyer later before you undertake a full search for the proposed mark. You will know that your search through the search engines is nearing completion when the search results produced start turning up information that was produced by earlier searches. After you have searched for mentions of existing marks that your remaining proposed mark or marks would infringe, you still have one step left in your search of nongovernmental records: a search of domain names.

Your Internet search effort should examine domain names because even though domain names are not necessarily trademarks, they may be and may represent an ongoing business effort your proposed mark would conflict with. Search the records of InterNIC (an accredited domain-name registrar) for any domain name that matches your proposed mark by searching the various forms of domain names that could be formed from it. You can do this through a Whosis search on the InterNIC site (*www.internic. net*) for the domain-name forms of your mark that end with these suffixes: .aero, .arpa, .biz, .com, .coop, .edu, .info, .int, .museum, .net, and .org. Again, save information on any match for later evaluation by your lawyer. You can perform the same sort of search of domain names with any accredited domain name registrar. For a list of these, go to *www.icann.org/registrars/ accredited-list.html*. ICANN is the Internet Corporation for Assigned Names and Numbers; it is the organization that, among other functions, accredits domain name registrars.

The Full Search

It is very important to realize that although a screening search can be very useful, it can only short-circuit further pursuit of unavailable marks; it *cannot* finally clear a mark for use. For this, you must hire a "full" trademark search. A full trademark search will cover much the same ground as your scanning search, but a full search will be performed by highly trained people who maintain databases that are much more comprehensive than those available to the ordinary marketer. In addition, the results produced by the full search will be interpreted by a lawyer who knows just what weight to give each piece of information produced and what to do about any seeming or actual conflicting marks. At this point, your primary job is to make sure that you hire a qualified trademark lawyer who will select a reliable trademark search firm. Your lawyer will question you about your proposed mark (the one that survived the scanning search) and your plans for it.

Then she or he will instruct a reputable search service as to the direction and scope of the search when commissioning it, will evaluate the raw data in the search report, and will give a legal opinion assessing the degree of risk, if any, involved if your proposed mark is adopted.

Caveat Emptor

Don't just hire one of the many search services eager to sell you their services through Internet ads; it is very unlikely that you will be able to determine the proper extent for the search or that you'll be able to properly evaluate the information produced by it. Consider the following list of search options offered by a company that maintains searchable trademark records for the use of its subscribers:

> **Platinum Plus** – U.S. Federal, State, Common Law, ccTLDs
> (Domain Names from 233 countries), gTLDs (.aero, .biz, .com,
> .coop, .info, .museum, .name, .net, .org, and .pro) and
> International files (Canada, WIPO, EC, and UK)
> **Platinum** – U.S. Federal, State, Common Law, Domain Names
> (.com, .net, and .org) and International files (Canada, WIPO, EC,
> and UK)
> **Gold Plus** – U.S. Federal, State, Common Law, Canada, ccTLDs
> (Domain Names from 233 countries) and gTLDs (.aero, .biz,
> .com, .coop, .info, .museum, .name, .net, .org, and .pro)
> **Gold** – U.S. Federal, State, Common Law, Canada, and Domain
> Names (.com, .net, and .org)
> **Silver** – International files (Canada, WIPO, EC, and UK)
> **Bronze** – U.S. Federal Only

Notice that you now know how to access some of this information for free for your screening search. And don't feel bad if you can't figure out which of these databases need to be searched to clear your proposed mark. That's the point: nobody but a trademark lawyer can reliably make that decision. That's why you need advice from a lawyer who has significant trademark experience. See chapter 6 for tips on finding one.

Be prepared to find out that your favorite proposed mark is already being used by someone else; it happens every day to someone who spent weeks developing what she or he believed to be a unique new mark. The good news is that it is much easier and much less expensive to discard a proposed mark before any money is spent advertising it than to abandon a new trademark six months into your first big promotion of it.

Of course, if you own or work for an ad agency or graphic design studio and are given the task of creating a mark for a client, you can't compel your client to hire a trademark search. However, you can make sure that you formally recommend, in writing, that your client conduct a search to "clear" the mark you suggest. Your job is to help choose a mark that works for the new product or service and, above all, doesn't cause problems. At the very least, you want to avoid being blamed for any problems that may result from the new mark. If you routinely recommend trademark searches, you won't lose the confidence of your clients because of what they perceive to be your negligence. Although it is not your *legal* responsibility to determine that any mark you propose to a client will not infringe someone else's mark, a client who has been hit with a trademark infringement suit may fail to make that distinction. Clients will always be fickle, but trademark searches give them one less basis for deciding that you should be replaced.

All this is also true for in-house creative and marketing people, except that for them the stakes are higher. If you work for a company and are asked to name a new product or service, failing to recommend a trademark search could cost you your job. Unless you know that your company's legal department, if there is one, or an outside law firm is handling a search, recommend one at the very beginning of the trademark selection process. The least that will happen is that you will look like you are doing your job; the best result of your recommendation may be that you save your employer a great deal of money by averting an avoidable problem.

Most experienced marketing people view trademark searches as a necessary part of the process of launching new products or services. It's your obligation to point out the pitfalls inherent in ignoring the fact that adopting a trademark without investigating its availability can result in real trouble. Any professional learns that part of success in business is "encouraging" clients and employers, in a loud voice if necessary, to do what is best. This is your line: "Mr. Jones, I'm sure a man of your experience understands the necessity for a search to clear this proposed mark for use before you invest a zillion dollars in it.

When may I expect to see a copy of the search report?" Nobody is happy with anybody else after any business dispute, and trademark infringement lawsuits are likely to have everyone involved in the creation of the offending trademark pointing an accusing finger at everyone else. Luckily, you can help eliminate much of the risk in adopting a new trademark simply by remembering that the risk exists and advising your client or boss to take steps to avoid it.

Trademark Clearance Checklist

If you carefully follow each instruction listed below, your chances of adopting a trademark that leads to a dispute or lawsuit is very small. Think of the whole clearance process as insurance against trouble that no business needs.

50

1. **Find out where proposed marks come from.** Ask everyone on the task force you create to select a new trademark to propose one or more names for your new product or service. And ask them to briefly describe the sources of the names they propose. For example, for a fashion doll, "MIRANDA (after the heroine of Shakespeare's play *The Tempest*)," or for a stuffed toy dog, "PUPSY (my best friend's dog's name in 1965)." Reject any proposed name that derives from the name of *any* commercial product or service, previously or currently in use, or the name of any person alive during the last one hundred years.

   Further, because one of your primary goals in selecting a new trademark should be to select one that is capable of being protected and registered with the U.S. Patent and Trademark Office, eliminate any proposed name that transgresses one of the Ten Deadly Sins of Trademark Selection (statutory bars to federal trademark registration) discussed at some length in chapter 4.

2. **Narrow your list of proposed marks to five or fewer marks.** Pick your favorite marks for further consideration. You can do this by polling your creative team or asking the opinion of the management of the company whose product or service the new mark will name. This is also the time for focus groups or consumer surveys regarding your proposed marks. This step allows you to put your efforts into marks that are likely to succeed from a marketing

standpoint. However, don't undertake any test-marketing of the new product or service under any proposed name at this point, since such marketing on even a small scale may lead to liability for the infringement of an established mark.

3. **Conduct a screening search for each proposed mark.** A screening search (described earlier) is a stage of preliminary trademark searching during which you check your list of proposed marks against easily available data on existing marks and halt consideration of any mark that would likely infringe an established mark. Eliminate any proposed mark that is similar to 1) any mark registered in the same class as the one your new mark would be registered in, even if the established mark is used for goods or services that are dissimilar to yours, or 2) any mark used for goods and services that are related or similar to yours, even if the established mark is registered in a different class.

    Further, abandon any proposed mark that is at all similar to any famous mark, since it is possible that such a proposed mark could lead to liability under the Trademark Dilution Act, even if it is used for vastly dissimilar products or services than those named by the famous mark. At this stage of clearing a mark, "famous" can be described as any mark that is immediately recognized by 30 percent or more of your creative team. (See chapter 5 for a detailed discussion of the Trademark Dilution Act.)

4. **Find a trademark lawyer.** Unless an attorney in your company's legal department or your regular lawyer is well versed in trademark law, find a trademark lawyer. Trademark law is a narrow specialty and most lawyers who do not regularly practice trademark law find it confusing and even infuriating. Just by reading this book you will have learned more than many lawyers know about trademark law. You wouldn't ask an auto mechanic, however competent he is, to fix your stereo—so hire the right kind of lawyer to help clear your new mark. Consult chapter 6 for tips on finding a trademark lawyer. And if you don't have one at the start of the clearance process, move this step in the process to the top of the list and begin there.

5. **Commission a trademark search.** Have your lawyer hire a trade-mark search firm to conduct what is called a "full" trademark search for the most promising proposed mark on your short list. A full search is a search of the trademark records in the U.S. Patent and Trademark Office, all the state trademark offices, phone directories, trade directories, and other databases that offer information on unregistered but valid marks. If you are in a real hurry, commission searches for two or three of your proposed marks at the same time so as to get the news about the availability of these marks all at once rather than searching one mark and then searching another if the first proves to be unavailable. So that your lawyer may instruct the search firm correctly as to the scope of the search, make sure that you give him or her the following information:

   a. **A copy of the proposed mark, spelled as you intend to use it.** The actual verbal content of the proposed mark is very important. A word spelled one way may be available while the same word spelled in another way may not be.

   b. **An accurate and full description of each product or service that the proposed mark will name.** That is, if you intend to market action figures, comic books, a board game, and children's videos under the mark JUSTICE CRUSADERS, your memo to your lawyer on the subject would describe these products as "toy action figures, named collectively 'Justice Crusaders,' based on the characters of the 'Justice Crusaders' series of comic books, and a board game and video-tapes featuring these characters." Because a trademark naming these products would have to be searched in four classes to compare it to established trademarks for goods similar to the JUSTICE CRUSADERS products, the search will be much more extensive and complicated, and generally more expensive.

   c. **A list specifying the anticipated territories where the products to be named by the proposed mark would be marketed.** Most trademark searches are of U.S. records only. This is fine, as far as it goes. However, many marketers, especially those who market easily exportable services or goods, want, at least eventually, to expand their market to other countries. If you have any plans at all for such expansion, let your lawyer know, since clearing a mark for international use involves searches of records in the other countries where it will be used. Failure to clear a mark in another country where marketing is planned can result in a suit for trademark infringement in that country, which is as much of a problem, or more, as a U.S. suit.

6. **Follow your lawyer's advice.** Lawyers' fees buy not only legal services, but also the informed judgment that good lawyers develop over the years of their practice. Your lawyer's evaluation of the likelihood that your proposed mark will conflict with an established mark is the heart of the opinion letter that he or she will write after carefully reviewing your search report. In formulating this evaluation, your lawyer will weigh many factors, large and small, gleaned from the information in the search report. Your lawyer should try to accurately assess the chances of conflict, but most lawyers will be conservative in this assessment. If you feel that your lawyer is being overcautious in recommending that you abandon your plans to use a proposed mark, get another trademark lawyer to evaluate your search report that is, since you pay for it, yours.

53

Whatever you do, however, don't just ignore your lawyer's reservations and cautions about a mark. This is reportedly what the marketing department at Nike did when it named a new women's running shoe INCUBUS®. The Nike legal department had apparently advised the marketing department that the word "incubus" means, "an evil spirit believed to seize or harm sleeping persons" and had recommended that another mark be chosen. Marketing ignored the advice. After the INCUBUS shoe was introduced, somebody noticed that Nike had chosen a bad name for the shoe and stories started appearing in the press. The shoes were recalled at some expense. Nike was embarrassed. It's a safe bet that the folks in Nike's marketing department wish that they had not ignored the advice of the company's trademark lawyers.

7. **Register your proposed mark(s).** After you have cleared one or more of your proposed marks for use, file an intent-to-use application to register any mark that you think you may use. This serves several purposes:

   a. Filing an intent-to-use application, in effect, "reserves" any mark you file such an application for. As soon as you file, your application becomes a part of Trademark Office records and will begin to turn up in other people's trademark searches, resulting in their avoidance of your proposed mark.

   b. Filing an intent-to-use application extends your rights in your trademark. Once you have begun to use the proposed mark and your registration application is granted, the date of first use of the mark is presumed to be the date you filed the registration application, even if that is months or even years before you actually began to use the mark. And because you can postpone the deadline for filing proof of your actual use of the mark for up to thirty-six months after the filing date of your application, you can take your time developing the new product or service the mark will name, as well as the marketing campaign for it, secure in the knowledge that no one else can register your mark before you begin to use it. If you file to register more than one mark and end up using only one, you can simply abandon the applications to register those you do not intend to use. When you decide to abandon a mark that you have previously filed to register, you will have lost only your filing fee and the fee your lawyer charges to prepare the application.

   c. Filing an intent-to-use application negates the biggest unavoidable drawbacks of trademark searches. Because trademark searches report the status of the trademarks they include as of the date the search was conducted, they become outdated quickly. This cannot be helped. Like a weather report, a trademark search that is accurate today may be inaccurate tomorrow. However, if you file an intent-to-use registration application as soon as your trademark lawyer lets you know that a proposed mark appears to be available for use, you negate the danger that the report will soon be "stale." Filing to register your proposed mark gets your name in the hat as the owner of that mark ahead of anyone else who may decide to adopt it because, when your application is eventually granted, you will be able to use, as your date of first use of the mark, the date you filed the application to register it. Priority of use is usually determinative in questions of trademark ownership, so filing an intent-to-use application can effectively eliminate any competition for ownership of your mark.

Design Trademark Clearance

A trademark can be a symbol or a name or word. The best trademarks are visually memorable, even if they are primarily verbal. Think of the familiar, distinctive-typeface trademarks for COCA-COLA®, KLEENEX®, and L'EGGS®. As famous as these marks are, even more effective are the symbols that immediately communicate, without words, that the products to which they are applied originated with their manufacturers. A good example of this is Apple Computer's striped apple-with-a-bite-missing logotype. Computer consumers in any part of the world are likely to recognize the Apple logo and to know that it guarantees high-quality products. In an era when many marketers aspire to market their products internationally, symbol trademarks are more important than ever before. Unfortunately, the continuing proliferation of trademarks has made it difficult to create a trademark that is safe to use.

As we have seen, in order to avoid creating trademarks that infringe existing marks, you must know something about the standard used to judge trademark infringement. Trademark infringement is evaluated by applying the "sight, sound, and meaning test." That is, the proposed mark is compared to established marks for similarities of appearance, sound when spoken, and meaning. If there are enough similarities between the proposed mark and an established mark that consumers are likely to confuse the two marks if they are used for similar goods or services, the proposed mark is said to be "confusingly similar" to the established mark and cannot be used without the risk of a lawsuit for trademark infringement. While it is easier to compare verbal marks for confusing similarity, it is equally important that the evaluation of similarities be made for trademarks whose impact is

55

primarily visual. This group of marks includes marks that consist of a name or word that is rendered in a distinctive typeface and marks that include or consist of logotypes.

Available for Use

Obviously, when comparing design marks for similarities, the "sound when spoken" part of the three-part infringement test does not apply. However, the absence of this part of the infringement evaluation test makes the other two-thirds of the test proportionately more important. With design marks, whether you will face a federal lawsuit for trademark infringement after just spending most of your advertising budget for the year to introduce your new logo depends equally on what the logo looks like and what it "means."

The evaluation of a proposed logo starts with a consideration of the broadest possible group of established marks that are similarly configured. For instance, if Texaco were only now considering adopting its familiar five-pointed-star-in-a-circle logo, all established star and star-in-circle marks would be examined to determine if the "new" Texaco logo infringed any of them. All marks that included other prominent visual elements besides star designs could be eliminated from the universe of marks examined for confusing similarity because such additional elements would eliminate any real probability that consumers would confuse the Texaco mark with them.

Similarly, all star marks that consisted of realistic drawings of stars could be dropped from the ongoing comparison; all such logos would be dissimilar enough to the highly stylized Texaco star design to eliminate any real chance of consumer confusion. Any remaining star marks would be scrutinized carefully to judge whether the "proposed" Texaco logo would be likely to be confused with them. If such marks were used to market products or services that were remote from petroleum products or gas station services, any similarities that existed would be of less concern. However, if the products or services named by an established mark were to be close Texaco's, the established mark would be a more serious an impediment to the adoption of the Texaco mark. Even if the proposed Texaco mark were nearly identical to an established mark used to market sophisticated medical apparatus to hospitals and physicians, the hospital-equipment star trademark could be of very little concern to the petroleum company. This would depend largely on whether there was any overlap in the marketplace between the two marks; if not, they could coexist comfortably in American commerce without bumping into each other.

Image Plus Word

These same evaluations would be made in clearing for adoption and use a mark that consisted of a name or word rendered in a distinctive typeface. The difference, of course, is that there would be an additional important element in the search—the verbal content of the mark. The verbal content of a mark is usually considered to be its dominant element for purposes of comparing it to existing marks to determine confusing similarity. However, the visual impact of such a proposed mark is by no means immaterial, especially in a situation where the verbal content of the mark is not so different from that of other marks used for similar products.

57

For example, if a shoe manufacturer adopted the name SWEET FEET for its new line of ladies' shoes and printed the mark in a script typeface in navy blue ink on the insoles of its products, it might encounter some opposition, in the form of a cease and desist letter, from the marketer of the SUGAR FOOT line of women's footwear, especially if the SUGAR FOOT mark were applied to SUGAR FOOT products in the same location and with the same color ink in a similar typeface. The verbal elements of these two marks do not sound alike when spoken and do not have identical meanings. However, the products they name are identical. The choice of a script typeface for the new SWEET FEET mark is all that is necessary to push SWEET FEET into "confusing similarity" territory, where the SUGAR FOOT manufacturer will have no choice but to challenge it.

The good news for the SWEET FEET graphic designer is that, although the designer may not have been consulted about the name of the new shoe line, which, of course, contributed to the problem with the SUGAR FOOT people, the designer is not helpless when it comes to protecting the Sweet Shoes Company from a trademark infringement suit. The designer can insist on seeing the report for the trademark search that the Sweet Shoes marketing department had performed before it chose the name SWEET FEET. (And the SWEET

FEET designer wants the *report*, which consists of fifty to one hundred pages of data, including reproductions of design marks, produced by a trademark search firm on similar marks already in use, rather than the opinion letter, based on the search report, written by the trademark lawyer who interpreted the report data but only in terms of the verbal elements of established marks versus those of the proposed mark.) And the designer can, using what can be learned by looking at the existing, established design trademarks in that report, steer clear of any design for the SWEET FEET name that is at all similar to any established mark with any similar meaning.

SWEET FEET, rendered in a block, serif typeface with each letter in a different bright color, may be dissimilar enough to the SUGAR FOOT mark to avoid any potential problem with the SUGAR FOOT folks, who may ignore it and never even think of calling their lawyer. This depends in part on factors that no one connected with the new mark can really predict. One such factor is the plans its owners have for the SUGAR FOOT mark. (Do they plan to expand their use of it or is it an old mark for an unprofitable line of shoes that they intend to phase out?). Another is the vigilance of the SUGAR FOOT lawyers, who may be in the habit of suing any competitor who adopts any mark that is at all similar to the SUGAR FOOT mark or may, instead, take a more laissez-faire approach to the inevitable elbowing between competitors that occurs in a free market economy. The same clearance process is possible for design trademarks that include no verbal elements, but the evaluation of similarities is a little more difficult because confusing similarity may result from more subtle similarities between proposed marks and established marks.

Searching Design Marks

The time to perform a trademark search for a design-only mark is after the field of proposed designs has been narrowed to three or fewer logotypes. The U.S. Trademark Office now has an online design search database that you can search and has categorized registered design marks to help you search those that are similar to your proposed mark, but searching to clear a design trademark (including design marks that include or incorporate words) is complicated. Go to the Trademark Office's online Design Code Search Manual (*www.uspto.gov/tmdb/dscm*)

to start your search. The Trademark Office's database can be helpful in steering you away from existing marks and can help you avoid trite designs. But don't rely too much on what you can find out from the Trademark Office's design mark database. Even if you can figure out how to use the search system well enough to completely avoid stepping on any of the design marks it includes, remember that the database includes federally registered marks only. That means that while your newly created design mark may not infringe any federally registered design mark (this is good!), you still have the rest of the design marks in the world to worry about and you can't get information about the others out there without a full trademark search. So create your mark, check it out online, and, if it looks all right to you, call your trademark lawyer for a full search before your new design mark makes its first public appearance.

A full search for a design trademark may cost a little more than that for a word mark, but the extra expense is definitely worth it. If you don't hire the trademark lawyer yourself, ask whoever does to furnish you with a copy of the search report and the trademark opinion letter. Whether or not your proposed mark proves to be too close to an existing mark, you will gain valuable information about other existing marks already in use for similar goods or services by looking at the search report. You may be able to modify your proposed mark by changing typefaces, colors, or design elements enough to eliminate any chance of conflict. However, show the modified mark to your lawyer and if your lawyer deems the design you create unavailable for use, move on to the next proposed mark on the short list of those under consideration.

U.S. Trademark Office FAQs

How do I find out whether a mark is already registered?
You may conduct a search free of charge on the USPTO Web site using the Trademark Electronic Search System (TESS) at *http://tess2.uspto.gov/bin/gate.exe?f=login&p_lang=English&p_d=trmk*. If your mark includes a design element, you will have to search it by using a design code. To locate the proper design code(s), please consult the Design Search Code Manual [*accessible on the USPTO Web site*].

You may also conduct a trademark search by visiting the Trademark Public Search Library, between 8:00 A.M. and 5:00 P.M.

at 2900 Crystal Drive, 2nd Floor, Arlington, Virginia 22202. Use of the Public Search Library is free to the public. You can also conduct a search at a Patent and Trademark Depository Library near you. For locations, click PTDL [*on the USPTO Web site*].

Private trademark search firms will conduct searches for a fee. The USPTO cannot aid in the selection of a search firm. Search firms are often listed in the yellow page section of telephone directories under the heading "Trademark Search Services" or "Patent and Trademark Search Services."

Is it advisable to conduct a search of the Office records before filing an application?

Yes. You may conduct a search free of charge on the USPTO Web site using the Trademark Electronic Search System (TESS) at *http://tess2.uspto.gov/bin/gate.exe?f=login&p_lang=English&p_d=trmk*.

You may also conduct a trademark search by visiting the Trademark Public Search Library, between 8:00 A.M. and 5:00 P.M. at 2900 Crystal Drive, 2nd Floor, Arlington, Virginia 22202. Use of the Public Search Library is free to the public. You can also conduct a search at a Patent and Trademark Depository Library near you. For locations, click PTDL [*on the USPTO Web site*].

Can the Office conduct a search for an applicant?

No. After a trademark application is filed, the U.S. Patent and Trademark Office (USPTO) will conduct a search of the records as part of the official examination process. The official search is not done for the applicant but rather to determine whether the mark applied for can be registered.

Can trademarks be searched online?

Yes. We now offer online searching through the Trademark Electronic Search System (TESS) database, at *http://tess2.uspto.gov/bin/gate.exe?f=login&p_p_lang=English&p_d=trmk*.

Where can I conduct a trademark search?

You may conduct a search free of charge on the USPTO Web site using the Trademark Electronic Search System (TESS) at *http://tess2.uspto.gov/bin/gate.exe?f=login&p_p_lang=English&p_d=trmk*. If your mark includes a design element, you will have to search it by using a design code. To locate the proper design code(s), please consult the Design Search Code Manual [accessible on the USPTO Web site].

You may also conduct a trademark search by visiting the Trademark Public Search Library, between 8:00 A.M. and 5:00 P.M. at 2900 Crystal Drive, 2nd Floor, Arlington, Virginia 22202. Use of the Public Search Library is free to the public. You can also conduct a search at a Patent and Trademark Depository Library near you. For locations, click PTDL on the USPTO Web site.

What are common law rights?

Federal registration is not required to establish rights in a trademark. Common law rights arise from actual use of a mark. Generally, the first to either use a mark in commerce or file an intent to use application with the Patent and Trademark Office has the ultimate right to use and registration. However, there are many benefits of federal trademark registration. [For a list, see chapter 5 of this book.]

What is a common law search? How can I do one? Is doing a common law search necessary?

A common law search involves searching records other than the federal register and pending application records. It may involve checking phone directories, yellow pages, industrial directories, state trademark registers, among others, in an effort to determine if a particular mark is used by others when they have not filed for a federal trademark registration. A common law search is not necessary but some find it beneficial. Telephone numbers for search firms that perform these searches for a fee can be found in the yellow pages of local phone directories and through an Internet search.

In searching the trademark database on the Web there are records that appear to be a registrations but the registration numbers are shown as 0000000. Is this an error?

No, this is not an error. The registration number 0000000 is associated with USPTO records that have serial numbers that begin with "89-". The prefix "89-" is assigned to material that the PTO is obligated to protect either by law or treaty. However, since this material is not actually registered under the Trademark Act, it is not issued a registration number.

There are two types of material that are assigned "89-" serial numbers. One type is material that is used by U.S. federal agencies that should not be registered as trademarks unless the agencies themselves are filing the trademark applications. The second type is material we are obligated to protect under various international treaties. The entities holding this material may be international organizations or foreign governments. These filings are not assigned registration numbers because the "89-" materials are not "registered"; they are only deposited in the USPTO for reference and informational purposes. During the USPTO examination of pending applications, the "89-" material will be referenced as a bar to the registration of a mark undergoing examination if it is determined that the mark in the application creates a false association with entity holding the "89-" material [15 U.S.C. 1052(a)] or if the "89-" material is the official flag, coat of arms or other insignia of a country or other political entity [15 U.S.C. 1052(b)].

Chapter 4
Trademark Selection

In addition to coming up with a new trademark
that will grab the attention of consumers of your product and determining that it will not infringe an established trademark, it is important to consider whether the name or symbol you choose will be eligible for federal trademark registration.

There are two types of trademark registration: 1) state trademark registration, which is cheap and easy to obtain and confers some benefits, and 2) federal trademark registration, which is not easy to obtain, but which confers much greater benefits. Since most trademark owners want to be able to register their marks federally, that is, with the U.S. Patent and Trademark Office, we will discuss restrictions on federal trademark registration.

The federal trademark statute, which governs trademark registration, imposes certain restrictions on which marks can be granted federal registration. The inherent characteristics of the mark determine whether these restrictions will prevent the eventual registration of the trademark. The problem of these restrictions can be largely eliminated by careful avoidance of a few varieties of marks that can cause the Trademark Office to deny a registration application.

The Ten Deadly Sins of Trademark Selection

There are ten reasons the Trademark Office will deny federal registration to a trademark (other than defects in the form of the application or some other procedural problem). They are the following:

1. **The mark is confusingly similar to a trademark that is already federally registered.** The test the Trademark Office uses to determine whether your mark is "confusingly similar" to a registered mark is the same "sight, sound, and meaning" test used by judges in trademark infringement suits to decide whether the plaintiff does indeed have grounds to complain about the defendant's use of its name, but the only thing the Trademark Office will do to you if you adopt a name that's too close to a registered trademark is deny your application to register your name. Any liability that may be incurred by the infringing use of the previously registered mark is beyond the purview of the Trademark Office; it remains the job of the owner of the registered mark to sue you.

2. **The word or, more typically, the symbol for which registration is sought does not function as a trademark—that is, does not act in the marketplace to identify the source of the goods or services to which it is applied.** This basis for refusing federal registration is most often cited in applications for design marks that the Trademark Office believes are being used on goods merely for purposes of ornamentation rather than in any way that indicates the source of the products. In other words, the famous JORDACHE® jeans hip pocket embroidery designs may not have achieved federal trademark registration if they had not become "distinctive of the goods," that is, if they had not begun to function to indicate to consumers that the jeans that bore them were manufactured by Jordache.

3. **The mark is "immoral, deceptive, or scandalous."** To be rejected for registration on this ground, a name has to be blatant. Some marks that are slightly risqué make it to registration, but none that are really off-color or offensive will be granted registration. Usually mild double entendres, obscure sexual slang, and all but the most shockingly vicious phrases or symbols will pass muster

with the trademark examiner who reviews your registration application, even though it is the examiner's job to try diligently to figure out why it should not be granted. Before you cry "First Amendment" and "government censorship," bear in mind that the Trademark Office will not, no matter how much it hates your trademark, tell you not to use it; the government just draws the line at registering any immoral, deceptive, or scandalous name. In any case, you should avoid any really offensive name for your product or service because consumers may object to it and may have an aversion to requesting it from retailers. Moreover, some advertising media may refuse to air or publish ads that include the offending name.

The "deceptive" part of this restriction is usually not much of a problem unless your mark is going to get you in hot water anyway. For instance, if you get the bright idea to call your line of cubic zirconia jewelry BUDGET TIFFANY because you intend to copy the famous jewelry retailer's designs and to use the same famous robin's-egg-blue packaging, the Trademark Office will deny your application to register the name on the ground that, because you have no connection whatsoever with the famous jeweler, your name is deceptive. But by the time the Trademark Office's rejection of your application reaches you, your mark will already be in litigation initiated by the lawyers for Tiffany's, for the offenses of trademark infringement and trade dress infringement.

Ordinarily, trademark infringement is a civil offense, which means that infringers are sued in civil courts, not brought up on criminal charges by the district attorney. Infringers pay for their transgressions in dollars, not days in jail. Which is funny, if you think about it, because if someone breaks into your apartment and steals your stereo, he can be imprisoned, but if he infringes your hard-won trademark, which is like stealing your reputation, he won't go to jail, even though his infringement of your trademark may have cost you a lot more than your stereo was worth. However, remember that the wholesale counterfeiting of a product that bears a famous name or mark is potentially a criminal offense under both state and federal statutes. This can result in jail time and large fines, in addition to the destruction or impoundment of the counterfeited products. (See the end of chapter 2 for information on online Department of Justice reports of criminal trademark infringement prosecutions.)

4. **The mark disparages or falsely suggests a connection with persons, institutions, beliefs, or national symbols, or brings them into contempt or disrepute.** This restriction is similar to the "immoral, deceptive, or scandalous" restriction. For example, if you want to call your rock band TRICKY DICK in honor of the only U.S. president ever to resign from office, that's your business, but the Trademark Office may deny your application to register that name on the ground that it disparages Richard Nixon. It doesn't matter that TRICKY DICK is merely a nickname for Richard Nixon. It doesn't even matter that he is now deceased. And your arguments that Mr. Nixon's reputation would be hard to hurt aren't going to make the slightest difference to the Trademark Office.

Applications that imply nonexistent connections with particular well-known institutions will also be denied. For instance, the Trademark Office would not grant a registration to a home-security company called F.B.I. SECURITY; call your company LAW ENFORCEMENT ALARMS, though, and you may be able to register the name. Ditto for a restaurant named SEARS AND ROEBUCK, or HARVARD for scholastic aptitude tests.

And no matter how clever you think it is, the Trademark Office will refuse to register any name or logo that disparages any belief or national symbol.

If you're a group of Jewish cantors who sing traditional Jewish songs at wedding receptions, you may be able to call yourselves STARS OF DAVID and convince the Trademark Office to register the name, since your use of it would not be disparaging. However, you wouldn't be able to register that name for any rock band without running into some trouble from the Trademark Office, which could reasonably interpret your use of the name or symbol as disparaging.

The same goes for crucifixes. If you manufacture and sell white chocolate crucifixes under the name IMMACULATE

CONFECTIONS, don't expect the Trademark Office to allow you to register that mark. In fact, the same obstacle will be encountered by anyone who attempts to register any name or symbol dear to the adherents of any religion, including Eastern religions as well as more familiar Western belief systems.

All this is also true for "national symbols." If you apply to register as the trademark for a night club a logo depicting Uncle Sam wearing red lipstick and rouge, white theatrical makeup, and blue eyeshadow, the Trademark Office will turn you down, even if your only goal in depicting Uncle Sam in such a manner is to make him look like the female impersonators who appear at your club. Your manner of using the famous American symbol will be interpreted by the Trademark Office as bringing it into contempt or disrepute.

5. **The mark consists of, or simulates, the flag or coat of arms or other insignia of the United States or of a state or municipality or a foreign nation.** The American flag, for instance, belongs equally to every American citizen. Since trademark registration gives the registrant the exclusive right to use the registered mark, the trademark statute prohibits the registration of any mark that consists of the American flag. This doesn't mean you can't use the American flag as a part of your logo; you just can't register your flag logo as a trademark. (If your logo includes the American flag only as a small part of a larger design, you may be able to register the entire design by disclaiming any exclusive right in the flag portion of it.)

   The same holds true for other official symbols from just about everywhere. The manufacturer of a line of women's dresses named LA FRANCE cannot register the French flag as its trademark. Nor can a restaurant called THE LONE STAR CAFÉ register the state flag of Texas as its logo.

6. **The mark is the name, portrait, or signature of a particular living individual who has not given his or her consent for use of the mark; or is the name, signature, or portrait of a deceased president of the United States during the life of his or her surviving spouse, unless that spouse has given consent to use of the mark.** The Trademark Office cannot grant exclusive rights in the name or likeness of a living person without the consent of that person.

This is an easy restriction to understand. How would you feel if you woke up one morning and found that the Trademark Office had given somebody else the exclusive right to use your name for a product or service without your permission? You'd be upset, right? Well, everybody feels the same way, which is why you have to prove to the Trademark Office that any living person whose name you use as a trademark consents to that use before you can register the name.

However, you can call your outdoor-equipment shop DR. LIVINGSTONE, I PRESUME, after the famous Englishman who explored Africa, or name your line of women's cosmetics CLEOPATRA'S SECRET or bottled olive oil DA VINCI. David Livingstone, Cleopatra, and Leonardo Da Vinci were all real people, but "were" is the operative verb. They are no longer living and are, therefore, no longer in a position to object to your use, without permission, of their names or to profit themselves from such uses. (Consider, for example, SHAKESPEARE fishing rods; no one had to ask the famous bard for his permission to use his name as a trademark.)

A caveat, however: There is something called the "right of publicity" that famous people acquire with their fame, and sometimes it can be inherited by descendants. Basically, the right of publicity is a celebrity's right to be the only person who profits from the use of her or his famous name. This means that you should not only avoid choosing as a trademark the name of any living person but should also be very careful about adopting the name or even the nickname of any famous figure who died after, say, 1900.

Remember that this restriction applies even if you own the company that owns the trademark. Honest. Dolly Parton had to give her written consent before the trademark used to market the DOLLYWOOD® amusement park could be registered. Ditto for Oprah Winfrey and the popular OPRAH® television show.

So much for living people. The dead presidents restriction is sort of a leftover from when companies were likely to name their products after popular politicians in an effort to appeal to the people who made the politicians popular—you know, "TEDDY ROOSEVELT MOUSTACHE WAX." This restriction is of less concern to marketers than many of the others in the Trademark Office's long list of types of unregistrable marks, but it could play a role in your choice of a name for a new product. For example, during the lifetime of Jacqueline Kennedy Onassis you could not have registered the name JFK for rocking chairs similar to the one used by the late president without her permission. The trademark statute doesn't say what happens if the dead president is female—presumably, her widower would have to consent to any use of her name. Apparently the men (they were men) who wrote our trademark statute back in the forties thought that the possibility of a woman being elected president was so slender as to be nonexistent, so they specifically worded the statute in terms of deceased male presidents.

7. **The mark is "merely descriptive" of the goods or services it names.** Many marketing people hate this restriction and make rude noises when their lawyers remind them of it, since they believe that the more a new product name describes the product or service it names, the better a trademark it is. If you think about it, you will realize that this is not the case.

In actuality, the best trademarks are fanciful, that is, they don't mean anything much; they just capture the imagination and come to signify the particular product they name rather than being equally applicable to any product of the same kind, which is the case with marks that are descriptive. Think of KLEENEX® or EXXON® or WISK®; none of those marks mean anything as ordinary English words, but they each immediately bring to mind the specific products marketed under them.

Besides this important consideration, there is the fact that the Trademark Office almost always disallows an application to register a descriptive mark. It will not allow, by virtue of a federal trademark registration, one company to bar all others from using what are simply ordinary words to describe a product or service. If you ask yourself whether a proposed mark would tell consumers what a product or service is, or in the case of names for publications, by whom the publication is intended to be read, you can eliminate descriptive marks before they are adopted and later turned down for federal registration.

Now, it must be said that there are many trademarks that are very descriptive that are currently registered in the U.S. Patent and Trademark Office. These marks, for the most part, started out as unqualified for registration because of their descriptiveness but later, because of the fame they acquired as the names of well-known products or services, came to signify to consumers the products or services of their particular companies. In short, after a while the Trademark Office will reconsider allowing registration of descriptive marks that have achieved some fame. But at the trademark-selection stage in the history of a product, this exception to the descriptiveness restriction should not make any difference to anyone who wants to come up with a mark that won't have to work at becoming eligible for federal registration.

8. **The mark is "deceptively misdescriptive" of the goods or services it names.** This restriction on registration is akin to some of those mentioned above, designed to deter the adoption of misleading or distasteful trademarks. "Deceptively misdescriptive" means a mark that falsely suggests that a product or service has some characteristic that it does not indeed possess—in other words, the mark describes what it names, but falsely.

For example, LAPIS for a line of blue glass-bead jewelry would not be granted registration, since the Trademark Office would hold that the word "lapis," when used for blue jewelry not made of the semiprecious stone lapis lazuli, was a "deceptively misdescriptive" name that could mislead consumers. The same argument would apply to, say, TOP GRAIN for vinyl luggage, SILKSHIRT for women's polyester blouses, or PURE GOLD for jewelry that is merely gold-plated.

This restriction against registering deceptively misdescriptive marks is intended primarily to discourage actual attempts to mislead consumers, but it should not be disregarded if you consider choosing an ironic name. You may get the joke in your new mark, but the Trademark Office will not be persuaded to register it by the mere fact that the name is funny if it transgresses one of the trademark statute's restrictions on registrability. For example, DR. FEELGOOD'S HEALTH TONIC used for bottled beer may not be registrable, no matter how much you or consumers like the name for its wackiness.

9. **The mark is "primarily geographically descriptive or deceptively misdescriptive" of the goods or services it names.** When the name of a product or service includes a geographic term or place name, such as the name of a river or mountain, that either tells where the product or service comes from or suggests falsely that it comes from a place that it does not, that name will run afoul of this restriction when its owner seeks to register the mark federally. The general rule has long been that if the Trademark Office can find a geographic term in any atlas or gazetteer, registration will be denied to the mark that contains it.

The reasoning behind the first part of this restriction is that if a product comes from the geographic region named in the mark, registration for one mark that includes a geographic term that is equally applicable to all products of the same sort produced in that region would unfairly deny other manufacturers the right to use the term to describe their products. For example, CARRARA STONE for marble from Italy would be unregistrable because more than one company markets marble building materials quarried from the famous deposits at Carrara and the phrase "Carrara stone" applies equally to all such products.

The reason for the second part of the restriction—that registration will be denied to any mark that suggests a nonexistent geographic origin—is similar. If the marble were not quarried in Italy at Carrara, the name CARRARA STONE would be geographically deceptively misdescriptive because it would lead consumers to a false conclusion about the origins of the stone. This restriction has more application to manufacturers of cheese, wine, bottled water, and other products tied to certain regions than it does to the marketers of most other products, but it can have an unexpected effect on the uninitiated.

The restriction on registration of geographic marks also applies to graphic representations of a state or country. If your entire logo is the map of a state or some other recognizable representation of a piece of the world, the Trademark Office will deny it registration.

Now bear in mind that you can make up fictitious place names all day long and register them as trademarks; EMERALD CITY for mobile homes or BIG ROCK CANDY MOUNTAIN for sugar cubes would be registrable. And you can use actual place names in purely fanciful ways because no one will be likely to believe that they are used to indicate the origin of a product or service; KENYA for safari-style sport clothing would be registrable and BLUE DANUBE® has long been used for a china pattern.

And remember that, as is the case with some other restrictions on registration, famous marks enjoy different rules. (Consider the country music stars, the group ALABAMA®, for example.) When a geographically descriptive name that the Trademark Office considers unregistrable comes to signify only the product or service it names, it becomes registrable because, in effect, its fame enables it to escape the anonymity inherent in a geographic name and to function as a trademark. But trademark fame is not always easy to achieve and it is a much better idea, when adopting a new mark, to choose one that won't have to outshine competing marks before achieving registrability.

10. **The mark is primarily a surname.** Personal names have long been considered not to be inherently distinctive when used as trademarks, which is another way of saying that they are descriptive or generic and can't, in and of themselves, point to a particular source for a product.

Think of this example: there are four zillion people in the United States named Smith, so the source of SMITH'S SOCKS for children could be anyone in the country whose name is Smith. Moreover, until one SMITH'S SOCKS became well-known enough to transcend the anonymity of most surname marks, all the Smiths in the United States could market socks using their mutual surname without infringing each other's trademark rights. In other words, surname marks do not work as trademarks until they have achieved something called "secondary meaning," which is a term trademark lawyers use to mean "Everybody knows that trademark because it's so famous."

Now, obviously, there are many famous surname trademarks that have been granted federal trademark registration by the Trademark Office. That is because WATERMAN® for fountain pens, SMITH BROTHERS® for cough drops, CAMPBELL'S® for soups, LIPTON® for tea, WILSON® for sporting goods, HOOVER® for vacuum cleaners, and CRANE® for stationery are all trademarks that have risen above anonymity by virtue of having achieved strong reputations in the marketplace. Since a trademark represents the reputation of a product or service in the market, this is just a way of saying that over the years these surname marks have achieved trademark status sufficient to persuade the Trademark Office to allow their registration.

In addition to the potential for difficulty in registration, surname marks sometimes present an additional problem: Before naming a product for a real person, determine whether the founder of the company who wants his name on the product is a discreet and honorable person. All it takes is one brush with the law or the tabloids to diminish the credibility—and market share—of a surname mark. Think of Martha Stewart and what happened to the value of stock in Martha Stewart Living Omnimedia, Inc. when she ran afoul of the law.

Marks formed from first names are equally problematical. Whether any name mark succeeds is largely a matter of chance, even if the mark is the name of the CEO's child—SARA LEE® baked goods and WENDY'S® hamburgers immortalized those two little girls, but not even Ford likes to think about EDSEL® automobiles anymore.

Design Elements of Marks

It is important to remember that all the restrictions on registration listed above can also apply to design trademarks or trademarks that combine graphic elements and words. You may be able to get away with registering BON VIVANT for a "parfum" that is actually manufactured in New Jersey without running into the geographically misdescriptive restriction on registration, but use a map of France as the background for the words BON VIVANT on the perfume bottle labels and the Trademark Office will reject the application to register the mark.

Similarly, although ASTRONAUT for children's pajamas would, alone, be registrable, the use of sketches of Alan Shepard and Sally Ride in conjunction with the word ASTRONAUT, without their permission, would cause the registration application to be rejected. (In addition, this use would probably result in a suit for infringement of the astronauts' right of publicity.)

Another caveat—despite having a whole book of written-down rules to operate by, the Trademark Office, like God, often moves in mysterious ways. This means that all of the above statements about what are and are not registrable trademarks are subject to some Trademark Office exceptions, whims, and inconsistencies. However, it is important to choose a trademark that can be registered, because many unregistrable marks are also all but unprotectable. That is, if you adopt an unregistrable mark, it may be next to impossible to prevent someone else from using your mark, depending on the characteristics of the mark. Use the "Ten Deadly Sins of Trademark Selection" list as a guideline in selecting proposed marks and leave the final opinion as to the registrability of any proposed mark to someone who pays for malpractice insurance, your trademark lawyer. You don't have to function as a trademark lawyer in order to do your job, but you can forestall a great many problems if you know a little about what you are doing when you create a new trademark.

Naming Names

Because a trademark may be unregistrable on the basis of any of the ten registration restrictions, it may seem unreasonably difficult to find a trademark that will work. It is really easier than you think, especially if you keep in mind a few principles of trademark creation.

Trademarks that are coined out of thin air or consist of existing words used in uncharacteristic ways are referred to as "arbitrary" or "purely fanciful" marks. Arbitrary or fanciful marks are the most registrable and the most effective as trademarks. Marks that are what the Trademark Office calls "suggestive" are nearly as desirable. This is not the kind of "suggestive" you think; suggestive marks are marks that call to mind—or suggest—an association related to the product they name. They imply strength or softness or freshness or flavor, depending upon the product; they are subtle marks, created by marketers and ad people who are very skilled at making artful associations. Think of TORO® lawn mowers, DOWNY® fabric softener, IRISH SPRING® deodorant soap, and ZESTA® saltine crackers. None of these marks is obvious, but we perceive nonetheless the strength of TORO lawn mowers, the softness DOWNY fabric softener imparts to laundry, the fresh scent of IRISH SPRING soap, and the zesty taste of ZESTA saltines.

The least protectable and effective marks are "descriptive" marks—they merely describe what they name. For example, THE HOT DOG SHOPPE for a café that specializes in hot dogs will immediately let everyone who sees its marquee know what sort of dinner he or she can buy there, but it is hardly memorable or distinctive. HOT DOG HEAVEN would be somewhat less descriptive. THE DOG HOUSE would be better still. HOT DIGGITY DOG would be the most memorable and registrable of all. If you think up a proposed mark that is too descriptive to register, start substituting words for some of the elements of the descriptive mark. You may be able to move the mark from "descriptive" to, at least, "suggestive" by simply using one different word.

Twelve Steps to Creating a Winning Trademark

Now that you know what to avoid in creating a new trademark, you're ready to actually begin. Any method for coming up with new trademarks that works, works. However, the steps listed below are a good place to start in your quest to create a memorable and effective trademark:

1. **Assemble a creative team.** A study of four hundred U.S. companies by Rivkin and Associates, Inc., a New Jersey marketing and consulting firm, found that the most commonly used and most effective method for finding new trademarks is a task force assembled for the purpose. These committees usually consist of someone from the company's administration, someone from marketing, a PR person, someone from sales, maybe a trademark lawyer, etc. If no one proposes such a committee, be a hero and suggest that one be formed. Several heads are better than one, and people from different disciplines bring different talents to the task of choosing a new name.

2. **Think up a name that has never existed before.** Nobody had ever heard of EXCEDRIN® or CRAYOLA® until somebody named pain relief tablets and crayons those now-famous names. One way to create this sort of mark is to compose a long list of English-language syllables, each with a vowel and at least one consonant. Include some standard English prefixes and suffixes. Divide the list into three or four sections. Combine a syllable from the first section with any syllable from each of the other sections. Scramble the combinations you don't like, or flip them back to front. Replace syllables with others to make new combinations. Substitute a new vowel for one in a syllable that is not euphonious. Add syllables or whack them off. Be bold. It is a rule of physics that you will come up with approximately forty-seven bad combinations for every good one you stumble onto. Ignore the prevalence of bad combinations and look for the pearls. Your working list will look like this:

RE	GO	WAN	VA
SAR	SI	CO	LA
CO	WET	MA	EY
FA	SIR	RA	MAX
DEN	SO	VA	CAM
PRO	BEN	MO	EX
NO	TA	RON	TER
BE	TAR	NAM	MA
XE	WES	ER	DOM
YO	WA	TOM	WAN
SO	CA	RAK	AL
EM	VEN	PO	SON

Your list will look like so much nonsense, and so will most of the combinations of syllables you come up with. However, play with the combinations that best roll off your tongue until you create some promising ones, then post a list of two or three over your desk and look at them for a while. Remember, the combination CO-CA-CO-LA would seem strange to anyone who had never heard of COCA-COLA®.

You can buy software programs that can help you create potential new trademarks. To find available programs, search for "naming software" or "branding software" on the Web. No naming programs will tell you which of the many names they generate is the best—your own taste and marketing savvy will have to do this—but they can provide you with a multitude of possibilities. These programs are cheap enough that you may want to try two or three of them—spending even a hundred dollars or so to help you generate a list of potential new trademarks is much cheaper than hiring a consulting firm at $25,000 or more. (However, if you want to hire such a firm, go to *marketingadvertisingseek.com* and click on the "Branding" category to be taken to a list of nearly three hundred marketing and advertising consultants' Web sites.)

3. **Use a common word in an uncommon way.** "Apple" once meant only a kind of fruit. Now we know it also means a particular, famous brand of computer. The word "windows" has gone through a similar transformation; it now signifies a particular brand of computer software while retaining all its previous meanings. Be creative. Be silly. Mine your dictionary.

4. **Use an uncommon word in a new way.** "Oreo" is the Greek word for "hill." The original plan was to market mound-shaped cookies as OREO® cookies. The cookies were flattened in the process of development, but the name stuck—enough so that every kid in America, and most adults, ask for these particular cookies by name. There are other familiar uses of unfamiliar words: VOLVO® means "I roll" in Latin; REEBOK® was the name of a particular kind of fleet-footed African gazelle before it became a brand name for running shoes; and NIKE® was the name of the Greek goddess of victory long before it was the name of one of Reebok's competitors.

5. **Marry two or more words.** Some of the most famous marks in the world were formed by constructing a new word by combining others, usually descriptive terms, either as whole words or in a truncated form. NABISCO® was formed from "National Biscuit Company" in this manner. Other examples include CITIBANK® ("city" plus "bank"), SPAM® ("spiced ham"), and

NYQUIL® ("night" plus "tranquil"). One way to begin creating a mark of this sort is to list all the words you can think of that favorably describe the product you are naming. Then stick them together in combinations of two or three. Eliminate syllables here and there to create snappy combination words that are easy to say, spell, and hear.

6. **Look at the forms, shapes, and inhabitants of nature.** Inspiration for a new trademark or logo may be as close as the seashore, the woods, the skies, or your backyard. The Texaco star logo is one of the simplest commercial designs on the cultural landscape, but it has also outlasted a lot of fussier, more pretentious logos and has for a long time signified only that company and its products to most Americans. Consult field guides and nature encyclopedias. Look at books on symbols. Study reproductions of cave paintings and hieroglyphics. Look at maps of the constellations.

   Think, too, of the traditional meanings or mythological significances of certain natural objects and animals. Tradition has it that owls are wise, bulls are aggressive, lions are proud, bees are busy, turtles are slow, ants are industrious, dogs are faithful, cats are aloof, mice are quiet, and monkeys are playful. An owl logo could serve as the trademark for a textbook company. A bee logo would signify the busyness of the personnel of a housecleaning service. A monkey logo could signal visually to kids and their parents that there is fun to be had at an amusement park or a fast-food restaurant. Read Aesop's fables and the Uncle Remus tales. Peruse books of folk tales from other cultures.

7. **Study world cultures.** Study English heraldry or Scottish tartans or Celtic symbols. Get a book on origami or Japanese art or Chinese symbols. Read Shakespeare or Chaucer (that's where Toyota got CRESSIDA®) or Bullfinch's mythology. Ask your librarian for books on African art. Find out about the Olmecs, the Toltecs, the Aztecs, the Mayas, and the Incas. Study Inuit art. Read up on other native cultures of the Americas. More than one product has successfully borrowed the symbols or legends or literature from another culture or the past to create a memorable trademark. The famous automobile trademark

THUNDERBIRD® had its origins in the name Native Americans gave to the large woodpeckers they heard in the forests of precolonial America.

8. **Consider meanings, translations, and cross-cultural meanings.** Browse your biggest dictionary and check your thesaurus. Both may give you ideas for names. But make sure you know the meaning and all the connotations for any word you consider using as a trademark. Remember Nike's INCUBUS? Enough said. (However, INCUBUS did apparently work as the name of a rock band, which presumably didn't mind its connotations. Go figure.) The famous bad example of a mark that worked in English but failed spectacularly in another market is NOVA®. "Nova" means "a star that suddenly becomes very bright"—in English. This is certainly an acceptable association for an automobile, which is what the NOVA mark named when it was introduced some years ago. However, "no va" in Spanish, means, unfortunately, "no go," which is certainly a less-than-wonderful name for a car south of the border and in other countries where Spanish is spoken.

79

The moral to this little story is to have someone who knows languages translate your proposed mark before you start printing up your packaging materials. And don't assume that your proposed mark is safe to use because it won't be used outside the United States. More than one language is spoken here and this country shows every sign of becoming more multilingual in the future. You don't want to end up with a successful product named by a trademark that offends any segment of this society or subjects your company to ridicule. Call the languages department of the nearest large university and enlist the help of a couple of professors to check your proposed marks for hidden meanings. Better still, ask a native speaker of the language to review your mark for connotations that may not be apparent to even a scholar of that language. And if you are adopting a symbol from another culture or from history, check it out with historians of that culture and religion professors. After all, once upon a time even the swastika had no evil connotations.

9. **Choose a name that fits your commercial personality.** No hot new club is going to be called ETHEL'S NITE CLUB. Not anymore. An evaluation of the "personality" of a proposed mark should be made for any product or service name. If the product is fun and friendly, choose a fun and friendly name. But nobody wants a bank to be too funny or too friendly—reliability and convenience are the qualities that sell bank services. Figure out the commercial image your product or service must project and then make sure your new mark matches it. And make sure that the vibes your name conveys are distinct *enough*. There are lots of cowardly marks in the marketplace that are so worried about sticking out that they fade into the background. This is related to the "dilute verbal element" problem and presents the same sort of difficulty. You may remember a STARBUCKS® coffeehouse after hearing of it or seeing it only once, but is BREWS a coffeehouse or a microbrewery? Coffeehouses are hip, casual, fun, and friendly. Try JAVA or CUPPA JOE or BUZZ instead.

10. **Avoid "dilute" verbal and visual elements and stay away from initials and numbers.** Some words that may have once implied something to the consumer are today so diluted by overuse that they now mean, essentially, nothing. Try for a memorable mark that is, by its verbal and visual content, distinctive.

    Who can distinguish one "NATIONAL" company from another? Think of ACE, ACME, BEST, CONSOLIDATED, EXCELSIOR, FEDERATED, PREFERRED, etc. Verbal elements like this will sink without a trace in the ocean of mass communication. Design elements of marks can be as mundane—the American flag used as the background for a product name disappears into invisibility in most marks.

    IBM®, AAA®, and CBS® are certainly well known and successful trademarks, but before those companies bowed to common usage and adopted and began to use these alternate forms of their names in addition to their more formal names, they were called INTERNATIONAL BUSINESS MACHINES®, the AMERICAN AUTOMOBILE ASSOCIATION®, and the COLUMBIA BROADCASTING SERVICE®. The point is that trademarks comprised of initials really only work when they are derived from actual company names that have been shortened in common parlance. J&T TOWING is, by comparison, a less distinctive mark because no one knows, of course, who "J" and "T" are and were before they were reduced to their initials. The exception to this is acronym marks. Consider MADD® (Mothers against Drunk Driving), VISTA® (Volunteers in Service To America), and NOW® (National Organization for Women). However, acronyms must be memorable to be good trademarks; this means that they should have some meaning as acronyms that relates to the cause or goals or product characteristics of what they name. Only the most talented marketing people can create acronym marks that are not strained or obscure.

The same goes for numbers. There are well-known number marks, but their fame may attest to the excellence of the products they name rather than to the memorability of the marks. FORMULA 409® and X-14® have established profiles in the market as names for household cleaning products, maybe because they are marketed by large companies that can afford to advertise them widely. You would do less well with "1234 BAR-B-Q SAUCE," however, especially if you didn't have the money to advertise and distribute it nationally.

11. **Misspell it in an engaging way**. Every kid—and parent—knows TOYS "R" US® (even though the company will never win an award for grammar and it is impossible to render the backward R correctly using an ordinary font). JELL-O® is a fractured form of "gelatin." NYTOL® is a creative rendering of "Night, all." And L'EGGS® is a "French" form of "legs."

Marks that are spelled in unusual ways can be memorable because they approach the novelty of coined marks. However, there is nothing more old hat than a too-cute misspelling used as a brand name. No examples of these marks are necessary; you can see them in any grocery store. And don't let your enthusiasm for your clever misspelling lead you to choose a name that is hard to understand, to spell, or to say. A good recent example of a difficult trademark is VAIO for computers. It means nothing in particular, which isn't necessarily bad, but how do you spell it and how do you say it? And the stylized typeface in which the name is rendered is cool looking but not immediately obvious as English-language letters. Sony should have gone back to the drawing board on this. Your product may be so popular that no one cares that it is hard to spell or write—it happens, but usually only after a lot of heavy lifting from the marketing departments that get stuck with obscure trademarks.

12. **Choose a name that can become an Internet address.** You've lost half the battle if your new trademark can't become an identical Internet address. This criterion was once of *some* importance; it is now critical for the success of any product or service marketed to consumers. Determine early in the selection process whether a proposed mark is available as a domain name; if it's unavailable, abandon it as a possibility. Aside from the unavailability of the domain name you want, you face the potential for infringing the rights of whoever already owns the domain name if you adopt a similar mark (you can read more about trademarks in cyberspace in chapter 10). You can check the availability of a domain name through any Internet registrar. And remember that having to insert an extra word or so in order to secure a domain name is like having two names in any context—confusing for anyone who must remember which name applies when.

New Protection for Famous Marks

Owners of famous trademarks gained substantial new protection from the federal Trademark Dilution Act of 1995, which was signed into law by the president and became effective in January of 1996. The act formalizes and makes a part of the federal trademark statute a principle of trademark law that had been available as a ground for suit in only about half the states. It allows the owners of an existing "famous" trademark to ask the court to enjoin the use of the same mark by another company—even if there is no likelihood of confusion between the marks—on the ground that the defendant's use of the mark, even for noncompeting goods or services, "dilutes" the distinctive quality of the famous mark. This allows the owners of truly famous marks to stop the use of their marks by the marketers of noncompeting goods and services as well as by competitors.

One of the first lawsuits brought under the new act was initiated by Hasbro, Inc., which owns the trademark CANDY LAND® for the famous children's board game, against a company that had adopted the domain name *candyland.com* for a sexually explicit Web site. Hasbro was successful in having the domain name enjoined on the basis that its use would dilute the strength of the CANDY LAND mark. Other, similar cases have followed. One example is the suit brought by Federal Express to halt the use of FEDERAL ESPRESSO as the name of a Syracuse coffeehouse.

The act defines "dilution" as "the lessening of the capacity of a famous mark to identify and distinguish goods or services, regardless of the presence or absence of 1) competition between the owner of the famous mark and other parties, or 2) likelihood of confusion, mistake, or deception." Although most really famous marks are registered in the U.S. Patent and Trademark Office, federal registration is not a prerequisite for protection of a mark under the act, which protects registered and unregistered marks equally, given an equal degree of fame.

The Trademark Dilution Act enumerates several factors to be considered in evaluating whether the mark owned by a plaintiff in a suit under the act really is distinctive and famous enough to be protected under its provisions. These include the following:

1. The degree of inherent or acquired distinctiveness of the "famous" mark
2. The duration and extent of use of the "famous" mark
3. The duration and extent of advertising and publicity for the "famous" mark
4. The geographical extent of the trading area in which the "famous" mark is used
5. The channels of trade through which the product or service named by the "famous" mark is sold
6. The degree of recognition of the "famous" mark in the trading areas and channels of trade used by both the owner of the "famous mark" and the defendant against whom the injunction is sought

7. The nature and extent of any use by third parties of marks that are the same as or similar to the "famous mark"
8. Whether the owner of the "famous" mark has a valid federal registration

These factors are not exclusive; that is, they are specifically not the only factors that may be considered.

For most trademark owners, the Trademark Dilution Act will not offer any more protection than the federal trademark statute offered before the new act was passed. This is understandable; very few marks can hope to reach the level of fame required to trigger protection from trademark dilution under the new law. For an understanding of the sort of fame that courts are likely to require before invoking the penalties of the new law, we have only to look to the LEXIS® case, decided not long before the new act was passed. The manufacturer of the automobile LEXUS® was sued by the owners of the online legal research service LEXIS on the ground of dilution. LEXIS lost. The court held that LEXIS was not well-known enough outside the legal community to have suffered dilution at the hands of the automobile manufacturer.

In other words, the sort of fame necessary to support a claim of trademark dilution is what used to be known as becoming "a household word." When the great majority of consumers are aware of a mark and the products or services it names, it is "famous" in the sense meant by the Trademark Dilution Act. If only some people are aware of the mark, or if almost everyone in a certain profession or industry is aware of it but practically no one outside that group is, the mark has not (yet) achieved the degree of fame necessary to command this very broad protection under the law.

Most marketers need only remember that a long-standing guideline for trademark selection is even more important since the passage of the Trademark Dilution Act. "Stay away from famous marks" is better advice than ever. Now owners of famous marks have a more direct and powerful way to stop you from naming your motor oil COORS® or your new detergent CLEAN-X (KLEENEX®).

The statute specifies several legitimate uses of famous trademarks that will not create any liability under the law. These exclusions from the proscriptions of the act are a response to legitimate First Amendment concerns. The new act expressly exempts:

1. Fair use of a mark in comparative advertising
2. Parody, satire, editorial commentary, and other noncommercial uses of a mark
3. Any form of news reporting or commentary that mentions a mark

(See chapter 9 for a more detailed discussion of the use of trademarks that belong to others.)

Chapter 5
Trademark Protection

Once you have settled on a mark, chosen from a list you or your ad agency proposed after careful consideration of the aforementioned dreaded Ten Deadly Sins of Trademark Selection, and have conducted a trademark search to determine whether the mark is available for use, the next step is the registration of the trademark. Every trademark wants to be registered after it is born. There are two options for trademark registration, state trademark registration and federal trademark registration.

State Trademark Registration

We will consider state trademark registration only briefly, for two reasons. First, state trademark registration offers much less protection to a mark than federal registration. Second, state registrations do not involve nearly so many rules and regulations as federal registrations and are usually easy to obtain.

You can almost certainly handle state registration of your trademark without a lawyer. The first thing to do is to call or write the trademark department of the state in which you want to register your mark. (State trademark departments are usually part of the secretary of state's office; you can find a list of these agencies for each state in appendix B.) Request a printed trademark registration form or download it from the state's Web site. When the form arrives, carefully read it and the instructions that will come with it, fill in the blanks, sign it, send it back with the proper application fee (fees are usually $50 or less, depending on the state) and with the specimens of use of the mark required. You will have to specify in what class of goods or services you want to register your mark. This may be one of the classes of the old U.S. classification system for trademarks. You will be sent a copy of this list of categories, which is different from the one that the U.S. Trademark Office uses, with your blank registration application or will find that it is a part of a registration form that is available online.

All the states have some sort of trademark statute; most are based on a model trademark statute. The provisions of state trademark statutes largely echo those of the federal statute. However, the federal trademark statute only applies to trademarks that are used in interstate commerce. The state statutes are designed to regulate the use of trademarks and protect the rights of trademark owners within each state.

Although some states offer more protection to trademark registrants than others, it is never a bad idea to apply for and secure a state registration for your trademark. Among other benefits, state trademark registration:

- Documents your ownership of your mark before you have used it in interstate commerce and are able to apply for federal registration
- Offers protection against infringement within the state where your mark is used
- Causes your mark to show up in the trademark search reports other people commission

You can apply for state trademark registration only in the state or states where you are *currently* using the mark. As with federal registration, "use" of a mark in a specified territory is defined as the offering for sale of the product to which the mark is applied or the advertising of and readiness to offer the services the mark names. The difference is that you may apply for state trademark registration based on your use of a mark *within* a state; federal trademark registration requires use of the mark in *interstate* commerce.

A good strategy is to apply for state registration for your mark as soon as you begin using it. This may be before you have begun to use the mark in interstate commerce or concurrent with your use of the mark in interstate commerce. You should file a federal use-based application or intent-to-use application at the same time. File to register the mark in every state where you are using it; apply to register your mark in additional states when you expand your use of your mark to those states. This plan will give you as much protection as possible as early in the life of your mark as possible, at the lowest possible cost.

In most cases, state trademark registrations endure for five years. As with federal registrations, you must renew state registrations prior to the expiration of the initial term of registration. If you have secured federal registration for your mark since filing for state registration and the federal registration is current and in effect at the end of the initial term of state registration, you can safely let your state registration lapse, since a federal registration offers much broader protection.

Even if your mark is only registered in one or more states, you should be careful to follow the rules for proper use of trademarks discussed in chapter 7. However, *do not* use the ® symbol or any other form of notice that indicates federal trademark registration until and unless your mark is registered federally. Ignoring this restriction on the use of notice of federal registration can seriously damage your right to stop infringers or later register your mark with the U.S. Trademark Office. Use the ™ (or SM) freely, but stay away from the ® symbol unless you have earned the right to use it by virtue of having been granted a federal registration.

Federal Trademark Registration

Any company that is serious enough about a new mark to spend any time or money developing it and clearing it for use will want to file as soon as possible for federal trademark registration, which means registration of the trademark in the U.S. Patent and Trademark Office, in Washington, D.C. (Ignore the fact that the name of the office includes the word "patent"; the Trademark Office and the Patent Office are entirely separate government departments that were mistakenly joined at the hip by a Congress that got confused and thought that they had something to do with each other.)

The federal trademark statute, the Federal Trademark Act of 1946 (also called the Lanham Act), gives to the U.S. Patent and Trademark Office, which is a division of the Department of Commerce, the power to regulate the registration of trademarks that are used in interstate commerce or commerce between the United States and another country. The Trademark Office consists of several divisions, each of which handles a different function; most trademark owners will be concerned with only one of the various offices that reviews, or "examines," applications to ascertain whether registration will be granted—the office that examines applications for the particular goods or services that the trademark owner offers under its trademark.

There are now two types of federal trademark registration: 1) the use-based application, which is based on current use of the trademark in interstate or international commerce, and 2) the intent-to-use application, which is based on a "bona fide intent" to use the mark in interstate or international commerce. At one time, every U.S. trademark application was based on current use of the mark; since a change in the law, this is no longer the case.

Use-based Applications

There are several requisite elements for a use-based federal trademark registration application. These include the following: the written application in proper form; a "drawing" sheet, on which the mark is reproduced according to the Trademark Office's specifications; your declaration, made under penalty of perjury, that you believe that you (or your company) own your mark and are entitled to register it; a date of first use of the mark anywhere; a date of first use of the mark in interstate or international commerce; a description of the goods or services marketed under your mark; specimens of ads, packaging, labels, etc., proving your use of your mark; and the proper filing fee, which is (at this writing) $335 per class of goods or services.

When your registration application is received by the Trademark Office, it is preliminarily reviewed for its sufficiency as an application, i.e., whether it includes all the components necessary to allow the examination process to proceed, and is given a serial number. (If you have omitted one or more important elements of your application, you will be notified.) This serial number remains the way the application is identified throughout the process of examination to ascertain whether a trademark will be granted. After assignment of a serial number, your registration application is forwarded to the correct law office within the examining section of the Trademark Office and is assigned to an examining attorney.

The Trademark Office classifies all goods and services according to the International Schedule of Classes of Goods and Services. The descriptions of goods and services may seem unfamiliar. For example, the REVERE WARE® trademark is registered in International Class 11, which includes "apparatus for lighting, heating, steam generating, cooking, refrigerating, drying, ventilating, water supply, and sanitary purposes." The lists of goods registered in other categories are sometimes longer. The International Schedule of Classes of Goods and Services classification list appears at the end of "Basic Facts about Trademarks," which is reproduced in appendix C. In addition to the list at the end of "Basic Facts about Trademarks," there is an expanded version of the International Schedule of Classes of Goods and Services, taken from the Trademark Office Web site's FAQs; this version of the list includes the Trademark Office's notes about what is and is not included in any given class. Read this version of the list to figure out where your product or service would be classified and what products or services fall into the same class. You may not think that personal deodorants and scouring powder belong in the same class, but the Trademark Office does and it will deny your application to register FRESHEN for a new antiperspirant if it already has a registration for FRESHEN for a bathroom cleaner.

The Trademark Office examining offices are numbered: Law Office 1, Law Office 2, etc. Each law office handles all the applications made in the classes of goods or services assigned to that office. Each application is handled by one examiner, who is a lawyer, according to the provisions of the Trademark Manual of Examining Procedure (TMEP). The examining procedures are logical and are designed to carry out the intent of the Lanham Act, but the logic of examiners' decisions is not always apparent to applicants. If you are curious, you can read the TMEP—even download it—at *www.uspto.gov/web/offices/tac/tmep*.

Other than a communication that notifies them of the serial numbers assigned to their applications, most applicants will receive no word from the Trademark Office for several months. You will probably not receive a Filing Receipt for your application for two to three months after filing it. It will take about six months more until you receive the first communication from the examining attorney who has been assigned your application file; this may be an Office Action or a Notice of Publication. An Office Action will either reject your application for registration or will ask you to furnish more information or correct or clarify statements made in the application. A Notice of Publication will notify you that your mark will be "published for opposition," which means that it will be published so that other trademark owners will know that your mark is being considered for registration.

It is an extremely common occurrence that an examiner will, at least initially, reject an application on one or more bases. The simplest is that the examiner points out a small technical problem with the form of the application and suggests a small change in the language of the application to correct some technicality, such as asking for a clarification of the description of goods or services named by the mark; sometimes this sort of small amendment can be authorized by the applicant in a phone call to the examiner.

A more difficult sort of rejection to overcome is a substantive rejection based on the failure of the mark to meet one or more of the legal requirements for registration. Substantive rejections are commonly based on the trademark examiner's decision that a mark embodies one of the statutory grounds for denial of registration; for example, that it is confusingly similar to a registered mark or that it is descriptive or deceptively misdescriptive of the goods or services it names. (See the Ten Deadly Sins of Trademark Selection in chapter 4 for the entire list of statutory grounds for rejection of an application.) The reason or reasons for the rejection will be described, and one or more Trademark Office rules or court decisions in trademark cases will be cited to support the examiner's rejection of the application. Whatever the examiner's objections, the applicant has six months to respond to the rejection. Such responses answer questions the examiner may have raised and present counterarguments to the grounds cited for rejection of the application, as well as amending the application to clear up technical problems. Even if your application is initially rejected on a substantive ground, it is possible to persuade the examiner that registration should be granted. However, this can be difficult or impossible, depending on the ground for rejection. Further, this is not a do-it-yourself job.

Like all documents filed with the Trademark Office in the process of pursuing a registration, responses to rejections must fulfill strict requirements in order to suffice. Filing an application to register a trademark is like appearing in a regular court and asking the judge to rule in your favor; the applicant states that he or she believes the mark that is the subject of the application is entitled to registration under the law, presents evidence sufficient to prove that to the Trademark Office, and answers questions and presents arguments to support the granting of the registration. These are difficult procedures that take lawyers years to master. Even an application that is eventually granted can require several carefully composed replies to the Trademark Office.

If, even after you present arguments to overcome the examiner's denial of registration, your application is "finally" rejected by the examiner, there are several courses open to you. You can simply abandon your effort to register your mark, which will not affect whatever rights you have or will gain in it. You can file an appeal with the Trademark Trial and Appeal Board, which is a complicated formal undertaking somewhat like appealing an ordinary court case after an adverse verdict of the trial court. Or you can amend your application to ask that registration be granted on the Supplemental Register rather than the Principal Register (see page 93 for an explanation of the difference between the two types of registration).

If your application is not rejected or if you overcome the examiner's initial rejection of your application, the trademark examiner is satisfied that your trademark is entitled to registration. Your trademark will then be subjected to the next step in the process of qualifying for registration. It is "published for opposition." This means that your mark is reproduced (in the case of purely verbal marks, this means only that it is printed to show its exact verbal content) in the *Trademark Official Gazette*, which is published weekly. (You can view and, if you wish, download the *Trademark Official Gazette* at *www.uspto.gov/web/trademarks/tmog.*) Anyone who believes that registration of your mark will harm him or her has thirty days to file an objection to the registration, called an "opposition." Many opposition proceedings are settled; some are fought hard through the Trademark Office's in-house court, called the Trademark Trial and Appeal Board. If no one objects to the granting of your registration within the prescribed period, a certificate of registration will be mailed to you as soon as the Trademark Office's slow machinery can produce one. The whole registration process can literally take years, especially if there are rejections to be countered or if an opposition proceeding is filed. During this process, you can check the status of your application online or by calling the Trademark Office. The Trademark Office moves slowly; even applications that encounter no such problems routinely take year or eighteen months to result in a registration.

There are two varieties of federal trademark registrations: an applicant may be granted a registration on either the Principal Register or the Supplemental Register. Principal Register registrations bestow the most benefits and are the goal of every federal trademark applicant. (When the term "federal registration" is used in this book, registration on the Principal Register is meant.) However, if a mark is unable to qualify for the Principal Register, a Supplemental Register registration also has its uses. Most marks on the Supplemental Register are descriptive, surname, or geographic marks that do not yet function as trademarks, in the eyes of the Trademark Office. That is, they do not point to *one* source for the goods or services they name because they are not distinctive and have not yet acquired the degree of fame necessary to result in "secondary meaning." Marks registered on the Supplemental Register are entitled to use the ® notice of registration and gain some benefits of federal registration, such as access to federal courts, and are presumed, after a period of five years, to have gained enough fame to qualify for an upgrade (upon request by the registrant) to the Principal Register.

Intent-to-Use Applications

Once upon a time in America, it was necessary for trademark owners to have used their trademarks in interstate commerce before applying for federal trademark registration, and trademark rights began to accrue from the date a trademark owner actually began to use a mark in the marketplace. However, it is now possible for a trademark owner to apply for registration before actually beginning to use the new trademark, so long as the trademark owner has a "bona fide intent" to begin to use the mark in interstate commerce within six months of the date the registration application is filed. (The period of time for beginning use of the mark may be extended, in six-month increments and upon making the proper filings, to a total period of thirty-six months.) Registration may then be granted after use of the mark is made in interstate commerce.

This system of registration represents a big change in the law. It is not quite the same as the system that exists in certain European countries, which allows marketers to "reserve" a trademark for use before actually adopting it, but it is close, since now U.S. companies can put everyone on notice that they intend to use a mark before they actually do so. This change should eliminate the situation that formerly existed, where two companies that had to begin using their new marks before they applied for trademark registration began to use the same mark for similar products—each discovering the existence of the other only upon filing their applications, after they had expended the time and money necessary to launch a new mark. In this situation, only one of the two companies could end up owning and registering the mark—the company that began using it first.

Now, when a company files an intent-to-use application to register a mark, stating that it will begin using the mark within six months, its intentions become part of the official records maintained by the Trademark Office and are included in the data searched by trademark search firms. This means that when a second company conducts a search to ascertain the availability of the mark, the first company's application for that mark, indicating that it has already "staked a claim" to the mark, will appear in the search report and warn the second company away from the mark.

Intent-to-use applications confer one other benefit on trademark owners that was not formerly available: when a registration is eventually granted to an intent-to-use applicant, the date of the applicant trademark owner's rights in the mark is deemed by the new rules to commence from the filing date of the application to register, rather than just from the date of the applicant's first actual use of the mark. This means that early filing of a trademark registration application can now give additional months or even years of ownership rights, on the front end of the ownership period, to a trademark owner who had not even begun to use the mark on the date of filing.

All this complicated stuff boils down to this for businesspeople: you should know that it is possible to file for federal trademark registration just as soon as a search has cleared a new mark for use. Speed is important because the earlier the date of filing, the sooner ownership rights in the mark will, eventually, be deemed to have begun. In addition, early filing removes some of the danger that two companies will be competing for registration and ownership of the same mark.

Intent-to-use applications require essentially the same components as use-based applications. However, instead of a declaration that the mark that is the subject of the application was first used in interstate commerce on a certain date, the statement in an intent-to-use application is that the applicant has a bona fide intent to use the mark for the goods or services specified. Further, there is no requirement that specimens of use of the mark be furnished until the applicant is able to file a "Statement of Use" attesting to the fact that the mark has begun to be used in interstate commerce.

95

Maintaining Your Registration

Federal trademark registrations endure for a term of ten years. However, because all trademark rights are based on use of the mark, between the fifth and sixth anniversaries of the date a registration is granted, the registrant must formally attest to continuing use of the mark by filing an affidavit describing that use and furnish a new specimen of use of the mark. Further, at the end of the initial ten-year registration period, but no sooner than six months prior to the end of the period, you may file to renew your registration. You may renew the registration for your mark at ten-year intervals as many times as you want, so long as you continue to use the mark. In theory, a trademark can live in perpetuity in the marketplace. There are some trademarks that are still active after a hundred years or more of service in commerce.

Apply at Your Own Risk

It is one thing to know that federal trademark registration is desirable and to know something about the registration process, but filing for federal trademark registration is, like searching a trademark to clear it for use, not a do-it-yourself project. The Trademark Office allows trademark owners to file their own applications for registration, without the help of a lawyer, but satisfying the complicated filing requirements imposed by the Trademark Office is not easy and filing without the help of a trademark lawyer is likely to result in the rejection of the application.

The Trademark Office now prefers the electronic filing of trademark registration applications rather than the paper application that was formerly the norm, so it may seem that filing for trademark registration is easier than ever. (Go to the U.S. Patent and Trademark Office home page at *www.uspto.gov* and click on "File" under the "Trademarks" heading to see the beginning page for the Trademark Electronic Application System (TEAS).) However, remember that with electronic filing, as with paper applications, it is hard for an applicant, without the advice and help of a trademark lawyer, to create an application that will not present obstacles to the registration process. A trademark registration application is not a long or complicated form, but what is said and where is important and unless you understand the rules and reasons behind each representation you make on an application, it is very likely that your application will be denied, for one or several reasons. Lawyers do have their uses; filing for trademark registration is one of them.

However, for the brave, the registration forms prescribed by the Trademark Office are available online through the Trademark Office Web site. Directions for filling out registration applications are included with each question on the registration form, in the pamphlet "Basic Facts about Trademarks," which is reprinted in the appendix C and in the Trademark Office's FAQs beginning on page 99 of this book.

Most experienced trademark lawyers would tell you that filing for federal trademark registration is not a do-it-yourself job. Even if you manage to meet the requirements of the Trademark Office for a registration application, you may still be confronted with the need to keep your application on track by filing a response to some complicated objections to registration raised by the trademark examiner who reviews and evaluates your application. That is, even if you manage to file a proper application without a trademark lawyer, you still may need to find one, because almost no one who has not done it before can successfully respond to a complicated Trademark Office rejection of an application. Failure to respond will result in the abandonment of your application; failure to respond fully will result in a final rejection of your application.

Federal trademark registration offers several important advantages to trademark owners, among them:

- A federal registrant has rights in the registered mark superior to anyone else except prior users of the mark.
- The owner of a federally registered trademark is in a much better position to quash infringers than if the mark were not registered, since federal registration offers immediate access to a federal court, where a federal registrant can obtain an injunction with nationwide effect to stop infringers.
- A federal trademark registrant who sues an infringer in federal court may be entitled to recover profits, damages, and court costs, including attorney's fees. In some circumstances, the registrant may be awarded "treble damages," which are damages three times the amount that would ordinarily be awarded.
- Moreover, because a federal registration gives the registrant the benefit of the presumptions that the registrant owns the registered mark and that the registration is valid, registrants who end up in court have a powerful advantage over any challenger who also claims ownership.
- A federal registration serves as "constructive notice" to any subsequent user of the registered mark that the registrant claims ownership of it. In other words, the presence of the registration in the public records of the Trademark Office is presumed to make any other would-be user of the mark aware of prior ownership claims of the registrant. This eliminates any defense raised by an alleged infringer that the mark was adopted in good faith.
- After five years, a registered mark may become "incontestable"; that is, the registration becomes conclusive evidence of the registrant's right to use the mark.

Even better, federal trademark registration helps trademark owners avoid the necessity of bringing suit to stop trademark infringers in two important ways. First, once a trademark is registered in the Trademark Office, any other companies that conduct searches to clear proposed new marks will know that the registered mark is already in use for the goods and services it names and will stay clear of it or any confusingly similar mark. Secondly, even if some company does infringe the mark, it is likely to agree to stop using the mark

97

immediately upon the receipt of a cease and desist letter from the trademark owner's lawyer, since the infringer will know that the owner of the registered mark does, indeed, have the clout to prevent the continued infringing use of the mark. These circumstances have the effect of stopping trademark infringement lawsuits at the optimum time— before they start.

International Protection

The Protocol Relating to the Madrid Agreement Concerning the International Registration of Marks (Madrid Protocol) is an international treaty that allows a trademark owner to seek registration in any of the countries that have joined the Madrid Protocol by filing a single application, called an "international application." The International Bureau of the World Property Intellectual Organization (International Bureau) in Geneva, Switzerland administers the international registration system. Since late in 2003, a United States trademark owner can submit an international application to the United States Trademark Office for forwarding to the International Bureau. The U.S. Trademark Office does not *grant* the international registration but, rather, certifies the suitability of the application before forwarding it to Geneva. The Madrid Protocol is an efficient way to file for trademark registration, with one application, in multiple countries. U.S. trademark owners can save time and money through this registration mechanism.

You can read the Trademark Office's list of FAQs about the Madrid Protocol on the Trademark Office Web site (*http://uspto.gov* then click on "Trademarks" then click on any of the "Madrid" links that appear on the page). You can find out what the International Trademark Association has to say about it (thumbs up) at *www.inta.org/madrid*. It's interesting reading—a primer on the increasingly international nature of commerce and the reach of the commercial efforts of even ordinary citizens into the markets of the world.

However, bear in mind that if filing a United States trademark registration application is too complicated for the average businessperson to accomplish successfully, international trademark registration is even more complicated. Remember that international registration is now possible with less effort and expense than formerly and educate yourself, if you wish, to the steps in obtaining such registration, but call your trademark lawyer to guide you through the process of registering your mark through the Madrid Protocol.

U.S. Trademark Office FAQs

Do I have to register my trademark?

No, but federal registration has several advantages, including notice to the public of the registrant's claim of ownership of the mark, a legal presumption of ownership nationwide, and the exclusive right to use the mark on or in connection with the goods or services set forth in the registration.

What are the benefits of federal trademark registration?

1. Constructive notice nationwide of the trademark owner's claim.
2. Evidence of ownership of the trademark.
3. Jurisdiction of federal courts may be invoked.
4. Registration can be used as a basis for obtaining registration in foreign countries.
5. Registration may be filed with U.S. Customs Service to prevent importation of infringing foreign goods.

Do I have to be a U.S. Citizen to obtain a federal registration?

No. However, an applicant's citizenship must be set forth in the record. If an applicant is not a citizen of any country, then a statement to that effect is sufficient. If an applicant has dual citizenship, then the applicant must choose which citizenship will be printed in the Official Gazette and on the certificate of registration.

Where can I find trademark forms?

You can access forms through the Trademark Electronic Application System (TEAS), at *www.uspto.gov/teas/index.html.* TEAS can be used to file an application for registration of a mark, response to examining attorney's Office action, notice of change of address, amendment to allege use, statement of use, request for extension of time to file a statement of use, affidavit of continued use under 15 U.S.C. §1058, affidavit of incontestability under 15 U.S.C. §1065, combined affidavit under 15 U.S.C. §§1058 and 1065, or combined filing under 15 U.S.C. §§1058 and 1059. Additional forms may be available through the Trademark Assistance Center at 1-800-786-9199 (or (703) 308-9000 if you live in Northern Virginia).

How do I obtain a federal trademark registration?

You can fill out an application online, check it for completeness, and file it over the Internet using the Trademark Electronic Application System (TEAS), at *www.uspto.gov/teas/index.html.* You can also respond to Office actions and file, notices of change of address, allegations of use and requests for extension of time to file a statement of use through TEAS. You can check the status of your application through the Trademark Applications and Registrations Retrieval (TARR) database at *http://tarr.uspto.gov.* If you do not have access to the Internet, you can call the Trademark Assistance Center at 1-800-786-9199 (or (703) 308-9000 if you live in Northern Virginia) to request a paper form.

What is the Trademark Electronic Application System (TEAS)?

The Trademark Electronic Application System, at *www.uspto.gov/teas/index.html,* allows you to fill out an application form online, check it for completeness, and file it over the Internet, paying by credit card or through an existing USPTO deposit account. TEAS can also be used to file a response to examining attorney's Office action, notice of change of address, amendment to allege use, statement of use, request for extension of time to file a statement of use, affidavit of continued use under 15 U.S.C. §1058, affidavit of incontestability under 15 U.S.C. §1065, combined affidavit under 15 U.S.C. §§1058 and 1065, or combined filing under 15 U.S.C. §§1058 and 1059.

Who may file an application?

Only the owner of the trademark may file an application for its registration. An application filed by a person who is not the owner of the mark will be declared void. Generally, the person who uses or controls the use of the mark, and controls the nature and quality of the goods to which it is affixed, or the services for which it is used, is the owner of the mark.

Do I have to use the application form provided by the Office?

No, but filing electronically through the Trademark Electronic Application System (TEAS), at *www.uspto.gov/teas/index.html* is strongly encouraged, to avoid the omission of important information. Also, applications filed electronically are processed faster than paper applications.

Can a fax copy or photocopy of an application be filed?
You cannot transmit an application by means of facsimile transmission, i.e., by "faxing" it to the Office, but you can file a photocopy or a fax copy by U.S. mail or hand delivery.

Can I fax in my application?
No.

What constitutes interstate commerce?
For goods, "Interstate commerce" involves sending the goods across state lines with the mark displayed on the goods or the packaging for the goods. With services, "interstate commerce" involves offering a service to those in another state or rendering a service which affects interstate commerce (e.g. restaurants, gas stations, hotels, etc.). See TMEP section 901.03.

What is a specimen?
A specimen is a real-world example of how the mark is actually used on the goods or in the offer of services. Labels, tags, or containers for the goods are considered to be acceptable specimens of use for a trademark. For a service mark, specimens may be advertising such as magazine advertisements or brochures. Actual specimens, rather than facsimiles, are preferred. However, if the actual specimens are bulky, or larger than $81/2'' \times 11''$, then the applicant must submit facsimiles, (e.g., photographs or good photocopies) of the specimens. Facsimiles may not exceed $81/2'' \times 11''$. ONE SPECIMEN IS REQUIRED FOR EACH CLASS OF GOODS OR SERVICES SPECIFIED IN THE APPLICATION.

Specimens are required in applications based on actual use in commerce, Section 1(a), 15 U.S.C. §1051(a), and must be filed with the Amendment to Allege Use, 15 U.S.C. §1051(c), or the Statement of Use, 15 U.S.C. §1051(d), in applications based on a bona fide intention to use the mark in commerce, Section 1(b), 15 U.S.C. §1051(b). Specimens are not required for applications based on a foreign application or registration under Section 44 of the Trademark Act, 15 U.S.C. §1126, or for applications based on an extension of protection of an international registration to the United States under Section 66(a) of the Trademark Act, 15 U.S.C. §1141f.

What is the drawing?

The "drawing" is a page which depicts the mark applicant seeks to register. In an application based on actual use, Section 1(a), 15 U.S.C. §1051(a), the drawing must show the mark as it is actually used, i.e., as shown by the specimens. In the case of an application based on a bona fide intention to use, Section 1(b), 15 U.S.C. §1051(b), the drawing must show the mark as the applicant intends to use it. In an application based on a foreign application or foreign registration, Sections 44(d) or 44(e), 15 U.S.C. §§1126(d) or (e), the drawing must depict the mark as it appears or will appear on the foreign registration. The applicant cannot register more than one mark in a single application. Therefore, the drawing must display only one mark.

If an applicant submits a specimen, is a drawing still required?

Yes. A drawing is required in all applications, and is used by the Office for several purposes, including printing the mark in the Official Gazette, and on the registration certificate. A specimen, on the other hand, is required as evidence that a mark is in actual use in commerce.

Do I need an attorney to file my application?

No, although it may be desirable to employ an attorney who is familiar with trademark matters. An applicant must comply with all substantive and procedural requirements of the Trademark Act and the Trademark Rules of Practice even if he or she is not represented by an attorney. The names of attorneys who specialize in trademark law may be found in the telephone yellow pages, or by contacting a local bar association. The USPTO cannot aid in the selection of an attorney.

On what bases can a foreign applicant file an application for registration?

1. Use in interstate commerce or commerce between the United States and a foreign country.
2. Bona fide or good faith intention to use the mark in interstate commerce or commerce between the United States and a foreign country.
3. Ownership of an application filed in a foreign country (if within six months of the foreign filing date).

4. Ownership of a foreign registration (with a copy).
5. Extension of protection of an international registration to the United States under the Madrid Protocol, pursuant to section 66(a) of the Trademark Act. See *www.uspto.gov/web/trademarks/madrid/madridguide.htm* for further information about the Madrid Protocol.

Can the Office refuse to register a mark?

Yes. The Office will refuse to register matter if it does not function as a trademark. Not all words, names, symbols or devices function as trademarks. For example, matter which is merely the generic name of the goods on which it is used cannot be registered.

Additionally, Section 2 of the Trademark Act (15 U.S.C. §1052) contains several of the most common (though not the only) grounds for refusing registration. The grounds for refusal under Section 2 may be summarized as:

1. The proposed mark consists of or comprises immoral, deceptive, or scandalous matter;
2. The proposed mark may disparage or falsely suggest a connection with persons (living or dead), institutions, beliefs, or national symbols, or bring them into contempt or disrepute;
3. The proposed mark consists of or comprises the flag or coat of arms, or other insignia of the United States, or of any State or municipality, or of any foreign nation;
4. The proposed mark consists of or comprises a name, portrait or signature identifying a particular living individual, except by that individual's written consent; or the name, signature, or portrait of a deceased President of the United States during the life of his widow, if any, except by the written consent of the widow;
5. The proposed mark so resembles a mark already registered in the Patent and Trademark Office (PTO) that use of the mark on applicant's goods or services are likely to cause confusion, mistake, or deception;
6. The proposed mark is merely descriptive or deceptively misdescriptive of applicant's goods or services;

7. The proposed mark is primarily geographically descriptive or deceptively geographically misdescriptive of applicant's goods or services;
8. The proposed mark is primarily merely a surname; and
9. Matter that, as a whole, is functional.

Can I get a refund of monies paid to the Office?

Not usually. Only money paid by mistake or in excess (that is, paid when not required, or not required in the amount paid) may be refunded. A filing fee will be returned if submitted with a defective application which is denied a filing date. However, once the application receives a filing date, the filing fee will normally not be returned. All requests for refunds should be referred to the Finance Office, or the Examining Attorney assigned.

How can I check on the status of a pending U.S. trademark application?

Once you receive a filing receipt containing the serial number of your application, you may check on the status of your application through the Trademark Applications and Registrations Retrieval (TARR) database on the Office's World Wide Web site at *http://tarr.uspto.gov*. If you do not have access to the Internet, you can call the Trademark Assistance Center at 1-800-786-9199 or (703) 308-9000 if you live in Northern Virginia to request a status check. Applicants should check on the status of their pending applications every six months.

How long does it take for a mark to be registered?

It is difficult to predict how long it will take for an application to mature into a registration, because there are so many factors that can affect the process. Generally, an applicant will receive a filing receipt approximately six months after filing. The filing receipt will include the serial number of the application. All future correspondence with the PTO must include this serial number. You should receive a response from the Office within six to seven months from filing the application. However, the total time for an application to be processed may be anywhere from almost a year to several years, depending on the basis for filing, and the legal issues which may arise in the examination of the application. Current status information on trademark

applications and registrations may be obtained through the
Trademark Applications and Registrations Retrieval (TARR)
database on the Office's World Wide Web site at
http://tarr.uspto.gov. If you do not have access to the Internet,
you can call the Trademark Assistance Center at 1-800-786-9199
or (703) 308-9000 if you live in Northern Virginia to request a
status check.

How long does a trademark registration last?
For a trademark registration to remain valid, an Affidavit of Use
("Section 8 Affidavit") must be filed: (1) between the fifth and
sixth year following registration, and (2) within the year before
the end of every ten-year period after the date of registration.
The registrant may file the affidavit within a grace period of six
months after the end of the sixth or tenth year, with payment of
an additional fee.

The registrant must also file a §9 renewal application within
the year before the expiration date of a registration, or within a
grace period of six months after the expiration date, with payment of an additional fee.

Assuming that an affidavit of use is timely filed, registrations
granted PRIOR to November 16, 1989 have a 20-year term, and
registrations granted on or after November 16, 1989 have a
10-year term.

This is also true for the renewal periods; renewals granted
PRIOR to November 16, 1989 have a 20-year term, and renewals
granted on or after November 16, 1989 have a 10-year term.

When did the renewal period change from twenty to ten years?
November 16, 1989. Registrations issued on or after November
16, 1989 have a ten-year term, renewable every ten years.

**How long does an Intent-to-Use applicant have to allege actual
use of the mark in commerce?**
An applicant may file an Amendment to Allege Use any time
between the filing date of the application and the date the
Examining Attorney approves the mark for publication. If an
Amendment to Allege Use is not filed, then applicant has six
months from the issuance of the Notice of Allowance to file
a Statement of Use, unless the applicant requests and is granted

an extension of time. If the applicant fails to file either an Amendment to Allege Use or a Statement of Use within the time limits allowed, then the application will be declared abandoned. No registration will be granted.

Is a federal registration valid outside the United States?
No. However, if you are a qualified owner of a trademark application pending before the USPTO, or of a registration issued by the USPTO, you may seek registration in any of the countries that have joined the Madrid Protocol by filing a single application, called an "international application," with the he International Bureau of the World Property Intellectual Organization, through the USPTO. [More information about the Madrid Protocol is available on the Trademark Office Web site.]

Also, certain countries recognize a United States registration as a basis for filing an application to register a mark in those countries under international treaties. See TMEP Chapter 1000 for further information. The laws of each country regarding registration must be consulted.

What are some suggestions to facilitate filing a trademark application and/or contacting the Patent and Trademark Office (PTO)?
File electronically through the Trademark Electronic Application System (TEAS), at *www.uspto.gov/teas/index.html*, whenever possible. TEAS can be used to file an application for registration of a mark, response to examining attorney's Office action, notice of change of address, amendment to allege use, statement of use, request for extension of time to file a statement of use, affidavit of continued use under 15 U.S.C. §1058, affidavit of incontesta-bility under 15 U.S.C. §1065, combined affidavit under 15 U.S.C. §§1058 and 1065, or combined filing under 15 U.S.C. §§1058 and 1059. When a document is filed electronically, the USPTO receives it within seconds after filing, and immediately issues a confirmation of filing via e-mail that includes the date of receipt and a summary of the submission. This confirmation is evidence of filing should any question arise as to the filing date of the document. Also, documents filed electronically are processed faster than paper documents. The data provided by the applicant

is entered directly into the Office's databases, so data entry errors are unlikely. When documents are filed electronically, it is very unlikely that they will be lost or misplaced within the Office.

Carefully review all documents before filing to make sure all issues have been addressed and all the necessary elements are included.

Do not file large or "bulky" specimens. Rather, submit a picture of the mark on the specimen. Bulky specimens are specimens that are larger than 8 1/2″ by 11″ and which do not lie flat. The USPTO encourages applicants to send photographs of the goods, as long as the mark is clear from the photograph. If filing electronically, the specimen should be submitted as a digitized image in jpg format.

Place the serial number or registration number (once known) on each paper or exhibit filed, including any required checks. If, for some reason neither number is available, please put some other identifying information on the correspondence (e.g., mark, name of applicant, filing date). Promptly inform the USPTO of any change in correspondence address. This can be done through TEAS at *http://eteas.uspto.gov/V2.0/ca200/WIZARD.htm.*

Use the Trademark Applications and Registrations Retrieval (TARR) database at *http://tarr.uspto.gov* to check on the status of any application. You should check the status of your application every six months.

Chapter 6
Trademark Lawyers

In a world where people find their mates through newspaper ads, it is not surprising that businesspeople sometimes select their lawyers from the Yellow Pages. Like marriage, the relationship between lawyer and client is often contracted with too little thought. Of course, your relationship with your lawyer isn't as important as marriage, but when you choose a lawyer to handle a legal matter, you do entrust an important part of your life to him or her for a while. This means that you should use at least as much care in selecting your lawyer as you devoted to buying your last car.

This is especially true with regard to any legal matter related to trademarks. Trademark law is a narrow area of the law about which most lawyers are content to remain ignorant, because it is confusing and sometimes even infuriating and resembles semantics more than it does other areas of the law. Very few lawyers who do not regularly practice trademark law are competent to handle even the most minor trademark matter. This means that you will need a *trademark* lawyer in any of the following situations:

- When you choose a new trademark
- When you expand the use of an existing trademark to additional products or services
- When you file for federal trademark registration
- When you believe that someone is infringing your trademark rights

- When you are accused of infringing someone else's trademark
- When you want to license your trademark to someone else

The first thing to know about finding a lawyer is that the lawyer referral services offered by local bar associations are practically worthless. These services include many fine lawyers in their listings, but they also include more than a few lawyers who are badly educated, inexperienced, predatory, unethical, or all of the above. This is because these services ordinarily refer callers, on a rotating basis, to lawyers who are members of the bar associations that sponsor them, without attempting to evaluate the abilities of the attorneys who are listed. You may be referred to a lawyer who has signed up for the referral service as a "trademark lawyer," but that is probably the lawyer's own evaluation, so you really won't know how extensively the lawyer has practiced trademark law or what level of competence he or she has reached. In other words, these services really offer no more information to the consumer than the Yellow Pages.

109

Most bar associations are like clubs; usually, such an association will accept as a member any lawyer who will pay the association's annual dues and is licensed to practice law where the association is located. The fact that a lawyer possesses a license to practice law is *not* enough to ensure that he or she will give you the help you need in handling a particular matter or treat you fairly. A law license means only that the lawyer who holds it graduated from a law school, passed a character review and the bar exam for the state that issued the license, and has not been disbarred since.

There's a big difference between being the kind of lawyer everyone wants to hire and simply avoiding disbarment. A lawyer with a valid law license may have graduated at the bottom of his class from an unaccredited law school and have passed the bar exam only on the third try. He may be inexperienced, inept, ignorant, and disorganized. He may be an alcoholic or a drug addict. He may be dishonest or greedy. However, unless these failings have so harmed a client that the client filed a formal complaint with the licensing body in the state where the lawyer practices and that body found, after investigation, that the lawyer should be suspended or disbarred, he or she can hang a valid law license on the wall and continue to accept new clients.

Another poor method for finding a lawyer is lawyer advertising. Some good lawyers advertise. However, many lawyers who hawk their services through broadcast and print ads run their practices like factories. You are unlikely to get much individual attention from one of these lawyers. And although the content of lawyer advertising is regulated to some extent, ads for lawyers, which often depend on cheap theatrics for their effect, are really no more reliable than any other sort of advertising. That is, they *may* advertise the services of competent, trustworthy lawyers, but there's no way to tell from the ads whether they actually do. Further, it is unlikely that most firms that advertise will employ any lawyer who is qualified to practice in a highly specialized area such as trademark law.

This means that you should find your trademark lawyer through some means other than the Yellow Pages, a bar-association referral service, or lawyer advertising. These are the easiest methods for locating a lawyer, but they are also the least effective in terms of finding a good one who is suitable for your needs. Compiling a list of trustworthy, qualified lawyers requires some work, but, after all, either the matter for which you need a trademark lawyer is important enough to approach seriously, with some forethought, or it isn't. If you are not willing to expend the time and effort that such an initial screening process requires, you should reconsider whether you really want to pursue a legal solution to your problem or would rather forget the whole thing. There are several ways to come up with a list of good trademark lawyers; none of them is especially difficult.

Perhaps the best way to find a competent, ethical trademark lawyer is to call a lawyer you know and trust for help. If you already have a relationship with a lawyer you like who doesn't practice trademark law, ask that lawyer to recommend three other lawyers who *are* qualified to help you. Most lawyers know, or can find out, which other lawyers are considered able, honest, and experienced in their fields, even if they are not familiar with the specialized work of those other lawyers. And a lawyer whose client you have been and who you trust is likely to be careful in making such recommendations; in fact, if you ask a lawyer for three or four names and he or she responds with only one or two, he or she is being scrupulous by refusing to refer you to someone about whom he or she knows too little.

The best referral is from a lawyer who personally knows the lawyers to whom he or she refers you. This is because most lawyers will be especially careful of their treatment of a client when they know—or think—their actions are likely to be judged by another lawyer. However, a subclass of lawyer referrals to watch out for is the referral to another lawyer in the same firm. It is very possible that the lawyer to whom you are referred under such circumstances will be a paragon of skill and knowledge. It is also possible that you will be referred to a lawyer in the same firm simply because the referring lawyer is more concerned with the firm's income than with your getting the best possible recommendation. Don't reject such referrals out of hand, but make your own judgments. Nothing obligates you to engage the services of any lawyer to whom you are referred—lawyers speak of "their" clients; in reality, their clients should think of "their" lawyers, because the client is the person who calls the shots, although many lawyers forget this fact of capitalism.

If you don't know a lawyer who can recommend one or more trademark lawyers to you, ask several other people whose opinions you respect for a similar list of lawyers. But don't only ask your friends; even if they are true-blue, they may have very little information concerning trademark lawyers. Instead, ask other businesspeople in your town, especially those who own or manage businesses similar to yours. They may have had to solve trademark problems themselves.

Ask three questions of everyone you approach for names of lawyers: 1) "How do you know these lawyers?" 2) "What do you know about them?" and 3) "Why do you think one of them could help me?" Enter the name of any lawyer who is recommended by a reliable source on your master list. After you have three or four names of trademark lawyers, start investigating them.

You probably want to hire a trademark lawyer near you. Although it is easier to work with a local lawyer, trademark lawyers are urban creatures and are seldom found outside sizable cities. You may not be able to find one near you. However, since trademark practice is mostly a matter of specialized paperwork, it is likely that you can successfully manage your lawyer's work through the mail and on the phone, at least after your initial meeting. It is also possible that you will need to hire a lawyer in the same locale as that where suit has been brought against you or where you want to sue someone else. The matter of venue in trademark lawsuits is influenced by several factors, so if you are involved in a trademark dispute, one of your first questions to any lawyer you interview is whether he or she is located and licensed in the right place to defend or bring a suit for you. Any trademark lawyer can handle trademark searches and registrations or other matters in the Trademark Office in Washington, D.C., from anywhere in the United States. This means that a trademark lawyer you hire to advise you in these matters can live near you or in another city altogether—it really doesn't matter.

Your primary tool for investigating the lawyers recommended to you is Martindale.com. This is a free online lawyer-locator service; listings are organized by lawyer name, law firm name, area of practice, and state and city. Historically, this database and its predecessor, the multivolume *Martindale-Hubbell Law Directory*, are very reliable and complete; any lawyer who is actively engaged in practice in the United States will be listed in the Martindale.com database. Lawyers use the Martindale.com database to investigate their adversaries. But there's no reason you can't use it, too. The Martindale.com database is not the best *starting* place for someone in search of a lawyer (unless you find that you need to hire a lawyer in another city). However, it is a very good place to gather information on lawyers; most of this information is self-evident from the entries in the directory.

When you go to the Martindale.com home page, you can click on the "file folder" categories in the middle of the page to organize your search by lawyer name or area of practice. If you want to investigate a particular lawyer, use the "Lawyer" tab and enter her or his name; if you want a list of trademark lawyers in your area, click on the "Location/Areas of Practice" tab. Because lawyers who furnish the information regarding their practice areas tend to be optimistic in naming these areas, you want to be as precise as possible in specifying the practice area name when you search. "Intellectual Property" is one of the category choices under "Select general area of practice"; entering "trademark" in the blank "Or enter specific area of practice" space is better. When you enter your city or state and click on the "Search" button, you will have a list of trademark lawyers in your area. Then you can find out more about the lawyers who have been recommended to you.

If you read a few Martindale.com listings carefully, you can gain some valuable insights into the qualifications of the lawyers on your list, such as:

- **What law schools they attended**—The differences in law school training diminish in importance in direct proportion to the number of years a lawyer has practiced, and, in any event, the good reputation of a school does not ensure that all its graduates are paragons of the legal profession. However, you should at least make sure that any lawyer you consider hiring graduated from an accredited law school, as opposed to one of the numerous unaccredited schools that still operate around the country.

  Ask a reference librarian to tell you whether a law school unfamiliar to you is accredited; you can probably also get this information by calling the administration office for the law school in question.

- **Whether they were members of their law-school law review or moot court team**—Law review membership and moot court experience are earmarks of smart, capable lawyers. Law students compete among themselves to earn a place on their schools' law reviews, which are respected legal journals written, edited, and published by students, or moot court teams, which are like debate teams that compete by trying fictitious lawsuits. A spot on either results in extra training in an important area.

  (This is not the case with some other law school extracurricular activities. You don't have to be Albert Einstein—or Learned Hand—to become, for example, president of the student bar association or of a law fraternity. And despite the fact that lawyers list such memberships in their Martindale.com profiles as if they indicated some accomplishment, any law student whose body is still warm can become a member of a law fraternity.)

- **Where they worked previously**—Judicial clerkships are like finishing school for young lawyers, and former judicial clerks are usually bright, precise, and serious, with high ethical standards. Similarly, a lawyer who once worked for the state attorney general or local district attorney's office or local federal prosecutor is likely to know the players and the terrain of the local civil judiciary system.

- **Whether they have published scholarly articles**—Although most lawyers are technicians rather than scholars, it can't hurt to hire one who has earned the respect of his or her peers for expertise in some area, which is the chief result of publishing articles in law reviews or legal journals. Bear in mind, however, that a lawyer who has published articles on oil-and-gas law, for example, is unlikely to be interested in handling any trademark matter.
- **Whether they are partners or associates in their firms**—Partners in a firm are called "members." Other, often more junior, lawyers are called "associates." Partners have more experience than associates, but associates charge smaller hourly fees than partners. Perhaps the best solution is to hire a junior partner or a senior associate.

When you access the Martindale.com Web site, plan to spend an hour researching the lawyers on your master list and printing out their entries. Take your time. You're on a mission to perfect and protect your trademark, potentially one of the most valuable assets of your business, or to avoid being bested by the plaintiff who is suing you or the defendant you want to go after.

There is one other good online resource for finding trademark lawyers, though the information given is more limited. This is a publication called *Intellectual Property Today*, which publishes the results of an annual survey called Top Trademark Firms. Go to the home page (*www.iptoday.com/index.html*) of this publication, which is geared toward trademark professionals, and click on the heading "The Top 2003 [etc.] Trademark Firms." You will be taken to a PDF-format list of names of law firms whose practice includes a significant percentage of trademark matters. Then you can look up these firms using the Martindale.com database. Or maybe the best way to use the list of top trademark firms is to check out the lawyers on the list your research produces against the *Intellectual Property Today* list.

Remember, though, that you don't have to hire one of the top trademark firms in the country in order to get good service from a trademark lawyer—what you most need is competent advice regarding your trademark concerns at a reasonable price and with reasonable convenience. However, finding that one of the trademark lawyers or firms you have been considering was voted one of the top trademark firms in the country by a group of trademark professionals (other lawyers, business executives, etc.) is a reliable indication that you will be in good, if perhaps costly, hands with that lawyer or firm. This is also a very good place to look if you want to file an infringement suit or if, heaven forefend, you have to defend one—litigation may take all the muscle you can hire to help you.

After you do your online research, you're ready for the next step in finding a trademark lawyer—the screening interview.

Employment Interviews

Clients often forget that their lawyers need them just as much as they need their lawyers. The practice of law is, after all, a way of earning a living. Almost any lawyer, given an appropriate case, will accept you as a client and be grateful for the fees your legal problem creates. This means that you should recognize your first meeting with each of the lawyers on your list of prospective lawyers for what it is, an employment interview. You won't be the only employer of the lawyer you hire, but you will be *an* employer of that attorney and should expect to be treated like the prospective source of revenue that you are.

The first thing to do is to call for an appointment with each of the lawyers on your master list of prospects. When you call, make sure that you mention two things to the people who answer the phone: 1) that you are a prospective client and 2) that you have been referred to the lawyer you are calling. These statements will get most of the lawyers you call to the phone. You can probably eliminate some of your prospective attorneys from consideration on the basis of these initial phone calls. If you like the sound of a lawyer during your first phone call to him or her, ask for a brief interview appointment. It may seem to you that it would be more efficient to interview the lawyers on your list by telephone, but you'll find out more about them and get a better feel for which one you want to hire if you visit their offices.

Any lawyer you call, or the lawyer's secretary, will tell you at the time you make the appointment whether there will be a charge for this initial consultation meeting. Don't interpret a fee for your first meeting as a sign that the lawyer who charges it is not for you. It is likely that any lawyer with whom you meet will give you some useful advice during the course of the meeting and, in any event, lawyers make money by selling their labor by the hour and some of the best charge for *every* hour they work. However, just as many good lawyers do not charge for initial meetings, regarding such meetings as a necessary predicate to a new client relationship rather than actual billable time.

Your screening interviews should be both short enough to be efficient and long enough to determine the answers to a few basic questions.

If you are involved in any conflict between two marks, it may be inevitable that your dispute will ripen into a lawsuit. Any lawyer who practices trademark law should be able to help you clear a new mark, file to register it, and use it properly. However, not all trademark lawyers have significant experience in trademark litigation, especially if they have been in practice only a few years. This means that you should hire a lawyer who has the ability to represent you in litigation or, at least, one who can call on the more extensive litigation experience of another lawyer in the same firm.

And although you should arm yourself for war, your goal should be a treaty; that is, you should try to settle any dispute on a satisfactory basis before it becomes a lawsuit. Litigation should be avoided because its costs so often outweigh its benefits, even for plaintiffs who prevail in court. To ensure that you will be able to achieve the results you want with as little expenditure of time and money as possible, you will want to hire an attorney who is open to the idea of settling your dispute without full-fledged litigation. Because litigators, like surgeons, often see the most extreme remedy available as the only one, you should also ask what success any lawyer you interview has had in settling disputes out of court, either by means of settlement agreements negotiated between lawyers or through some variety of alternative dispute resolution. Remember Ambrose Bierce's definition of litigation: "A machine which you go into as a pig and come out of as a sausage."

After you briefly describe the matter with which you need help, you should ask each lawyer you interview for a brief preliminary assessment of your chances of success. Pay attention to their answers; lawyers learn to make pretty reliable judgments even in on-the-spot evaluations. And remember that if a lawyer tells you that your mark is unregistrable or infringes another mark or that you are not likely to prevail in a dispute or lawsuit, he or she is obligated to give an honest opinion. You can do whatever you like with the information, but no lawyer can tailor an opinion just to tell you what you want to hear.

Besides what you can learn about a lawyer from the Martindale.com Web site, there are several other indicators that you will be pleased with an attorney. Keep the following guidelines in mind when you interview the lawyers you consider hiring.

Remember that many of the best lawyers do not practice in big firms with luxurious offices in ritzy buildings. Before you are too impressed by a lawyer's fancy office, remember that it is the clients of that lawyer who pay for the oriental rugs and original art.

Remember, too, that the standards for membership in most bar associations are lenient; i.e., any lawyer who is licensed in the locality for which the bar association is organized and will pay the requisite dues can become a member. This means that a lawyer's memberships in his or her local, state, and national bar associations mean very little as far as establishing whether he or she is the better-than-average attorney you want to hire. Lots of the framed certificates indicating membership in organizations with fancy names that you may see in the offices of the lawyers you interview mean absolutely nothing to you as a consumer of legal services. However, certificates that indicate further training past law school or certification by some national association show, at least, a lawyer who is concerned with keeping current and developing the abilities necessary to adequately represent his or her clients.

Pay attention to the support staff you see in each lawyer's office. Past a point, it is immaterial to most people who need a lawyer's services whether the lawyer commands a platoon of secretaries, paralegals, and associates, since no client except a big corporation that needs mountains of paperwork churned out before next Wednesday is likely to need the services of all those other people. However, a good secretary, a skilled paralegal, or a sharp associate can make a client's life easier and diminish legal fees by making or returning phone calls that would otherwise be billed by the lawyer and handling—without charge or at a reduced rate—the more routine work performed for a client. Ask any lawyer you interview which other people in the firm would be working on your case and what their qualifications are. Try to meet these people before you terminate the interview. Give the lawyer points for friendly, intelligent subordinates who look and act like professionals.

Even if you are impressed with an attorney after your meeting, don't hire him or her on the spot. Most successful lawyers are skilled at selling themselves to prospective clients; an honest lawyer won't make promises he or she can't keep, but you should make allowances for the mild sales pitch any lawyer who is interested in your business will make, if for no other reason than that lawyer enthusiasm has been known to wane after a client has been "landed"—like a fish. This means that you should give yourself time to reflect on the substance of your meetings with the lawyers on your list and to compare your impressions of all of them and their evaluations of your trademark problem. The bigger the problem, the longer you should consider how to handle it and who should help you. Even if you like a particular lawyer, things may look different after you meet with the next one.

Give yourself at least a week for your round of interview meetings. Your time and money will be well spent. By the time your meetings are completed, you will have had the advantage of the preliminary opinions of several lawyers about the cost of the work you need help with or your chances of success in settling or winning your dispute, and you will be considerably more educated about the issues involved and will have completed a crash course in Lawyers and Their Habitats.

When you make up your mind which lawyer you want to hire, call that lawyer to tell him or her that you want to engage his or her services. If you didn't like any of the lawyers you interviewed enough to hire one of them, repeat your research and start interviewing again. If any matter is too complicated for you to handle or settle on your own, it is important to get the right lawyer to help you, since the wrong one may be no help at all or even an impediment to your goals.

After you have hired a lawyer, you must know how to recognize common failings of lawyers to protect yourself against them. Regrettably, lawyers, as a class, are subject to most of the failings to which the rest of humankind is prey. Since lawyers are only human, you may never find one who doesn't displease you in some way. However, because lawyers *are* human, put up with your lawyer's foibles if his or her work is good and he or she seems truly concerned with your best interests. Good lawyers share most, if not all, the following characteristics.

Eight Signs of a Good Lawyer

1. **Your lawyer returns your phone calls promptly.** Lawyers are like dentists; they are paid only for the work they perform. This means that your lawyer tries to turn every moment of the workday into billable time and that he or she probably really is "on the phone" or "in a meeting" or "in court" when you call. Moreover, as a time management technique, many lawyers never *take* telephone calls but, rather, return their calls only during the periods of the day they set aside for *making* calls. Don't be offended if you can't get your lawyer on the line every time you call.

   However, pay attention and complain if your lawyer does not get back to you promptly. "Promptly" usually means a return call the same day you call. It certainly means a return call within twenty-four hours. It also means that your lawyer's secretary will call to let you know that your lawyer is traveling or otherwise unavailable if he or she cannot call you back within twenty-four hours.

2. **Your lawyer keeps you informed.** One of a lawyer's more important duties to his or her clients is to keep them well informed of the progress and status of the matters they entrust to him or her. Lawyers are simply skilled agents who act on behalf of their clients only to the extent that those clients direct and authorize them to do so. Therefore, the entire lawyer-client relationship is premised on the assumption that the client will be kept informed by the lawyer. This means that you should receive copies of any trademark searches conducted for you, any Trademark Office filings and correspondence, all of your lawyer's substantive communications with your adversary's attorney, and any documents such as court filings, depositions, responses to interrogatories, etc., as well as an occasional phone call or update letter. No important transaction should occur without your prior knowledge and consent.

   This does not mean that your lawyer must check with you every time he or she picks up the phone or writes a letter, but, rather, that he or she should act only within mutually agreed parameters. If your lawyer seems to have forgotten that he or she works for *you*, complain about it. If he or she doesn't reform after your complaint, get another lawyer.

3. **Your lawyer keeps commitments.** Every lawyer must reschedule a meeting or ask for an extension of a deadline occasionally, but there is no excuse short of being hospitalized or stuck in a blizzard that will suffice to explain away a lawyer's missing an important deadline or failing to show up for a meeting, deposition, or court appearance. Lawyers who miss deadlines and can't be relied on to show up when they say they will lose the respect of other lawyers and of judges, their credibility is damaged and, consequently, they may be less able to successfully negotiate on your behalf. You can lose important rights because of your lawyer's disinterest, disorganization, or overbooking.

If your lawyer misses (as opposed to rescheduling) any important commitment without a really good reason, view him or her as an unexploded hand grenade; that is, get as far away from him or her as possible, as soon as possible, to avoid the injury that *will* result from his or her inability or unwillingness to handle your business carefully.

4. **Your lawyer follows your instructions.** The word "attorney" means simply "agent." Lawyers stand in the place of their clients and speak and act for them only to the extent that they are authorized to do so. Any lawyer who loses sight of this fact has ceased to act as an agent for her or his clients and has become, at least potentially, a loose cannon. Don't expect a lawyer who views you only as a vehicle for exercising his or her bag of professional tricks to miraculously change. Cut your losses and find an attorney who will take instruction.

However, don't view your lawyer's resistance to particular directives as mutiny. Lawyers are supposed to exercise their own informed judgment and any lawyer who blindly follows the orders of a client has abdicated a large part of a lawyer's professional duty. Expect that your lawyer will, in any given situation, enumerate for you the alternatives available to you, evaluate the wisdom of each of those alternatives, and make recommendations for action. The final decision in any such situation should be yours.

You should expect that your lawyer will frankly tell you what is objectionable about any instruction that you give to which he or she objects, and you should know that any ethical lawyer will resign from representing you if you insist that he or she participate in any dishonest strategy. Watch out for a lawyer who doesn't object strongly to any suggestion that he or she stretch the truth or engage in any sort of monkey business. People seldom direct their dishonesty in only one direction; you may find that you are on the receiving end of your lawyer's lack of scruples if you expect or tolerate ethical corner-cutting from him or her.

5. **Your lawyer never makes inflated claims regarding his or her abilities.** As much as lawyers wish otherwise, no lawyer can really predict with certainty the outcome of any legal proceeding or negotiation. Regardless of how skilled your lawyer or how just your position, there are factors in any matter before the Trademark Office or in any trademark dispute over which neither you nor your lawyer has any control at all—the judgments of the Trademark Office or the attitudes and agenda of your adversary and of your adversary's attorney. No amount of skilled lawyering can persuade the Trademark Office to grant a registration when the trademark statute or the *Trademark Manual of Examining Procedure* dictates otherwise. And a really determined bad guy can derail even the most reasonable and competent attorney's strategies for a fair settlement of a dispute.

If you are in court, the number of important factors out of your attorney's control increases. Among the things that are uncontrollable, there is no more unpredictable and unassailable factor than the judge who hears your case. Many judges are wise and fair and struggle to mete out the justice that they are supposed to dispense. Others make arbitrary and unfair rulings that are, seemingly, based more on what they had for breakfast than on any reasoned interpretation of the law.

All this is by way of saying that no lawyer can make reliable claims of success. During the course of a dispute or lawsuit, events

121

can occur that no one can predict or control or mitigate; such events can defeat any lawyer. If you hear the words "I've never lost a suit," or "I've got that judge in my back pocket," or "This case is a cinch," issue from the mouth of your lawyer, pin him or her down before any such rash statement has evaporated. Your lines are "Is that so? It seems impossible that you've never lost a suit," and "What, exactly, makes you think you can persuade that judge to see things our way?" and "Really? If our winning is a foregone conclusion, then why didn't the defendant settle out of court?" Get another lawyer if you find that any large percentage of your lawyer's discussions embody such delusions of grandeur. One of the primary jobs of a lawyer is to communicate with precision. Your lawyer's routine overstatement of his or her abilities is likely to cause problems; at the least, such behavior makes him or her an unreliable advisor. Look for a sober, serious, careful lawyer instead. A serious lawyer may not be as entertaining, but he or she won't lead you down the garden path or out on a limb, either.

6. **Your lawyer is never overly aggressive or hostile.** Anyone who thinks that every good lawyer eats nails for breakfast should reconsider that assumption. Actually, there are very few lawyers for whom a consistent posture of aggression or hostility is effective for anything other than giving clients a false sense of security. As a practical matter, a lawyer who is always aggressive is not an effective representative for his or her clients. Lawyers should be fearless enough to ask for what their clients want, clever enough to figure out how to get it, and bold enough to engage in the occasional bluff. However, they also should keep in mind, *at all times*, the best interests of their clients. A lawyer who only knows how to fight and intimidate his or her adversaries is a hack who is lacking several of the tools a good lawyer knows how to use. The abilities to negotiate and strategize are at least as important to most lawyers as the ability to fight. Think about it. If your lawyer's actions only operate to activate the defenses of your adversary, it is much more likely that you will find yourself in a full-blown fight than able to make a reasonable settlement. Unless you want to spend your retirement fund paying the fees of an attorney who loves a good fight,

expect your lawyer to control his or her temper and to expend his or her aggression in some manner other than useless sparring on your behalf.

7. **Your lawyer is always frank when answering your questions.** Sometimes lawyers, who are prone to get carried away on the wings of their own oratory, forget the value of plain statements of fact. This sort of tin-pot eloquence will never be eradicated completely from the repertoire of most lawyers, and it is unlikely in the extreme that it will vanish from the armory of litigators, many of whom are hams at heart. Further, some of your lawyer's windy explanations may be necessary to convey the information you request. Clients always think that anything can be explained briefly; in reality, a long, confusing explanation may really be the best answer possible to a question, even though the necessity for its length may not be apparent to the client.

However, you should pay attention if the answers you get from your lawyer are always too vague to satisfy your inquiries. If this long-windedness is chronic, ask your lawyer to respond to your questions more plainly and with more brevity. If he or she won't or can't change, consider whether the long-windedness is really intentional obfuscation. Long, complicated answers may be simply an occupational trait of lawyers, but mendacity should not be. Regardless of this, some lawyers do engage in various sorts of prevarication, ranging from hedging to outright lying, even with their clients, to whom they owe *at least* the truth. Any evasion of the truth by a lawyer in any statement to a client is the sign of an incompetent lawyer who is covering up her or his inadequacies or a lawyer who, like a cat with a mouse, is manipulating the client for selfish ends.

Don't allow your lawyer to toy with you or the matter that you have entrusted to him or her. But don't discharge him or her until you have asked for an explanation of what you think is a lie. If your lawyer's explanation is not convincing, get another lawyer.

8. **Your lawyer never overbills you.** Because lawyers must make judgment calls at every turn in handling almost any client matter, it is often difficult to know when a lawyer is billing you for

123

make-work. However, it is important to question your lawyer if you think you are being billed for unnecessary work, because an uncomplaining client who pays excessive bills without question can count on receiving more and bigger bills from his or her lawyer, who may view the client as a fatted calf.

No fee statement should come as a surprise to you. When you engage your lawyer's services, you should receive a letter or be asked to sign a short agreement that specifies your lawyer's hourly rate and billing policies. If the matter you entrust to your lawyer involves a trademark dispute or lawsuit and your lawyer agrees to work on a contingency-fee basis, you should receive a detailed fee agreement specifying 1) what share of any award or settlement amount your lawyer will be entitled to; 2) what expenses you will be expected to pay; and 3) whether other expenses will come off the top of the judgment or settlement or will be deducted *from your share* of that amount.

Question any fee or expense you think is excessive. If your lawyer does not answer your questions frankly and to your satisfaction, don't pay the disputed amount until you are satisfied that the charge is fair, or offer to pay only what you believe is fair under the circumstances. Any lawyer with your interests at heart should be willing to explain any legitimate fee or billed expense that puzzles you and, within reason, to modify any billing practice to which you object.

Unless a lawyer has abandoned all pretense of living up to his or her professional and ethical standards, even a polite complaint letter or phone call from a client is likely to produce better behavior. In fact, any complaint, except one about truly outrageous behavior, should be polite and, to the extent possible, nonaccusatory. Despite occasional evidence otherwise, most lawyers will conduct themselves professionally if their clients make it obvious that they expect good treatment. The alternative, of course, is that a lawyer you reprimand, even mildly, will refuse to reform. If this happens and the transgression is substantive, find another lawyer. You get the behavior you put up with.

Off With Their Heads

And then there are the sins of lawyers that require summary execution, without discussion, without possibility of a reduced sentence. It may be unlikely that any lawyer you investigate before hiring will ever commit any of these sins, all of which are major breaches of a lawyer's duty to his or her client. However, although lawyers don't like to admit that any such breaches ever occur, they sometimes do. In the burgeoning population of American lawyers, there are bound to be some who are truly corrupt, because of alcoholism or drug abuse or gambling, because of ineptitude, because of depression or some other mental illness, or because of simple, garden-variety venality.

For lawyers, these mortal sins are failing to keep a client's secrets, stealing from a client, and lying to a client.

If at any time you find that your lawyer has committed any of these sins, terminate his or her services immediately by means of a hand-delivered letter in which you demand prompt delivery to you of your file and the return of any retainer or deposit against charges for legal work that has not yet been performed. Threats seldom produce the desired results and, if they are too rash, diminish the force of the threat, but you should include in your letter a measured statement that you will take your complaint to the lawyer-licensing board for your state if your lawyer fails to comply promptly with your demands. Then, if your lawyer's transgression was serious enough, or has caused you significant harm, file your complaint anyway. You will find that the lawyer-licensing board, which is a division of your state's supreme court, will take your complaint very seriously and that the only lawyer who will criticize your action is the one who will become the subject of the board's investigation.

Managing Your Lawyer

One important factor in obtaining satisfactory legal work that clients often overlook is that almost any lawyer's work will better satisfy his or her client if that person knows how to be a *good* client. Being a good client is part technique and part attitude.

Even a principled lawyer will represent you more satisfactorily if you know how to manage his or her work. There are several techniques that clients can employ to get the best services from their lawyers. Ordinarily, clients learn these lawyer management skills only after they have been through a few battles with the aid of several lawyers. Experience is a good teacher, but when it comes to figuring out how to manage lawyers, learning from experience is a bad method, because the information you need comes only after the fact and because your lawyer's meter is running while you learn.

Fortunately, many techniques for managing a lawyer's work can be employed as easily and effectively by anyone who understands them as by an "experienced" client—a category you may, in any event, want to avoid. Four of the most important lawyer management techniques are as follows:

1. **Give your lawyer the necessary information.** Your lawyer needs accurate information in order to represent your interests. The first thing your lawyer will do is ask you a long list of questions. The more pertinent information you can give your lawyer, the less time he or she will have to spend ferreting out the information, and the smaller your fee bill will be. Try to give your lawyer complete information in an organized form as soon as it is requested. If you don't have the information your lawyer needs but can get it as easily as your lawyer can, gather it yourself to save yourself legal fees.

    A corollary to the principle that your lawyer needs information in order to represent you is that he or she does not need a file cluttered with extraneous information. Points that you think are important may be, in actuality, beside the point. If your lawyer doesn't ask about some topics that you think are pertinent, ask whether the information will help. Save your tale to recount to your friends if your lawyer isn't interested, because the information you considered important is either immaterial, unreliable, inadmissible, or available in some better form elsewhere.

2. **Call your lawyer only when necessary.** It is important to remember that the mere fact that the telephone on your desk is connected to the one in your lawyer's office doesn't mean that it is a good idea to call your lawyer every time you have a question or think of something he or she needs to know. Among other drawbacks, if you are paying your lawyer on an hourly basis, calling him

or her every time you have the urge is likely to result in much higher legal fees. Most lawyers bill a minimum amount of time, usually a quarter hour, for any phone call and the time it takes to draft a file memo concerning the phone call. If your lawyer is working on a contingency-fee basis, too many calls from you will exasperate him or her, since he or she will not earn any more for the extra work you create by calling too often than the agreed-upon share of the settlement amount or judgment paid to you that he or she is already due.

One good technique for reducing time on the phone with your lawyer is to put your thoughts in a concise memo for your file. You don't have to hire a secretary or even learn to type to produce such memoranda—a legible handwritten memo will work. Even if your lawyer reads every word of your memo, less billable time will be consumed than if you furnish this information in the course of several phone calls.

Another good approach is to keep a running list of your thoughts and questions and look over and organize these notes before you call. Then, call your lawyer's secretary and make a phone appointment for fifteen minutes or half an hour in order to ensure that your lawyer will be waiting, with your file open, when you call. This saves endless games of telephone tag and won't create more fees than calling without an appointment. Of course, none of this applies to emergency calls, but in most trademark matters or disputes, there *are* very few true emergencies.

And remember that sometimes it is possible to address the questions you have to a lawyer's secretary or a paralegal or associate. These people are less difficult to get on the phone; if they can't answer your question, it may be possible for them to ask your lawyer the question you need answered and call you back with the answer.

3. **Don't quibble over ordinary charges.** It is understandable and appropriate that clients get upset over unreasonable bills from their lawyers. If you receive a statement from your lawyer that you consider excessive, you *should* complain about it. In fact, it is far better for the long-term health of your relationship with your lawyer to question bills you don't understand than to allow

them to go unchallenged. This does not mean, however, grilling your lawyer, or your lawyer's secretary, about every charge on your statement.

Part of the responsibility for ensuring that no part of your lawyer's statement comes as a surprise is yours. If your lawyer does not furnish you with a written description of his or her billing practices, including a list of the expenses incurred on your behalf that you will be expected to reimburse, ask for one so that you will know what to expect.

Expect to be asked for a retainer fee to cover the initial work that you hire your lawyer to perform and that you may be asked to make further occasional advance payments against fees and significant expenses. Expect to be charged a minimum of a quarter hour for any phone call made or taken by your lawyer on your behalf, including calls to and from you. Expect that all letters will be billed at a minimum of a half hour. Expect to be billed, at a reduced rate, for the services of paralegals. Expect to be billed for expenses incurred on your behalf, including postage, courier fees, long-distance telephone calls, photocopies, travel costs, trademark search fees, Trademark Office and court filing fees, and the costs of court reporters for depositions. In fact, at some firms, expect to be billed for all expenses that are even remotely attributable to work performed for you, including almost everything except the electricity consumed by the lights in your lawyer's office.

But, too, expect that your lawyer or his or her secretary will answer any questions you have about your bills and that, within reason, your objections will be taken seriously and your directions will be followed.

4. **Maintain the right attitude.** Despite what many people may believe, most lawyers don't want passive clients. Such clients often make unrealistic demands on their lawyers, expecting them to pull rabbits out of hats, sometimes in situations where there are no good remedies for the clients' problems. Instead, lawyers want their clients to be, to a large extent, partners in the effort to reach the clients' goals or the search for solutions to the clients' problems. This means that you should take the attitude that the legal matter or problem belongs to you.

This sounds like a restatement of the obvious, but it really isn't. Once you stop thinking of the legal matter or problem you entrust to your lawyer as a matter that will, as a matter of course, be satisfactorily resolved by your lawyer simply because you have turned it over to him or her, and begin to view it as a matter that you may be able to accomplish or solve satisfactorily with the assistance of your lawyer, you will have a realistic view of your situation and will be less likely to be surprised by developments or disappointed by results. Your legal concern is *yours*. Your attorney can help you, but only because you hire him or her, furnish the necessary information and direction, and make the correct choices when the available options are presented to you.

Chapter 7
Trademark Usage

Once a trademark is registered federally, and this means registered in the U.S. Patent and Trademark Office, not simply registered in one or more states or in another country, the trademark owner is allowed to use, and should use, a trademark registration notice in conjunction with the registered mark. Use of such notice warns others that the mark is registered and that ownership of it is claimed by the owner, and allows the owner to gain certain advantages provided by the federal trademark statute.

Notice of Federal Registration

The most familiar trademark registration notice is the "circle R" symbol, or ®; the ® symbol should be used "on the shoulder" of the registered mark (in the superscript position), or in the subscript position, very near it. Alternate forms of notice are "Registered in the U.S. Patent and Trademark Office," or "Reg. U.S. Pat. & Tm. Off."; these alternate forms of notice should be used with an asterisk placed close to the registered mark and a corresponding asterisk preceding the notice itself, which usually appears in a footnote position on the package or label or in the ad, etc.

It is important to know that the forms of trademark notice specified above are the only forms of notice that have the legal effect of proper trademark registration notice. You can't, in short, make up your own.

Not using the ® symbol (or one of the other prescribed forms of trademark registration notice, although they are generally used less often and may, in fact, be less likely to be recognized as notice of registration than the familiar ® symbol) in conjunction with a federally registered trademark will not invalidate the registration, but it can deprive the trademark owner of some very important advantages in the event that the registered mark is infringed.

If the Rounder Doughnut Company registers its trademark HOLE IN ONE for packaged doughnuts sold in grocery stores, everyone else in the world who wishes to adopt and use in the United States a confusingly similar trademark for doughnuts is presumed by law to have notice that HOLE IN ONE is owned by Rounder, even if they do not conduct a trademark search and discover Rounder's federal registration. If Burgerama, Inc., adds to the breakfast menu for its fast food restaurants a doughnut it calls HOLE IN ONE, the Rounder Doughnut Company will sue Burgerama, since consumers could easily confuse the fast food restaurants' doughnuts with those marketed by Rounder. By virtue of its federal registration, Rounder will be entitled to an injunction from the court ordering Burgerama to cease use of HOLE IN ONE.

But if Rounder also wants to be awarded an amount of money representing the damages it has suffered because of Burgerama's infringement or the profits of Burgerama attributable to the sale of doughnuts under the HOLE IN ONE name before its receipt of Rounder's cease and desist letter, Rounder must have used the ® symbol (or another prescribed form of notice) on its packaging. If Rounder did not use a trademark registration notice with its mark, the court is allowed by law to award only damages or profits that resulted from actions of Burgerama *after* it received actual, specific notice that the HOLE IN ONE mark was registered.

Now all this may sound like mumbo jumbo, but it's not. It may seem unlikely that something that a commercial artist does or does not do in creating the artwork for a new cereal box or an ad for a vacuum cleaner can determine how much money a federal court can award to the cereal company or the vacuum cleaner company, but that is precisely the case.

The responsibility to make sure that a trademark registration symbol is properly used with a registered trademark belongs ultimately to the trademark owner. If you are not the owner of a trademark or responsible for managing a company that owns it, you have no legal obligation to find out whether a trademark owned by your client or your employer is registered or to make sure that the trademark registration symbol is used. However, no client or employer is going to object to your raising the question of the proper use of a registered mark. If you want to keep your clients or employer happy, you must be at least conversant with the basics of proper usage of the trademark registration symbol and notations, since that usage so directly affects valuable rights of trademark owners.

An important related consideration is the improper use of the ® symbol (or another of the prescribed forms of trademark registration notice). If trademark registration notice is used in conjunction with a trademark that is not federally registered, or used with a trademark appearing in advertising for, or in conjunction with, goods or services for which it is not registered, serious consequences can result, including the loss of the trademark owner's right to recover for trademark infringement or to register the mark federally.

Many people, even people who should know better, think that the ™ symbol they often see printed next to trademarks is the equivalent of the ® symbol and has some legal effect. In reality, it does not. The ™ symbol is sometimes used by trademark owners as a "no trespassing" sign to indicate that someone is claiming ownership of the mark. It has no real legal effect but can be useful, since there are no requirements to be met before it can be used and there really is no such thing as misuse of it. In addition, many trademarks are not yet federally registered, or have been denied federal registration, or cannot be federally registered for one reason or another. Use of the ™ symbol, which usually appears in the same locations as those used for placement of the ® symbol, can warn others that the owners of these names consider them to be trademarks and claim ownership of them. (Another form of informal trademark notice, the ᔆᴹ symbol, is often used in the same ways that the ™ symbol is used when the mark in question names services.)

Similar to the ™ symbol is some statement such as "The name DENTAL ASSISTANT'S QUARTERLY is a trademark of the Dental Assistance Association of America." Statements of this sort have exactly the same effect (some) and uses (several) that the ™ symbol does; that is, they are another variety of informal trademark notice.

Use It Correctly or Lose It

Trademarks, whether registered or not, can theoretically last perpetually. As long as someone markets goods or services under a name or symbol, it has a legal existence as a trademark. However, trademarks "die" every day.

Trademark Abandonment

One of the ways a trademark dies is by "abandonment"; that is, the owner of the mark ceases using it. This ordinarily happens to trademarks owned by underfinanced or unskilled marketers and to those that name unsuccessful products or services. Such abandonment is, of course, a result of a decision of the trademark owner. (Does Ford use EDSEL for *anything* anymore?) Sometimes a mark is abandoned because of some spectacularly bad event associated with it. The 1996 Valu-Jet air disaster in Florida may have resulted in the abandonment of the cartoon-plane logo that became familiar to people who had never before heard of the airline through weeks of news footage about the crash; Valu-Jet was sold and merged with another company soon afterward, and the Valu-Jet name and logo fell into what will probably become permanent disuse. When a trademark really has been abandoned—that is, it has fallen out of use for a substantial period of time and its owner has no intent to revive it—it can be used by another marketer because it has ceased to represent the commercial reputation of the products of its original owner. (But remember that it is risky to adopt and use a mark that you believe to be abandoned without some investigation into the intentions of the original owner of the mark. Suspension of use of a mark may occur for several reasons other than the owner's intention to abandon it and, even if the owner does eventually abandon the mark, such intent cannot be deduced merely from a short period of disuse of the mark.)

133

Trademark Genericness

The second way trademarks die is almost the converse of the first situation, because such deaths often befall very famous trademarks and always occur against the will of the trademark owner. This form of trademark death results when a trademark becomes "generic," that is, when the word that formerly served as a trademark comes to signify to the general public the kind of product or service it names rather than representing a particular brand of that product or service. This form of trademark extinction should be of great interest to anyone who owns a trademark or participates in the marketing of the product or service it names. That is because loss of a trademark through its becoming generic is always a great financial loss to trademark owners, especially considering the fact that many trademarks become generic because they name extremely popular products or services; a mark that names a popular and successful product or service is a valuable mark indeed. Marketing people, graphic designers, and advertising creative people are the first line of defense against genericness.

"Escalator," "cellophane," "trampoline," "shredded wheat," "mimeograph," "linoleum," and "aspirin," all once named particular products of particular companies; they were trademarks rather than, as now, the generic terms for whole classes of goods. Because they became generic, they lost their status as the names of particular products of particular companies; they can now be used by anyone.

In the case of the former trademark ESCALATOR, a court held that because consumers thought of all moving stairways as "escalators," ESCALATOR had lost its ability to point only to products of the Otis Elevator Company. In the decision that canceled Otis's fifty-year-old trademark registration for ESCALATOR, the court stated that the fact Otis itself had used its trademark in its own ads as "escalator," that is, as a generic term for a class of products, supported the contention that the mark had become generic. Otis and its ad agency goofed, and they paid the price by losing one of the company's most valuable assets, its famous trademark ESCALATOR.

Similar scenarios surrounded the ends of all the former trademarks mentioned above, and others. Ironically, it is the names of unique and innovative products that are most at risk of becoming generic. This is because the name of the first version of a groundbreaking product can come to mean that *type* of product in the minds of consumers, who may refer to all products of the same sort by the trademark of the first one they encountered. XEROX® is one trademark that is presently in danger of becoming a generic term (for photocopy machines and photocopies). LEVI'S®, FORMICA®, WALKMAN®, TUPPERWARE®, KLEENEX®, ROLLERBLADE®, and POST-IT® are similarly endangered.

XEROX

Once a trademark, not always a trademark.

They were once proud trademarks, now they're just names. They failed to take precautions that would have helped them have a long and prosperous life.

We need your help to stay out of there. Whenever you use our name, please use it as a proper adjective in conjunction with our products and services: e.g., Xerox copiers or Xerox financial services. And never as a

verb: "to Xerox" in place of "to copy," or as a noun: "Xeroxes" in place of "copies."

With your help and a precaution or two on our part, it's "Once the Xerox trademark, always the Xerox trademark."

Team Xerox. We document the world.

135

Avoiding Genericness

In some cases, a company may be virtually powerless to prevent its trademark for a unique product that captures the public's imagination from falling into common usage as the name of the *type* of product rather than the name of one particular brand of that product. "Nylon," "yo-yo," and "zipper" may have been marks that no amount of care could have preserved from genericness. However, in almost every case a company can at least put up a fight to halt the fall of its marks into genericness, by care in its use of them and, when necessary, by ads that promote the names as trademarks.

A mark may become generic because consumers and the media begin to use it to refer to a class of products rather than to the products of one particular marketer, and it is important to take measures to squelch such incipient genericness. A bigger problem, however, is misuse of the trademark by its owner or those who use it under the owner's control, since such misuse can be a critical factor in a court's decision whether a mark has become generic, thereby losing its trademark significance.

The very least that is required of any trademark owner is that it police its own use of its trademark and the use of the mark by its licensees and agents, such as ad agencies and retailers. Proper use of a company's trademark can have very real dollars-and-cents consequences for the trademark owner. Trademarks are often considered to be among the most valuable assets of the companies that own them because they often represent a certain steady share of the market for the products they name. If a trademark becomes generic (and therefore available for use by anyone), that market identity and share are lost.

Proper trademark usage, crucial for protecting the exclusive ownership of a trademark, involves a few rules of "trademark grammar" that all marketing people should know and use. Remember that:

- **A trademark is always an adjective, never a noun**—It is "CHEER® laundry detergent," never simply "CHEER"; hence "Get your clothes clean with CHEER® laundry detergent." Think of "CAMPBELL'S® soups," "TOTES® umbrellas," "HOLIDAY INN® hotels," and "POLAROID® film."
- **A trademark is a proper adjective**—It is "ROLLERBLADE® in-line skates," never "I want some ROLLERBLADEs." Think of "LEVI'S® jeans," "EGG MCMUFFIN® breakfast sandwiches," and "CHANEL® perfumes."

- **A trademark is always singular, never plural**—It is "EASY SPIRIT® shoes," never simply "EASY SPIRITs." Think of CRAYOLA® crayons," "APPLE® computers," and "KLEENEX® tissues."
- **Trademark variations should be avoided**—Trademarks should never be made possessive, i.e., it is never "HEINZ's great taste" but is, rather, "The great taste of HEINZ 57® steak sauce." And if the mark is registered or ordinarily used in one typeface or format, don't change its customary appearance without careful thought; otherwise, how will consumers recognize their old friend? Similarly, avoid changes in the verbal content of the mark at all costs; it is "Fried to a golden brown with CRISCO® all-vegetable shortening!" not "CRISCO-ed to perfection again!"

Although these rules aren't really that difficult to remember or follow, not all trademark owners follow them religiously—maybe because they are uninformed or careless or because they think their marks are so famous they can ignore the rules. You, however, should tend to your own mark carefully, in the hope and expectation that someday it will become famous enough that you can hire a dozen or so trademark lawyers to do it for you.

The problem may not be remembering or following the rules in using your valuable trademark, but whether *others* do. If you own a trademark or are in a job that requires you to create or approve ads, packaging, signage, press releases, or other materials that embody a trademark, you owe a duty to yourself, or to your employer or client, to see that the mark is used correctly. There are several ways to do this.

Following the Rules

One of the best ways to avoid trademark genericness is to produce a set of trademark usage guidelines for your company. These guidelines can educate anyone who writes or produces any advertising or public relations materials for you in the proper use of trademarks in general and your mark in particular. It can also be furnished to journalists who write about your product or your company and can be made a part of any agreement to license your trademark to another company (see the discussion on trademark licensing). Your trademark usage guidelines should include a section on graphic standards for the use of anyone who reproduces your mark in any but purely verbal forms. This section should specify colors and typefaces and should give examples of the proper visual forms of your mark.

You can even get creative with these guidelines and print them on T-shirts that you use as trade-show giveaways, style sheets that you furnish to the media, and posters for your retailers. One of the best ways to promulgate guidelines on proper use of your trademark is to post them on your company Web site. (Go to *www.oracle.com/html/3party.html* to view a good example of online trademark usage guidelines. Another good example can be found at *www.mcba.com/general_legal.html#trademarks*.) The main thing is to get the word out to anyone who has or may have any reason to use your mark in or on anything the public sees.

Another good method for ensuring proper use of your trademark by your company and its agents and licensees is to appoint a trademark czar to review and approve any materials that embody your trademark before they are produced and duplicated. Anyone given this responsibility should be really capable of understanding and carrying out the job. This is not a task that can be delegated to a file clerk who doesn't have enough to do; your trademark enforcer should be a lawyer or senior marketing person who thoroughly understands trademark law and the purposes of correct trademark usage as well as the consequences of incorrect usage. Establish a formal system for review of anything besides internal documents and be consistent in enforcing the rules of usage that you have decreed apply to your mark. Treat the person who is charged with protecting your trademark with at least as much respect as you give your chief financial officer; if you have a hit product on your hands, the trademark that names it will be well worth the attention.

Fending Off Infringers

The law imposes upon trademark owners the obligation to police their trademarks. That is, the quid pro quo for the protection the law gives your commercial reputation is the obligation to protect that reputation from those who would damage it and to take action to ensure that the mark continues to point to *one* source for the goods or services it names. The trademark owner's interests are concurrent with those of consumers: if the trademark remains strong and distinctive, it will become more valuable and consumers may continue to rely on the mark as an indicator of a quality product.

Policing a trademark means keeping an eye out for marks that are similar to your mark and acting quickly to stop the use of any that you think infringe it. There are lots of ways to do this, and many degrees of vigilance. Most trademark owners watch the trade publications for their industry; consciously or unconsciously, one of their reasons for doing so is to discover whether any marketer of a similar product or service is using a name or symbol similar to their own trademarks. If they discover such uses, they will immediately take action, usually by calling their lawyers. All this is obvious. Any businessperson needs to keep up with what is going on in his or her area of commerce and most businesspeople know that a mark that is too similar to their own can present big problems, even if they don't know that what they would be complaining about is trademark infringement.

Finding out about less direct conflicts may be more difficult. Large corporations use in-house paralegals and employ "watching services" to discover the use of any marks that may conflict with their marks. These trademark owners review trade publications, of course, but they also carefully watch the weekly *Trademark Official Gazette* (TMOG), which you can access online, for free, at *www.uspto.gov/web/trademarks/tmog*. Searching the TMOG every week can be a tedious task, but your expenditure of time will be repaid if and when you locate a mark published for opposition that you feel infringes your mark. If you find a mark that is too close to your own, call a trademark lawyer to help you file a Notice of Opposition (to the registration of the mark) with the Trademark Office. This is not an unusual event.

Corporations typically challenge marks that are published for opposition if they seem at all close to those the corporations own. Sometimes big companies challenge marks that are *not* really similar to their own marks by filing or threatening to file opposition proceedings in an effort to halt the granting of registration for the new marks. Many such disputes, especially those involving marks that are not really threats to an established mark, are settled by mutual agreement before the opposition proceeding is actually commenced. The trademark owner's idea, in such a circumstance, may be to give itself time to investigate and to consider whether there *would* be an infringement. It may also be that the trademark owner wants to be able to demonstrate that it acts promptly to stop any threat to its established mark. Courts look at such evidence in evaluating whether a trademark owner has a history of protecting its mark from infringers.

Nevertheless, it must be said that nothing in the law requires a trademark owner to rush to the courthouse to file a trademark infringement suit every time there is a question of infringement. There are effective methods for settling trademark infringement disputes besides slugging it out in court. And quite often trademark owners may be unsure whether the actions of another marketer really do constitute infringement; for example, does the name of its software program infringe your registered mark for an LSAT review course? However, if you "sleep on your rights" long enough and fail to challenge an infringer, a court hearing your tardy trademark infringement suit may rule that your previous failure to object to the actions of the defendant you are suing for infringement has allowed that defendant to depend on your apparent acquiescence to its use of the suspect mark and that to enjoin that use now would be unfair.

All this means that there are two rules for policing trademarks. The first rule is "Rust never sleeps"; that is, vigilance against trademark infringers must be ceaseless and tireless to be effective—you must know what is going on in the marketplace, which is both the birthplace and the stomping ground for trademarks, which do not exist at all if they do not exist there. The second rule is "Walk softly, but carry a big stick"; that is, don't file a trademark infringement suit until you are sure of your facts, have tried to settle the dispute satisfactorily out of court, and have sought competent advice about the probable outcome of your suit, but be ready to act decisively if you determine that you *must* sue to stop the erosion of your own rights.

Although it is important from the inception of your trademark to use it correctly and to see that others do so, the more famous it becomes and the more successful the product it names, the more vigilance it deserves. A viable trademark, that is, a memorable mark that is capable of federal registration, is like a small savings account. If you tend it carefully, it will grow in value. This means that you should watch out for marks that are similar to your fledgling mark and act quickly to stop the use of any that you think infringe it. And if someone uses your mark in a way that could contribute to its becoming generic, take a cue from the owners of the most valuable trademarks and write a letter asking that person to reform—it can be a nice letter, but it needs to be firm and to give specific examples of correct use of your mark. Let them know that you are watching.

To find out more about trademarks and how to protect and manage them, call the International Trademark Association (INTA) at (212) 768–9887 or visit the INTA's Web site at *www.inta.org*. The INTA, an association of (mostly corporate) trademark owners, publishes a number of reliable publications that are useful to trademark owners, among them handbooks on trademark searching and trademark administration, which is the management and protection of a trademark. Many are written for marketing people and other business executives rather than for lawyers. Annual dues for the organization are $575 for companies that have annual sales of $100 million or less, $850 for larger companies, and $700 for advertising agencies. These fees may be prohibitive for anyone but prosperous trademark owners, but many of the INTA's programs, such as seminars on trademark law and trademark issues, and publications, are available to nonmembers. Ask the INTA to send you information about the association and a list of its publications.

Condemned to Anonymity

The following terms were held by the Trademark Office or a court to be incapable of serving as indicators of particular sources for the goods and services they named because they had become, in the minds of consumers, generic terms for those products or services. After being declared to be nontrademarks, these terms became free for anyone to use in describing products or services and ceased to be the exclusive property of their originators.

AL-KOL for rubbing alcohol
ASPIRIN for acetyl salicylic acid
BABY OIL for mineral oil
BATH OIL BEADS for bath oil, water softener, and perfume
BODY SOAP for body shampoo
BRASSIERE for women's bras

BUNDT for a type of ring coffee cake
CELLOPHANE for transparent cellulose sheets
COLA for a soft drink
COMPUTER LEARNING CENTER for computer courses
THE COMPUTER STORE for retail computer sales services
CONSUMER ELECTRONICS MONTHLY for a magazine for electronics enthusiasts
COPPERCLAD for copper-coated conductors
CUBE STEAK for tenderized steaks
DRY ICE for carbon dioxide in solid form
EASTER BASKET for an Easter floral basket
ESCALATOR for moving stairways
EXPORT SODA for an exported soda cracker
FLOR-TILE for wooden flooring
FLOWERS BY WIRE for intercity floral delivery services
FLUID ENERGY for hydraulic/pneumatic equipment
HAIR COLOR BATH for a hair-coloring preparation
HARD TO FIND TOOLS for a tool mail-order service
HOAGIE for sandwiches
HONEY BAKED HAM for honey-glazed hams
JUJUBES for gum candies
LIGHT BEER for a light-bodied beer
METALOCK for a metal repair method
MONOPOLY for a real estate–trading board game
MONTESSORI for an education method and associated toys
MULTISTATE BAR EXAMINATION for a bar examination given in several states
MURPHY BED for beds that fold into a wall or closet for storage
THE PILL for oral contraceptives
POCKET BOOK for paperback books
PRIMAL THERAPY for a type of psychotherapy
PROM for programmable read-only memory computer systems
RUBBER ROPE for an elasticized rubber rope product
SAFE T PLUG for electrical plugs
SHREDDED WHEAT for baked wheat biscuits
SOCIOGRAPHICS for a technique of management consulting
SOFTSOAP for liquid hand soap

SUPER GLUE for rapid-setting cyanoacrylate adhesives
SURGICENTER for a surgical center
THERMOS for vacuum-insulated bottles
TRAMPOLINE for rebound tumbling equipment
VIDEO BUYERS GUIDE for a magazine for videotape buyers
WORK WEAR for industrial clothing
YO-YO for return tops

Death of a Trademark

In 2000, in a very thorough opinion, a federal district court judge in Manhattan ruled that the name "Pilates" had become a generic term for exercise instruction services and exercise equipment.

Born in Germany, Joseph Pilates began developing the Pilates exercise system while interned in England during World War I. He and his wife Clara emigrated to New York in the 1920s and opened a studio at which they taught his method of exercise. After Mr. Pilates's death in 1976, his wife continued to teach the Pilates method, which became popular with dancers, especially for rehabilitation after dance injuries. They also trained other instructors. The exercise system has since become nationally very popular and prevalent.

The defendant in the lawsuit, a California company named Balanced Body, has since 1976 manufactured equipment for use by followers of the exercise system. The principal plaintiff in the lawsuit, Sean Gallagher, was involved in a business that owned studios that taught the Pilates method and sold Pilates equipment. In 1992, Gallagher acquired trademark registrations for the PILATES service mark and for PILATES STUDIO. Gallagher renamed his exercise studio The Pilates Studio, obtained a Pilates trademark for exercise equipment, started a certification program for Pilates instructors, and began trying to stop use of the Pilates name by anyone else. He sent many cease and desist letters to others who were using the name and brought numerous lawsuits against studios and individuals who taught the Pilates system without having obtained certification from him.

In ruling that Pilates had lost trademark significance, the court based its opinion on several factors, but noted that during their lifetimes Joseph and Clara Pilates had "promoted [the Pilates] method of exercise and attempted to increase its use by the public" and "never did anything to prevent others from using their name to describe what they taught." The court said that since "consumers identify the word 'Pilates' as a particular method of exercise [the] plaintiff cannot monopolize [it]." In consequence, the judge ordered the cancellation of the plaintiff's trademark registrations for the Pilates marks.

In other words, once a trademark has become generic and is used by consumers to denote a kind of product or service rather that a particular product or service, it cannot be retrieved from genericness and restored to trademark status. To some extent, whether a trademark becomes generic is out of the hands of the trademark owner and very much in the hands of those who write, speak, and otherwise use the mark, as the owners of numerous former trademarks, now ruled generic, have discovered.

The winning defendant company in the Pilates case, Balanced Body, has posted the well-reasoned opinion of Judge Miriam Goldman Cedarbaum in PDF format. If you want to read it, go to *www.balancedbody.com/pilates_decision.pdf.*

Chapter 8
Trademark Licensing

One of the best ways to exploit and profit from a trademark is to license it to someone else. Being asked to license your trademark is exciting. It means, among other things, that your mark has become famous enough to attract the attention of consumers and that it stands for a quality product that consumers desire. Since you, as the trademark owner, are paid for the use of your trademark and do not put up the money to manufacture the products or provide the services that you license to be offered in conjunction with your mark, trademark licensing can literally create income from thin air for you.

But the royalty income from any licensing agreement may be a relatively minor incentive to enter the deal compared to the added publicity that your trademark will receive; brand extension is one of the major reasons that the owners of famous trademarks license those marks for products that are unrelated to those that the trademark originally named. Licensing can help you spread the fame of your brand into territories and market segments you would never otherwise have entered. However, if you're not careful, licensing can also result in your killing the goose that laid the golden egg, since allowing anyone to use your trademark whose use of it, for whatever reason, is not controlled by you will result in your loss of your mark.

Because licensing your trademark means letting someone else use it, unless you control that use, you have no way to ensure that your licensee is maintaining the good reputation that your trademark represents. The law views your allowing someone else to use your mark without controlling that use in much the same way it views your acquiescing to use of your mark by infringers who use it without your permission. In either case, your mark has ceased to point to one source—you—for the goods or services it names because you have lost control of how it is used. Where control of the goods and services offered under a mark has been lost by the owner of the mark, the mark may be held to have been abandoned.

Whenever anyone approaches you with a proposal to license your trademark, the first thing you should do after hearing the proposal is to call your trademark lawyer. You can probably create a mark yourself, clear it for use—at least preliminarily—figure out how to use it properly, and maybe register it without the help of a lawyer. This is not the case with trademark licensing. No smart marketer would consider trying to license a valuable trademark without the advice and assistance of a trademark lawyer.

Licensing Agreements

At the very least, a trademark license must be documented in a written agreement. Any attempt at verbal licensing would be viewed by a court as merely "naked licensing," that is, as your having granted permission to someone else to use your trademark without any real effort to control that use. At the least, it is hard to determine just what the terms of any agreement are when they are not memorialized in writing.

And your written trademark licensing agreement must include some very specific language in order to suffice to control the use of your mark. In fact, the word "license" means a permission granted by one person, the "licensor," who owns a right, to another person, the "licensee," who is permitted to exercise some of the rights of the licensor. At a minimum, a trademark licensing agreement should include provisions governing the following important points of agreement:

- **The grant of license**—This provision is the heart of a trademark licensing agreement. It specifies by whom and to whom the right to use the trademark is granted and typically conditions the grant upon the licensee's compliance with the other terms of the agreement.

The permission to use the trademark is usually exclusive, that is, it is granted only to the person(s) or company(ies) specified and the right to use the trademark for the same goods or services is not granted to anyone else during the duration of the licensing agreement. Exclusivity is not, however, mandatory. If a licensor can find more than one licensee willing to pay for the privilege of using a mark for the same goods or services during the same time period and in the same territory, the licensor may make the license nonexclusive.

What is important is the control maintained by the licensor—that control over how the mark is used may be exercised with one licensee or more than one, so long as it is maintained by the licensor. Further, most good licensing agreements provide that if the grant of license is not exercised—that is, if the licensee fails to actually use the trademark in the whole territory and throughout the entire term of the agreement—the agreement may be terminated by the licensor. This serves to free up the valuable trademark for licensing to another company if the licensee fails to exploit it as agreed; in other words, a licensee must "use it or lose it."

147

- **The territory**—this provision specifies in which states or countries the licensee is permitted to use the trademark. You may, for instance, license one company to use your mark in the eastern United States, and another in the western United States. The countries of the world may be divided into whatever small or large territorial "slices" the licensor and licensee agree, but the agreed territory for the license should be specified.

- **The term**—this provision specifies the start and finish dates for the licensee's use of the trademark; usually, a renewal period is specified as available to the licensee if certain conditions are met. As with the territory provision, and just as occupying a rental property past the expiration of a lease is trespassing, any use outside the period specified in the licensing agreement is trademark infringement.

- **The product (or services) licensed**—this provision is also very important. It specifies the exact products or services that the licensee may market under the licensed mark. The more carefully drafted the trademark licensing agreement, the more specific this provision. In other words, a good agreement will specify that the licensed mark may be used in conjunction with "boys' red, blue, yellow, and purple two-eyelet, rubber-soled canvas play shoes, up to size 8, manufactured in accordance with the specifications set out in Exhibit C, attached hereto and made a part of this agreement by this reference." Typically and importantly, the licensee is required to obtain permission from the licensor before using the licensed mark on any other product or to advertise any other service or significant variation of the licensed product or service.

- **Quality specifications for the licensed product (or services)**—one of the ways the licensor controls use of its mark is to agree that the mark may be applied only to products or services of satisfactory quality. This protects the standing of the licensed trademark and the licensor's investment in it, since just as the good reputation of the product or services to which the mark was first applied will reflect favorably on the licensed product or services, an inferior licensed product would reflect badly on the well-regarded trademark and product. These quite detailed specifications are typically written separately and attached to the licensing agreement as an exhibit, that is, on an attached sheet that is specifically agreed to be part of the agreement.

- **Quality control**—a trademark licensor must be able to determine whether the licensee is living up to the quality specifications for the licensed product in order to protect the licensed mark. All proper trademark-licensing agreements contain a provision allowing the licensor, or the licensor's representatives, access to the manufacturing facilities of the licensee in order to ascertain whether the licensed product or service is and continues to meet those quality specifications. The licensor may specify that, in addition to its access to the licensee's facilities, it will have access to the manufacturing records of the licensee and to the personnel who staff the manufacturing operation.

- **Trademark usage**—the actions of a trademark licensee with regard to the way the licensed mark is used accrue to the benefit or detriment of the licensor. This means that the licensor must specify the manner in which the mark may used on the licensed product or in advertising the licensed services and on or in packaging, signage, advertising, etc. Again, such provisions for use of the trademark often appear in an attachment to the basic agreement; this is one very good use for the trademark usage guidelines that trademark owners write for their own use and that of their agents and retailers.

- **Termination provisions**—all good trademark-licensing agreements give the licensor the right to terminate the agreement if the licensee breaches any of the provisions of the agreement. Typically, small or accidental breaches may be "cured" within a specified short period and the agreement will continue if the licensor is satisfied that the complained-of actions or conditions have been remedied. In the event of really significant and intentional breaches of the agreement (such as using the licensed mark outside the agreed territory), the licensor usually may, at its option, immediately terminate the agreement.

- **Payment of royalties**—this is, of course, another of the most important provisions of any trademark-licensing agreement. Typically, the owner of the licensed trademark is paid an agreed fee per unit of the product that is sold in conjunction with the mark. For services, payment is usually a set fee paid periodically during the term of the agreement. Many agreements provide that if the licensee fails to make to the licensor more than one such payment, the licensor may immediately terminate the agreement.

  As for the amount of royalties that will be paid, there is no single standard for determining what royalty is fair. In fact, the most influential factor in determining the royalties a licensor charges a licensee may be what the traffic will bear. Royalty arrangements vary according to the popularity of the licensed mark, the sort of goods or services licensed to be offered in conjunction with the mark, the territory involved, and the competition from other would-be licensees, if any. Royalties do, however, tend to hover in the neighborhood of 10 percent, with some licensors able to command greater royalties and some licensees able to pay smaller ones.

  The best way to figure out what royalty is fair is to locate some other licensors and licensees for marks of similar fame and for similar products; a few phone calls to some of the licensing executives involved in licensing deals similar to yours will help you get a feel for what to ask for.

The best way to proceed with any proposed licensing is to ask the would-be licensee to state the basic terms of the offered agreement (term, products licensed, territory, royalty, etc.) in a letter to you. Before you respond, take the letter to your lawyer and ask for advice concerning the fairness of the terms of the agreement. In addition, get some information about the would-be licensee; it's a lot easier to work with a solvent company that can do what it says it can than to find yourself one of the creditors of an insolvent company. Ask for references from other companies that have licensed their marks to the company that wants to license yours. And make sure that your lawyer writes the licensing agreement or, at least, that the first-draft contract offered to you by your licensee is thoroughly negotiated by your lawyer before you sign it. There's a big difference between your paper and theirs—it's often much easier to get the deal you want when you start from a contract your lawyer drafted for you.

Call Your Lawyer

And don't get the idea that you can write your own trademark agreement. Any contract you write yourself is likely to be like an airplane that you build in your basement—you won't know whether it is constructed properly until it crashes and burns. Trademark licensing agreements are highly technical documents that can have dire consequences if they are not drafted properly—you can even lose your trademark by failing to maintain adequate control of its use by someone else. Really. The same goes for a licensing agreement that you buy from an Internet contract mill. Even if you successfully substitute the names, dates, etc., from your own deal for those in one of these prefab contracts that were originally written for who knows who, will you be confident that the provisions the modified agreement includes are sufficient for your deal? Such agreements may cost only thirty dollars or so (to begin with), but they can ultimately cost you ownership of one of your most valuable business assets, your trademark.

If you want to save yourself some time and money, you can preliminarily negotiate the terms of a licensing agreement yourself and reduce them to a memorandum that your lawyer can use to draft the full licensing agreement. When your discussions with your would-be licensee become definite enough that the potential licensee is willing to specify the offered terms of the license, you can negotiate the essential terms of your agreement: the territory for the license; the term of the license, including any renewals; exactly what trademark would be licensed; exactly what products or services would be offered in conjunction with the licensed mark; and what royalty would be paid and how often. If you can hammer out answers to most of these questions, you will have created the bones of your agreement. However, reserve the right to change your mind about an offered term after you consult your lawyer and don't sign any memo you write or agree in a letter or an exchange of letters to any terms of an offered deal.

Make sure in your discussions and correspondence with any would-be licensee that you neither say nor write anything that can be construed as a definite commitment on your part before you receive the go-ahead from your lawyer. In any communication, make it clear that any license would be reduced to a formal, written document before the license commences. Use contingent language in referring to any offered or expected deal: "I would consider granting a license . . ." "Any licensing offer would have to pay at least . . . " "In the event that we grant a license to use our trademark, we would expect . . ." and so on. It's not a bad idea to end every communication with a paragraph like this: "Thank you for your interest in licensing my trademark. However, it is important that you understand that none of our discussions or correspondence about a possible trademark license represent any commitment from me to grant such a license and that I will make no such commitment until both you and I have signed a formal, written document that includes all the terms of our negotiated agreement." More than one businessperson has been surprised when someone on the other side of a deal thought, prematurely, that an agreement had been reached. Take your time. Then, call your lawyer.

Chapter 9
Other People's Trademarks

Almost everyone knows that selling toothpaste or sneakers or brokerage services by using a trademark that belongs to someone else is a quick ticket to a federal suit for trademark infringement. The law allows marketers to protect themselves from interlopers who want a free ride on their commercial coattails; they do this by means of lawsuits to preserve the integrity of their trademarks, which represent them to the public. The penumbra of protection granted an established trademark extends to identical marks and to marks that, although not identical, are similar enough to confuse consumers.

Usually, the comparison to determine trademark infringement is made between marks used to market similar products or services. However, the more famous and unusual the trademark, the wider the scope of protection trademark law grants it; no one can use KLEENEX® or COCA-COLA® or EXXON® for any product without encountering serious opposition from platoons of trademark lawyers who work for those companies, especially since the Trademark Dilution Act became effective in early 1996. (See chapter 5 for a more detailed explanation of the Trademark Dilution Act.)

There are other ways to infringe a trademark besides adopting a name for a product or service that is confusingly similar to an established mark for a similar product or services. Because trademark owners are vigilant in protecting their trademarks, wariness in the matter of other people's trademarks is a very good idea. However, such wariness can lead to an exaggerated fear of trademarks that belong to others and unnecessary maneuvering to avoid any mention or depiction of them. Surprisingly enough, there are some circumstances when using someone else's trademark *is* safe.

Broadly speaking, the law gives a trademark owner protection against any action that creates confusion about that trademark in the minds of consumers. This means that the dividing line between safe and unsafe uses of a trademark is where consumer confusion begins. Determining whether a given use of someone else's trademark will lead to a lawsuit is simply a matter of determining, under all the circumstances, whether that use will confuse anyone.

There are two common varieties of use of someone else's trademark that are usually safe and one that is, by definition, almost never safe. An examination of each of these situations will demonstrate the considerations involved in using other people's trademarks.

Incidental Use of Trademarks

More than one creative director has called in a lawyer to evaluate whether the presence of a COKE® can sitting on a table in a photograph is enough to disqualify the photo for use in an ad that isn't supposed to advertise COKE products. Before the lawyer can answer the question, he or she will have to see the photograph in question and read the ad copy, because the two important factors in evaluating whether the Coca-Cola Company is likely to sue are the emphasis of the photograph and the context of the use of the COKE logo.

Trademarks are a part of our world; they so pervade every environment of modern life that it is next to impossible to walk down a street or visit a public place or sit in a room without being surrounded by trademarks of every sort. This means that any realistic depiction of a street scene or restaurant setting or home or office situation will include representations of the trademarks found in that environment. Even though the trademarks that appear in such depictions are the valuable property of the companies that own them, in a way they also belong to the rest of us because they are a part of our lives. The First Amendment protects commercial speech such as advertising as well as other sorts of speech. This means that, as a matter of free speech, we have a right to "mention" the trademarks around us, either verbally or visually.

Which brings us back to the COKE® can in that photograph. Although free speech gives us the right to talk about or depict the world we live in, including trademarks, trademark law limits that right to some extent by discouraging certain sorts of uses of trademarks. The law would allow the Coca-Cola Company to sue the ad agency and the agency's client for trademark infringement if anything about the photo that included the COKE can implied that there was some connection between COCA-COLA® and the product advertised in the ad for which the photo was used. The same would be true if consumers could infer from the ad that the Coca-Cola Company somehow sponsored the ad or the product it advertised. As a practical matter, it is not likely that either of these grounds for suit would exist unless the COKE logo was legible and the can on which it appeared was a prominent element of the photograph; a background depiction of the can wouldn't create a problem, especially if the can wasn't an emphasis of the photograph.

Similarly, the context of the appearance in an ad of a "borrowed" trademark is important. If the COKE can photograph depicted the scene around the pool at an upscale resort hotel in an ad for that hotel, implying, however obliquely, that COCA-COLA is a favorite drink of carefree, wealthy people who look good in stylish bathing suits, the Coca-Cola Company probably would not object to the incidental appearance of its name and logo in the ad. If, however, the COKE can appeared in an objectionable photograph or if that photograph were used in any unsavory context, the Coca-Cola Company would be inclined to take whatever action was necessary to halt further use of the photo, especially if the COKE can was prominent in the photograph. The Coca-Cola Company, along with everybody else in the world, knows that villains and heroes and every other variety of human being drink COCA-COLA soft drinks. However, it is understandable that no one in Atlanta except the lawyers who earn their keep by guarding the various valuable COCA-COLA trademarks would like to see an ad photo prominently depicting a COKE can lying on a heap of rancid garbage or a broken COKE bottle being wielded as a weapon in a bar fight. Similarly, an identifiable depiction of a COCA-COLA product used in an ad for a topless bar or cigarettes or a personal hygiene product could earn the animosity of the

Coca-Cola Company. Any use of a trademark in an unsavory context can lead to a claim of product disparagement, which is comparable to a defamation suit brought on behalf of a trademark.

Comparative Advertising

Strangely enough, there is one variety of calculated, obvious use of other people's trademarks that will seldom cause trouble if carried out carefully. This is the use of trademarks belonging to competitor companies in comparative advertising. Trademark law does not prohibit *non*trademark or informational uses of the trademarks of others but, rather, punishes uses that confuse consumers. Comparative advertising informs consumers by explicitly comparing the merits of one product with those of another. The competitor's product, which always suffers from the comparison, is mentioned specifically in the ad copy and its package is usually pictured beside the advertiser's product in a head-on shot. Such ads require by their very nature that the products compared be carefully identified before the distinctions between them are drawn; only a very clumsy ad would fail to make entirely clear whether JOY® detergent or IVORY® detergent "cuts grease faster in laboratory tests." The test for trademark infringement is whether the public will be confused by the use of the mark. Since the possibility of consumer confusion is eliminated in comparative advertising, so is the likelihood of any charge of trademark infringement.

However, only claims that are truthful and that can be substantiated are safe. Because exaggerated claims or claims that can't be documented can lead to false advertising suits or unfair competition claims, every statement in a comparative advertising campaign should be carefully documented and every element of the campaign should be carefully designed.

Comparative advertisements can safely make use of competitors' trademarks if they are carefully constructed. Using a photo of another company's product or mentioning the product by name in an ad that compares it to your company's product is not an infringement of the trademark rights of the other company if the ad truthfully compares the products named by the trademarks and if the character and arrangement of the visual elements and the content of the ad copy do not create any likelihood that consumers will somehow mistakenly believe that your company's product has some relation to the product of the other company. (See *The Advertising Law Guide* by Lee Wilson, published by Allworth Press, for more information on the sorts of trouble false advertising can create for advertisers and ad agencies.)

Although properly designed comparative advertising does not usually lead to trademark infringement suits, there is one caveat. Whenever you use a trademark belonging to someone else in an ad, it is only prudent to state who owns that trademark in order to emphasize that the mark has no connection with the advertiser's product. This is easily accomplished by means of a "footnote" ownership statement. That is, a short statement should be included somewhere along the bottom margin or up the side margin of print ads and at the bottom of the screen in television commercials to the effect that "DOVE® is a registered trademark of the Lever Brothers Company."

156 The competitor's trademark should be used in exactly the form it appears on the competitor's product; that is, if it is a federally registered trademark and bears the ® symbol, that symbol should be used in the ownership statement. If the mark is not registered, no such symbol will appear, or the ™ symbol will be used in conjunction with the mark. In this event, the usage as it appears on the product should be duplicated and the ownership statement should read something like this: "CRUNCHIES™ is a trademark of the Toasted Oats Company and is not owned or licensed by the makers of SWEETIES™ brand cereal." A statement that your client's competitor owns its mark should completely eliminate any valid claim that the comparative ad creates confusion regarding the ownership of the mark or the manufacturer of the product it names. However, because not just any such disclaimer will suffice, any such ad and proposed disclaimer should be reviewed, before the ad is published, by a trademark lawyer, who can evaluate the possibility that the ad will result in an infringement lawsuit.

It is important to remember that the laws regarding comparative advertising in other countries may vary considerably from those in the United States. Be especially sure that any ad you prepare that mentions another company's trademark and will be published or circulated outside the United States will not furnish the owner of the other trademark with grounds for suit. Marketers use comparative advertising because it is effective—a comparative ad can lure consumers away from a product they are in the habit of buying on the strength of its convincing claims of the benefits of a rival product that is "new and improved" or simply "more effective in 75 percent of laboratory tests." This is enough to make the owners of the product that fares badly in such comparisons want to do whatever they can to stop the further publication of the ad. A lawsuit can do this. If a competitor finds your comparative advertising objectionable and the law in one or more of the countries where the ad appears supports that viewpoint, you will be vulnerable in any country where your competitor can, with a straight face, file a suit. Maybe U.S. law, with its predisposition to allow free speech in all possible contexts, can't be used as a club to stop your trumpeting the better performance of your product, but it may be possible to use the laws of other markets for just such a purpose, and every segment of international commerce counts. Japanese or Swedish or German money can fatten the bottom line for marketers just as well as American dollars. It's possible that somebody who works for your competitor wouldn't mind a long trip abroad at company expense to hire and supervise the lawyers who will be suing you under laws that you never heard of. Since you can't keep a tame trademark lawyer in your desk drawer to consult whenever you need advice, put his or her phone number on your ROLODEX® rotary card file (this is an example of correct usage of a trademark) *and* on your speed dial.

157

Trademark Parody

When a company decides to market a product under a name that is a parody of another mark, it is engaging in trademark parody. Trademark parody is almost always a bad idea, for two reasons. The first reason is that one of the kinds of confusion that trademark owners can legitimately complain about in court is "dilution," which is a claim that someone's use of an established mark is eroding the mark's strength even though the complained-of use is made in connection with a product that is unrelated to the product named by the established mark. If this fact alone isn't enough to convince you that trademark parody is almost invariably a dumb idea, consider this: only very famous trademarks are parodied—a parody of an obscure mark just wouldn't work. This means that the parodist is picking on a company rich enough to finance a trademark infringement lawsuit out of its petty cash. And since the passage of the Trademark Dilution Act, suits for dilution are easier for owners of famous marks to file and win. (The Federal Express suit to stop the use of FEDERAL ESPRESSO for a coffeehouse is a good example of a parody use of a famous trademark that ran afoul of the Trademark Dilution Act's proscriptions soon after the Act became effective.)

Another factor in trademark parody that often contributes to the problems that parodists face is that the parodied mark is often the butt of a joke, which may be an off-color joke. Nobody likes wise guys. The owners of the parodied mark may be so enraged by the parody of their mark that they will rush to file a trademark infringement suit and ask for an injunction against the parodist. Courts are usually sympathetic to the interests of the owners of famous trademarks; as a result, trademark parodists are routinely enjoined from pursuing their bad jokes at the expense of the well-known marks they parody.

You can understand trademark parody better by considering a few trademark parody cases in which the parodists were ordered by the court to give up making jokes at the expense of the plaintiff trademark owners. The pairs of marks that were the subjects of these suits tell the story in themselves; if reading the list makes you wince, you're getting the right idea about trademark parody. Not surprisingly, all these defendants lost in court.

Plaintiff Company	Defendant Trademark
Coca-Cola Company	"Enjoy Cocaine" (used, on a poster, in a script and color identical to those used for the COCA-COLA® logo)
Anheuser-Busch, Inc.	"Where There's Life . . . There's Bugs" (for a combination floor wax-insecticide, in a parody of the Anheuser-Busch slogan "Where There's Life . . . There's Bud")
General Electric Company	"Genital Electric" (used, on men's underwear, in a script monogram similar to the GENERAL ELECTRIC® script logo)
Johnny Carson	"Here's Johnny" (used, as the name of a line of portable toilets, in a parody of the phrase associated with the famous comedian; no trademark infringement was found, but the court found that Mr. Carson's right of publicity had been violated)

Not every trademark parody is ruled a trademark infringement. For example, the use in a florist's ad campaign of the slogan "This bud's for you" was held not to infringe the trademark rights of Anheuser-Busch, Inc. In its ruling, the court specifically mentioned the innocuous and pleasant nature of the florist's slogan. As a practical matter, all this tells us is that *sometimes* parodists win in court. Since paying to defend a lawsuit is almost as much a misfortune as losing it, this is really no encouragement to would-be parodists. The best thing to do with famous trademarks is to steer clear of them, especially if your parody is smutty or would associate a famous mark with an unsavory product.

More than one trademark infringement lawsuit has been brought simply because the trademark owner was angry and felt like doing something about it. If this doesn't scare you, consider the fact that owners of famous trademarks have whole platoons of trademark lawyers who have to justify their existence by periodically going after evildoers. If they are short of true malefactors this month, you and your ad may look like very good targets. When it comes to using someone else's famous trademark in an ad without permission, discretion really is the better part of valor.

The Etiquette of Trademark Usage

The only thing left to say about using other people's trademarks is that you should do so carefully. This boils down to the following four rules:

1. **Trademarks are proper adjectives; remember to use them as such.** It is a "Kleenex® tissue," not just a "kleenex," and you wear "Levi's® jeans," not just "levis."
2. **Trademarks should never be used as nouns or verbs.** You do not "Xerox®" a document, you make a photocopy of it, and it *is* a "photocopy," not simply a "xerox."
3. **Spell it right.** Most importantly, capitalize trademarks; it is "Coke®," not "coke," and "Cuisinart®," not "cuisinart."
4. **Give a mark its due.** If it is a registered mark, use the ® symbol in conjunction with the mark in at least the two or three most prominent uses of the mark in a text or an ad. If it is not registered, use informal trademark notice, i.e., the ™ superscript or subscript, if the owner of the mark does so on its products. (If the mark names a service, the trademark owner may use ᔆᴹ to indicate this.)

If you are confused about the proper spelling of a trademark or whether it is federally registered and therefore entitled to be escorted by the ® symbol whenever it appears in print, you can research the mark on the International Trademark Association (INTA) Web site. Compiled to help journalists, proofreaders, and others with proper trademark usage, the INTA's Trademark Checklist exclusively lists trademarks federally registered in the United States (nearly 3,000 marks), along with the generic terms for the products and services they name and indicates proper spelling, capitalization, and punctuation. You can access the INTA's Trademark Checklist at *www.inta.org/tmchklst.htm*. If you can't find the mark you are investigating, call the INTA Trademark Hotline at (212) 768-9886 for proper-usage information or contact the Hotline at *tmhotline@inta.org*. The Hotline operates weekdays from 2:00 P.M. to 5:00 P.M. eastern standard time.

Your rights won't be affected if you fail to follow these rules in using other people's trademarks, but theirs may be diminished. A trademark that is used incorrectly can become "generic"; that is, the mark loses its ability to refer to a particular product or service and comes to indicate a whole class of products. If this happens, the original owner of the mark loses the exclusive right to use it. This happened to "aspirin," and "escalator," and "thermos" as well as numerous other once-valuable trademarks. In determining whether a mark has lost its significance as an indicator of *one* company's products or services, courts often consider whether a trademark owner has acted against infringers. You may have no legal *duty* to use the marks of others carefully, but they may have a very good legal reason—the preservation of their rights—to challenge any misuse of those marks.

Because a trademark represents the reputation in the marketplace of the products or services of the company that owns it, it may be that company's most valuable asset. It is understandable that trademark owners pay close attention when their marks are used by people they never met in ways they don't necessarily approve. That's why they spend time writing letters to people who misuse them and money to publish ads to explain proper trademark usage. The way to avoid trouble when using other people's trademarks is to handle them like you would handle other people's money—carefully.

Is It Infringement?

1. **Q.** In an article for a regional business magazine on a local manufacturing magnate, you write "McCarthy knew he had become famous the day he googled himself and the search produced 350 hits." You are pleased with the article. So is Mr. McCarthy, who calls to ask if you'd be available to help his public relations department prepare a longer biography of him.

   However, you receive a polite but forthright letter in the mail the next week tells you that Google, Inc., the California company that offers GOOGLE™ Internet search services to millions of people all over the world every day, is *not* happy with you and your story. It seems that you have committed a trademark-usage *faux pas*—you turned Google, Inc.'s well-known trademark into a verb when you said that McCarthy "googled" himself.

   You get a little huffy when you read the letter and are still cranky when you have lunch the next day with your old college roommate, who is now a lawyer. You tell him the whole tale, expecting him to laugh at Google, Inc.'s overzealous attitude toward its trademark. You are surprised when he doesn't laugh. You ask him: *Is it infringement?*

   A. No. Not exactly. Your pal tells you that he understands why Google, Inc. objects to your use of GOOGLE as a verb. He even says that if he were house counsel for Google, Inc., he, too, would have written you a letter, except, he says, that he may have been less polite and more threatening. When you ask why, he explains to you that you and every other thoughtless writer and editor who launches an article into the vast river of modern communication are, by ignoring proper use of Google, Inc.'s trademark, actually eroding the company's mark. You bluster that you don't see how one little freelance writer (you) can do anything to harm such a big company.

   Your pal tells you that that is just the attitude that helped to transform many former trademarks into ordinary English words that have lost their original function of pointing to the products of a particular marketer. While you are thinking about this, your old roommate tells you that GOOGLE™ for search engine services may be in danger of losing its trademark status *because* it has become such a well-known name and *because* people like you have begun to use it as a verb. He says, "Why do you think the Xerox Corporation has spent so much advertising money encouraging the correct use of its mark? They may have been able to stop enough people from saying, and writing, 'make a Xerox of this' to preserve the function of their mark. Courts look at things like that when they have to decide whether a mark has become generic, you know."

You didn't know, but you do now. And you feel guilty; after all, you are supposed to be a business writer. You promise your buddy that you will reform. He suggests that you go to the Web site mentioned in the letter from Google, Inc. and familiarize yourself with the rules for proper usage of the GOOGLE trademark. You read what Google, Inc. has to say at *www.google.com/permissions/trademarks.html* and vow to become more conscious of proper trademark usage. Then you realize that perhaps this is a new area of expertise that you can pitch to Mr. McCarthy when you meet with him—after all, as a businessman, he has to be aware of the worth of his company's trademarks.

2. Q. Before the annual match between the University of Tennessee Vols and the football team at the big university you attend, you and several of your fraternity brothers spend two whole evenings in the basement of the fraternity house working on the shirts you will wear to the game. You bought an orange UT T-shirt for every guy in your fraternity; then you used wide red tape to create an international "prohibited" symbol on top of the UT logo on each shirt, something like a "no smoking" sign. At the game you and the guys—and your shirts—are a hit. Two of your frat brothers sell their shirts to other fans that day, right off their backs, for fifty dollars each. When you return from the game, you are excited even though your team lost. You think you have figured out how to pay your tuition next term.

The following Monday you consult with a local printer. He agrees to print up five hundred orange tees for you, each bearing the UT logo with a big red "prohibited" symbol on top of it. You plan to sell them on the Internet to other UT football opponents and ship them from the frat house basement. The shirts are printed by the end of the week and before the month is out you have had to reorder your shirts, which you sell for twenty dollars each.

Then you get a call from the dean of men, who wants you to come and visit him, *immediately.* You figure that he's heard about your entrepreneurial acumen and that he wants to congratulate you, maybe even give you some kind of award. But he isn't happy when you go to his office. In fact, he calls you "boneheaded" and tells you that you are going to be sued by the University of Tennessee if you don't give up moonlighting as a T-shirt mogul. You're puzzled. You ask him "What did I do? Is it possible—could it be? *Is it infringement?*"

A. The dean tells you that for answers to your questions you need to see somebody in the university counsel's office and that you have an appointment there in five minutes. You figure that's as good a reason as any to cut your afternoon chemistry lab and you rush to the appointment that you didn't know you had with the lawyer for the university. He doesn't have much time for you, either, but he listens for a few minutes to your account of how your brilliant idea came about—the tale about the UT shirts and the red tape and the popularity of your homemade "anti-UT" shirts at the UT game. But he doesn't listen for even one minute to your claims that your shirts are just an example of harmless parody.

It seems that you have been guilty of trademark infringement, that your use of the UT logo on your shirts violates the valuable rights of the University of Tennessee in its trademark. He tells you that after you buy a shirt with a trademark on it, you can do whatever you want with it, including destroying it, except duplicate it. The red-tape shirts didn't violate anybody's rights and *were* a permissible parody. However, your manufacture and sale of the printed "anti-UT" shirts did violate UT's trademark rights, because you duplicated—and altered—the UT logo without permission and the only reason the shirts sold was that they bore a version, albeit altered, of the UT logo.

He tells you that you are a "young idiot" and that he will be expecting you to turn over all your unsold T-shirts by nine o'clock the following day and that if you have any real business sense, you'll do whatever you can to make UT happy with you. Further, he says that you probably owe UT every nickel of the money you made from sales of the shirt and that if UT will accept that amount as damages for your infringing action, you'll be lucky. Then he tells you he has more important things to do than to instruct young upstarts like you and tells you that you should come back the next day to sign the settlement agreement that he is almost sure UT will fax to him after he pleads your case—and your ignorance—to their university counsel.

You thank him and leave. You don't feel as grateful as he seems to think you should, but you do decide, privately, that you probably have to abandon your plans to ship some shirts to your brother at the University of Oklahoma before their big game with another "UT," the University of Texas. Ah, the vicissitudes of capitalism.

3. Q. You are a member of the board of directors for the local humane association and in charge of planning the publicity for the association's annual "Adopt-a-Pet" drive. You come up with a great idea to encourage local citizens to pick out a pet at the association's animal shelter. You get a local grocery store to donate free pet food for a year to the winners of a drawing; everyone who adopts a stray dog or cat during the "Adopt-a-Pet" drive is eligible to win. You prepare a big ad to publicize the prizes and run it four consecutive weeks in the local newspaper. Nearly fifty stray dogs and cats are adopted during the drive and one dog owner and one cat owner are awarded the free food.

You feel like a marketing genius until you get a message from one of the humane association staffers to call a lawyer in Chicago who is, in the words of the staffer, "like, really bent out of shape, man." You call the lawyer, even though you think that he must have confused you with someone else. But you find out he wasn't mistaken when he tells you that

he represents Purina Mills, which is unhappy with you—
specifically with the newspaper ad you wrote and designed. It
seems that a Purina brand manager spotted the ad and passed
it on to the Purina legal department, which forwarded it to
the Chicago lawyer, who tells you that you are in trouble for
trademark infringement.

Your use of the PURINA® PUPPY CHOW®, DOG
CHOW®, KITTEN CHOW®, and CAT CHOW® trademarks
in your ad has irritated Purina, partly because of the reproduction of those marks and partly because the entire ad is designed
in such a way as to leave the impression that Purina Mills was
the sponsor of your free pet food contest. You thought you
were very clever when you scanned the pet food logos into
your computer to reproduce in your ad; now, when you take
a look at the ad again, you see that readers could easily believe
that Purina sponsored the contest or was directly associated
with it. Now the Chicago lawyer is mumbling about suing the
humane association. You tell him that you'll get back to him
after you consult with another board member, who is a real
estate lawyer. He hands you off to a trademark lawyer in his
firm. You ask the dread question: *Is it infringement?*

A. Yes. Under most circumstances, you would have a lawsuit on
your hands. When the trademark lawyer sees the ad you fax
to him, he tells you that the mere prominence of the
Purina trademarks in your ad, along with the line of copy
beneath them reading "Free Purina pet food for a year!"
is enough to make Purina's complaint legitimate. He explains
that in your effort to create awareness of your pet-adoption
drive you have committed the commercial sin of trademark
infringement by trading on the excellent, well-established
reputation of Purina Mills for quality pet food. He tells you
that it makes no difference that you meant only to publicize
your drive and the associated free-pet-food contest—an inad-
vertent infringement is still an infringement.

He also tells you that it is immaterial that the humane
association is a nonprofit corporation and that you were acting for it without pay—apparently trademark infringement is

trademark infringement and there is no exception for charities or civic organizations or amateur advertising copywriters. However, after you tell him that your ad ran only four times in only one newspaper that has a circulation area of only two counties and that nobody made any money off the ad or the contest and that, like most nonprofits, the humane association has very little money, he says that he can get you off the hook. He makes you promise never to run the ad again or use it in any way. You promptly agree.

Later that day he calls back to say that he has talked to Purina's lawyer and explained the situation, that Purina is being a good sport and won't sue or ask for any monetary settlement, and that it has promised to donate the pet food for next year's "Adopt-a-Pet" drive if you will agree to let it review any ad you create to publicize the drive. You quickly agree, hang up the phone, shred the ad that got you in trouble, and vow never to buy any kind of food for your cat but Purina.

4. Q. You are certain that your laundry and dry-cleaning shop gets men's shirts cleaner than Shirts to Go, a similar business two blocks over. You know this because you have at least one businessman in your shop every week with a shirt laundered there that still shows food or ink stains.

These poor guys always ask, "Can you can do anything to save my shirt?" Usually, you can fix their problem with a little extra attention and by running the shirt through your usual laundry process.

One day when a Shirts to Go customer brings in a stained shirt still in the Shirts to Go wrapper and asks the familiar question, you decide to seize the opportunity and take "before" and "after" pictures of his shirt, which is much improved by being laundered by your process. Then you make the shirt photos the centerpiece of an ad. The shirt is anonymous, but you name your competitor in the ad, in a headline that tells it like it is: "Two Pictures Are Worth a Thousand Words—Mack's Laundry Outcleans Shirts to Go." Under the headline you print a photo of the stained shirt still in the Shirts to Go wrapper and one of the same shirt, minus the ink stain on the breast pocket, in a Mack's wrapper. There is no other copy except the name, address, and phone number of your shop.

You get a handful of new customers every day for the next month—most of them are former Shirts to Go customers who bring in their dingy and stained shirts to see if you can return them to wearability. But one result of the ad is a nasty phone call from the Shirts to Go owner, who also saw the ad and who threatens, loudly, to sue you for trademark infringement. You tell him you'll have to get back to him; then you call your lawyer, whom you ask: *Is it infringement?*

A. No, it's not. When you show your lawyer the ad and tell him the circumstances that led to it, he tells you that you have nothing to worry about, despite the threats of your competitor. You have simply told the truth in your ad. There is no basis for any complaint for trademark infringement because the ad doesn't trade on your competitor's name or attempt to imply some association with the business it names. Rather, anyone who sees the ad can quickly determine that Shirts to Go is not associated with you but is, rather, your competitor and that your ad distinguishes between that business and your own by contrasting the quality of the service offered under each name.

167

Your lawyer says that because the ad creates absolutely no likelihood of confusion between the two businesses, there can be no infringement. Further, he says there isn't even any argument that your use of the Shirts to Go name dilutes that name because the name is not famous enough to qualify for the protections of the Trademark Dilution Act. He says that your competitor's threats must stem from mere anger and jealousy because there is no legal basis for a lawsuit. You are relieved. You buy space to run the ad every Monday for the next six months and you don't hear from the Shirts to Go owner again, probably, you surmise, because *his* lawyer told him the same thing you found out from yours.

5. Q. You run an Italian restaurant in the small town where you've lived all your life. It's a profitable business, but you have to watch expenses. As an economy measure, you fire your ad

agency and hire your nephew, who has a degree in marketing. You figure that, unlike the ad agency, he'll follow your instructions, won't cost an arm and a leg, and will be at your beck and call every day, all day. The first project you give him is the Christmas card you send every year to your customers. Over the years people have come to value receiving your Christmas cards—partly because the cards are always attractive, partly because you enclose a coupon good for a spaghetti dinner for two with every card.

Your nephew has the idea of printing a photo of your restaurant on this year's card. He takes several photographs of the restaurant but you know the one you want to use as soon as you see it. It is an exterior shot taken at dusk on a Saturday night from the roof of the hardware store across the street. It's a good view of the front of your restaurant, the sign that says "Roma Ristorante," and the line of people waiting for a table on the benches in front of the restaurant. You like the fact that the photo includes the front of Tony's Spaghetti House two doors down where *no one* is waiting for a table.

You approve the photo for your Christmas cards and tell your nephew to build an ad campaign around it. You also frame an enlargement of the photo and hang it over the hostess station in the entryway of your restaurant. The Christmas cards go out, the ads begin running in local publications, people are asking for posters of the photo, and it's harder than ever to get a table at Roma. You think about giving your nephew a raise until the day you get a call from your lawyer, who has received, as registered agent for The Roma Corporation, the complaint in a lawsuit filed by Tony, the proprietor of Tony's Spaghetti House. He tells you that you have been sued for trademark infringement for using the photo you like so well in your ads and on your Christmas cards because that photo also includes a view of Tony's establishment.

You ask your lawyer whether Tony has a valid claim, but your lawyer tells you he doesn't know because he knows almost nothing about trademark law. Then he gives you the name of another lawyer in town who may be able to help you. You consult her as soon as you have a copy of the complaint in the lawsuit. Of course, you want to ask her: *Is it infringement?*

A. Your trademark lawyer is a nice young woman named Gina who looks like your sister and isn't wearing a wedding band. You wait anxiously for her to read the complaint and look at your Christmas card and newspaper ad. When she offers you some coffee, you think she's trying to make you comfortable before she tells you that you're in a lot of trouble. But instead, she hauls out some biscotti she says her mother made, tells you that Tony is her cousin but no one in her family likes him, and assures you that he has absolutely no ground at all for a trademark infringement suit and that she thinks she can get the suit dismissed on summary judgment.

169

You ask her "But what about the fact that you can see Tony's Spaghetti House in the photo we used? We did use the photo in an ad and that is his trademark, the name of his business." "Not to worry," Gina says, "You have the right to use a picture of your own business in advertising and the fact that Tony's restaurant is two doors down from yours makes it almost inevitable that it would be pictured in some of your advertising materials." She says that there's nothing in your Christmas card or ad that otherwise refers to Tony's—both are clearly promoting your Roma Ristorante—and that the inclusion in the photograph of Tony's is simply an "incidental" depiction of a business on the same street as yours.

"But," you say, "maybe the ad is some kind of defamation of Tony's. Anybody who sees the photos is bound to notice that there are two Italian restaurants practically next door to each other and that one has a lot of customers and one doesn't. Isn't that slander or something?" Gina tells you that there is such a thing as trademark disparagement, which is saying something derogatory and untrue about a product or service by name, but that this is not such a case. She says that you have a right to depict your business in your advertising and a right to publicize its success. You just can't say or print something negative *and* untrue about Tony's. Since you haven't done that, he cannot sue you—and win—just because he doesn't like your ad.

Then she asks, "Did you get releases from any of the people in your photo?" and says that someone whose image is used in advertising without permission can sue. You tell her you didn't because you didn't know releases were necessary and that you'll check into it. Then you tell her to take care of the suit, that no one in your family likes Tony either, and you ask her for two of her business cards. You give one to your nephew and suggest that he invite Gina to lunch at Roma to find out about photo releases for advertising. You also tell him that if he were to marry a nice Italian girl—say, a lawyer— you'd have to give him a big raise.

I'll See You in Court

The following are thumbnail accounts of actual trademark disputes between the owners of established trademarks and people who used identical marks for *unrelated* products or services. These accounts are proof that the owners of famous trademarks are serious—some would say overvigilant—about protecting their marks. Sometimes the owners of the famous marks won their suits against the accused interlopers, sometimes the courts sided with the junior user of the mark—either way, being the object of a lawsuit filed by a rich plaintiff is a memorable misfortune.

- The giant cereal manufacturer, the Kellogg Company, sued Toucan Golf, Inc., which marketed golf clubs and other golf products by using a depiction of a toucan and the words "Toucan Gold." Kellogg claimed that Toucan Golf infringed on Kellogg's Toucan Sam cartoon trademarks used to market cereals. The court did not agree.

- The online auction giant eBay has been active in challenging similar and parody names for unconnected trading sites. It sued BidBay, a rival auction site, sent a letter to AlternaBay, a gay auction site, and complained about a parody site called eGray.org, which was run by opponents of (then) California governor Gray

Davis. A Lego-trading site named BrickBay.com changed its name to BrickLink.com after eBay said that BrickBay infringed eBay's trademark rights. The famous eBay has staked its claim to a large hunk of cyberspace and intends to keep it.

- The World Wrestling Federation (WWF) wrote a letter to the independent record label that marketed the recordings of Wesley Willis, asking it to stop the sale and distribution of an album called "The Wesley Willis Fiasco Live E.P." The album cover featured a logo similar to the WWF logo. The WWF letter claimed that the album logo infringed upon and diluted the WWF trademark and asked that all copies of the album be recalled and destroyed or surrendered to the WWF.

- The World Wildlife Fund sued the World Wrestling Federation to compel it to live up to a 1994 agreement not to use the WWF abbreviation, which the World Wildlife Fund registered when it was formed in 1961. The wildlife group wants the wrestling group to stop using any domain name that includes the WWF mark and to stop selling merchandise bearing it.

- The large online merchant Amazon.com sued Amazon Cosmetics and Tan Products, the owner of Amazontan.com, saying that the beauty products company was infringing its rights; the suit was dismissed on jurisdictional grounds. It also sued the operator of Amazon.gr, which called itself "Greece's Biggest Bookstore; the Greek business was ordered by the court to stop using the Amazon name.

- The OCLC Online Computer Library Center, Inc. sued The Library Hotel, a boutique New York hotel near the main New York Public Library, for trademark infringement. It claimed that The Library Hotel was using the DEWEY DECIMAL CLASSIFICATION® trademarks without permission. The hotel features theme-based rooms and each room is stocked with books that relate to its specific DEWEY DECIMAL® theme. The suit was settled; the hotel was granted permission to use the OCLC's trademarks in its hotel and marketing materials and the hotel made a charitable contribution to promote children's reading.

Chapter 10
Trademarks in Cyberspace

Like all frontiers, cyberspace is largely populated by mavericks and rebels who like the cyber-atmosphere of "if you can imagine it, you can do it." Unfortunately, the very dearth of rules that makes cyberspace so intriguing to everyone who has something to say or sell electronically is also causing problems. Americans often complain about overregulation by local, state, and federal governmental agencies and authorities. But many who are familiar with the problems that have arisen as everybody and his brother scramble for domain names would agree that, in some corners of cyberspace, more rules are needed.

One aspect of cyber-commerce has produced disputes since the very early days of the Internet; this is the ownership of domain names. A domain name is the heart of an e-mail address. In the e-mail address *johnjones@jonesventures.com*, "jonesventures.com" is the domain name. Domain names tell Internet users where to find companies and individuals in cyberspace. They function like zip codes do for "snail mail"; they direct e-mail and other communications to the right cyber-space neighborhood to find the person or entity named in the first part of the e-mail address. They allow Internet users to visit World Wide Web pages.

The system of categorizing Internet user addresses according to type is familiar to most Net surfers. They are called Top Level Domain names, or TLDs. The original five major nonmilitary domains are .com for commercial entities, .gov for governmental bodies, .edu for educational institutions, .org for organizations, and .net for networks. ICANN, the Internet Corporation for Assigned Names and Numbers (found at *www.icann.org*), has also recently introduced seven new domain-name categories: .biz, .info, .aero, .museum, .name, .pro, and .coop. Not just anyone can use these new domain-name categories; .biz will be restricted to businesses; .aero is reserved for the use of airlines and similar organizations, .museum is limited to museums; .name is for personal names, .pro is reserved for doctors, lawyers, and accountants; and .coop is only for cooperatives. The additional domain-name categories will ease the competition for domain names to some extent by allowing individuals and organizations more elbow room in cyberspace.

Several new TLDs have been proposed: .arts for cultural and entertainment activities; .firm for businesses; .rec for recreation or entertainment activities; .store for businesses offering goods for sale; and .web for entities emphasizing activities related to the World Wide Web. Even if these or other TLD categories are instituted, the Internet is likely to continue to be a crowed place. And because marketers have found ways to sell everything from coffee to books to the stuff from your hall closet online, the most crowded part of cyberspace probably will continue to be the commercial district, where all the .com addresses are located.

173

Internet addresses are actually a series of numbers. However, because people who want to locate an Internet merchant are much more likely to remember a verbal address than a series of numbers, domain names are alpha and/or numeric names that a computer can convert to numeric addresses. This means that the best domain names look like the names of the companies that own them; this sort of domain name creates an expectation as to who is at the Internet address it names. If you are familiar with a company and its domain name resembles the name of the company, you know what you will find at its address on the Internet. Such Internet addresses are easy to guess and easy to remember. For example, because ibm.com is one of the elements of the Internet address for IBM, anyone can guess that that address belongs to that company.

And although multiple companies engaged in different sorts of business can share a name, or elements of their names, without confusion because people shopping for tires won't look for them in grocery stores, the same is not true for Internet addresses that are very similar. Because cyberspace isn't a physical space but is, rather, a conceptual place, the physical attributes of a product, such as where it is manufactured and in what stores it is sold do not mitigate any similarity between product or company names. That is, the Internet—the information superhighway—lines up businesses, along with other entities, *only* according to their addresses. And no factor besides addresses determines the accessibility of those businesses and other entities.

To understand this critical distinction between company names and domain names, consider the Johnsons. There are many Johnson companies in the U.S. and they offer everything from paint to accounting services. The products of two of them can be found in literally nearly every household in the country; they are the S.C. Johnson Company and Johnson & Johnson, which is really a family of companies. The S.C. Johnson Company manufactures and markets WINDEX®, ZIPLOC®, PLEDGE®, and GLADE® products, among others. Johnson & Johnson manufactures BAND-AID®, MOTRIN®, MYLANTA®, NEUTROGENA®, and ST. JOSEPH® products among many others, including JOHNSON'S® baby shampoo and other baby products. We distinguish one giant Johnson company from the other because we shop for WINDEX®, ZIPLOC®, PLEDGE®, and GLADE® products in different aisles of the supermarket from the ones in which we buy BAND-AID®, MOTRIN®, MYLANTA®, NEUTROGENA®, and ST. JOSEPH® products, and JOHNSON® baby products.

Further, because of the reputations of the different brands owned by these two companies, we shop for the brand names themselves rather than specifically for the products of one Johnson company or the other. This sort of differentiation is not possible in cyberspace. Neither company can use the dominant verbal element in its name for its Web address, so the S.C. Johnson Company uses *www.scjohnson.com* as its Web address and Johnson & Johnson's Web address is *www.jnj.com*. (The domain name johnson.com is the address for yet *another* Johnson company, the company that manufactures Johnson outboard motors.)

In cyberspace you can't stand in front of a store, look through the front window, and see that home-cleaning products or over-the-counter medications and cosmetics are sold there. Instead, you have to depend on the only indicator of source possible—the domain name or Internet address for that business.

Obstacles on the Superhighway

So far, trademark disputes have been one of the biggest impediments facing Internet marketers. The gist of trademark law is that every marketer is entitled to his or her own reputation in the marketplace. Any interference with this—any act that causes consumers to confuse the products or services of one marketer with those of another—is trademark infringement. Anyone who understands trademark law would agree that domain names are more than just virtual street addresses.

Problems with domain names have usually arisen when one company registered a domain name identical or similar to the name of another company. It is reasonable that a company whose name had been adopted as the domain name of another enterprise would feel that its rights in its trademark—the embodiment of its commercial reputation—had been infringed. One variety of trademark infringement is confusion of sponsorship or affiliation. If, on account of similarities between a domain name and the name of an unrelated company, consumers are likely to believe that there is some relationship between the owner of the domain name and the company, the company's trademark rights have been infringed.

Superhighway Robbery

Trademark disputes have, in recent years, resulted when competitors and pranksters have registered domain names that are logically related to the names of established companies. Many such domain-name registrations were apparently made for the purpose of extorting fat buyouts from rich corporations. In the early days of the Internet, a journalist registered the domain name mcdonalds.com as a part of his research for an article for *Wired* magazine. Needless to say, McDonald's was chagrined to find that the most obvious domain name it could choose had already been registered. Some overeager capitalist at Sprint Communications registered mci.com; not surprisingly, MCI Telecommunications objected. The Princeton Review, a leading test-preparation company, registered kaplan.com, a domain name based on the name of its competitor, Stanley Kaplan Review, and planned to set up a Web site that compared the two companies' products, presumably showing the alleged inferiority of the Kaplan products. The domain name mtv.com was registered and used by a former MTV employee. The domain names windows95.com and nyt.com were registered by people who were not connected with Microsoft and the *New York Times*. Although several of these early "land grabs" resulted in lawsuits, all four disputes were settled out of court.

Similar problems have arisen when companies have registered domain names they had no intention of using. This has been done in the hope that some company that does want to use one of the registered domain names will buy it from the original registrant. This sort of kidnapping has been fairly common.

Superhighway Patrol

The Internet grew—and grew big—before there were enough systems to control its growth. However, it may be that domain-name disputes will soon become merely a relic of the early, lawless days when the Internet was new and land grabs were still possible. Now ICANN has acted to settle, if not obviate, most domain-name disputes.

In late 1999, ICANN adopted the Uniform Domain Name Dispute Resolution Policy. The Policy has now been adopted by all accredited domain-name registrars for domain names ending in .com, .net, and .org and by some managers of country-code top-level domains. Among other important innovations, the Policy, which is employed by domain-name registrars, states that, in applying to register a domain name, a would-be domain-name registrant represents that:

1. The statements made in the registrant's Registration Agreement are complete and accurate
2. To the knowledge of the registrant the registration of the domain name will not infringe upon or otherwise violate the rights of any third party

3. The registrant is not registering the domain name for an unlawful purpose
4. The registrant will not knowingly use the domain name in violation of any applicable laws or regulations. The registrant is responsible for determining whether the domain name infringes or violates someone else's rights

These provisions should all but eliminate domain-name hijacking. In addition, they will reduce disputes between legitimate businesses by requiring a registrant to figure out, in advance of trying to register a domain name, whether the name will infringe the rights of anyone else. This would seem to make a trademark search a prerequisite for applying to register a domain name.

In addition, under the Policy a registrar may cancel any domain-name registration if a court, administrative body, or arbitrator determines that the registrant is not actually entitled to the domain name.

Despite these requirements to keep domain-name registrants honest, there is also a mechanism to allow an entity that believes its rights are being harmed by the use of a particular domain name to complain to the registrar. Any registrant accused of using a domain name to which it is not entitled must submit to a mandatory administrative proceeding conducted by an approved arbitrator.

To prevail, a complaining entity must prove to a registrar that a registrant's name is identical or confusingly similar to a trademark or service mark in which the complaining entity has rights, that the registrant has no rights or legitimate interests in the domain name, and that the domain name has been registered and is being used in bad faith. Bad faith is defined as:

1. Registering or acquiring a domain name primarily for the purpose of selling it to the owner of the corresponding trademark or a competitor of the owner for more than costs directly related to the acquisition of the domain name
2. Registering a domain name in an effort to prevent the use of the corresponding trademark by the owner, if the registrant has previously engaged in such conduct

3. Registering a domain name primarily to disrupt the business of a competitor
4. Intentionally using a domain name to attract traffic to a Web site by creating the likelihood of confusion between the registrant's site or products and the site or products of the complaining entity

In the early days of the Internet, the parties feuding over the right to a domain name sometimes sued the registrar. The Policy specifically excludes registrars from liability and takes them out of the business of settling such disputes. The remedies available to prevailing complaining entities are limited to the cancellation of the domain-name registration of any registrant found by an arbitrator or court to be in violation of the Policy.

The Uniform Domain Name Dispute Resolution Policy isn't exactly international law, but it is like a treaty between various domain-name registrars and it is likely to have far-reaching and beneficial effects. Maybe cyberspace isn't totally civilized yet, but it's on its way to being a more orderly place that is less hospitable to outlaws than it once was. You can read the entire text of the relatively short and clearly written Policy on the ICANN Web site at *www.icann.org/dndr/udrp/policy.htm*. And if you think someone is using a domain name that infringes your trademark rights, see a lawyer.

Signing Up and Signing On

You can find a directory of accredited registrars, the countries in which they operate, and the TLD categories for which they grant registrations on the ICANN Web site at *www.icann.org/registrars/accredited-list.html*. And as soon as you become the registrant who owns a new domain name, you should consider filing for U.S. trademark registration. Just be sure that you are, indeed, using the domain name as a trademark and not just as an address for your Web site. This can be a tricky determination. Here's what the Trademark Manual of Examining Procedure, the rulebook by which trademark registration is or is not granted, has to say on the topic:

When a trademark, service mark, collective mark or certification mark is composed, in whole or in part, of a domain name, neither the beginning of the URL (http://www.) nor the

TLD have any source indicating significance. Instead, those designations are merely devices that every Internet site provider must use as part of its address. Today, advertisements for all types of products and services routinely include a URL for the web site of the advertiser. Just as the average person with no special knowledge recognizes "800" or "1-800" followed by seven digits or letters as one of the prefixes used for every toll-free phone number, the average person familiar with the Internet recognizes the format for a domain name and understands that "http," "www," and a TLD are a part of every URL.

Applications for registration of marks consisting of domain names are subject to the same requirements as all other applications for federal trademark registration.

. . .

A mark composed of a domain name is registrable as a trademark or service mark only if it functions as a source identifier. The mark as depicted on the specimens must be presented in a manner that will be perceived by potential purchasers as indicating source *and not as merely an informational indication of the domain name address used to access a web site.* [italics added]

. . .

The examining attorney must review the specimens in order to determine how the proposed mark is actually used. It is the perception of the ordinary customer that determines whether the asserted mark functions as a mark, not the applicant's intent, hope or expectation that it do so.

You can read all of what the Trademark Office has to say on this topic at *www.uspto.gov/web/offices/tac/notices/guide 299.htm.* Just remember that the trademark you create for use on physical products or the services you offer must suit those uses and that the best domain names are versions of trademarks the public already knows. It doesn't work so well in reverse—naming a line of ladies' hosiery LADIESHOSE.COM probably isn't a great marketing decision. But registering the domain name SilkyLegs.com after introducing your new SILKY LEGS hose works.

Work in Progress

There are two misconceptions about cyberspace and the law. The first is that there *is* no law in cyberspace. The second is that our old, boring, existing laws don't apply in cyberspace. Neither assumption is true. There is no "cyberspace law," except for all our laws that apply to any activity that is carried out on or through the Internet. And our existing laws continue to apply. Any new activity, including marketing on the Internet, that is within the scope of existing law is regulated just like the behavior that the laws were designed to regulate. The courts must apply old laws to new activities and sometimes there is a gap between the behavior and the application, but the law is still there and new law is being written to cover gaps in existing law. This is a good thing. Sometimes individual freedom is hampered, but not much, and a society where the rule of law prevails over force or despotism or disorder is the reward for submission to the law. Like most modern innovations, the Internet can be used for good or evil ends. The growth of protocols for its use and for the protection of its users is a benign and desirable development.

Appendixes

Appendix A
Trademark Cease
and Desist Letter

Romano and Tortellini, Attorneys
205 Waterman Street
Belmont, CA 94002

October 6, 2004

Mr. Robert Wilson
Mountain Properties, Inc.
729 East Mountain View Drive
Williamsville, CO 80206

Via Registered Mail; Return Receipt Requested

Dear Mr. Wilson:

This firm represents Brown Management Corporation of Blair, Colorado. Brown Management owns three resort hotels in Colorado: the Brown House Hotel in Denver, the Greenview Hotel in Blair, and the Brownstone Inn in Hopewell, which is, as you know, just over the county line from Williamsville. It is with regard to the Brownstone Inn that I am writing.

Brown Management Corporation has owned and operated the Brownstone Inn since 1984. Over the years, Brown Management has expended a great deal of money to advertise the Brownstone Inn and to ensure that the services and facilities there are the finest available. Consequently, the Brownstone Inn has an excellent reputation, both within Colorado and nationally, as a luxury hotel. Brown Management is the owner of two service marks, both of which have been registered in the United States Patent and Trademark Office. These service marks are the famous name BROWNSTONE INN, which is the subject of federal registration 1,985,065, and the well-known Brownstone Inn script logo, which is the subject of federal registration 1,985,094. Copies of these two registrations are attached to this letter.

It has come to the attention of our client that your corporation has begun construction on a Williamsville time-share condominium development that you intend to call and, indeed, are already calling in advertisements in national travel magazines and in publicity of other kinds, "the Brown Stone Community." Your use of the name "Brown Stone Community" for your resort condominium development constitutes infringement of our client's registered service marks and unfair competition, since consumers may mistake your condominiums for our client's famous hotel or mistakenly believe that your condominiums and our client's hotel have the same owners or that your development is sponsored by or affiliated with Brown Management Corporation or the Brownstone Inn. Furthermore, your use of the "Brown Stone Community" for your development dilutes the strength of our client's famous marks and damages the business reputation and diminishes the good will of the Brownstone Inn, all of which were developed and acquired by our client at great expense and effort.

You should be aware that the United States trademark statute (15 U.S.C. 1051 *et seq.*) provides in part that:

> When a violation of any right of the registrant of a mark registered in the Patent and Trademark Office shall have been established in any civil action arising under this chapter, the plaintiff shall be entitled . . . to recover (1) defendant's profits, (2) any damages sustained by the plaintiff, and (3) the costs of the action.

The law also allows the court to award treble damages and reasonable attorney's fees to the prevailing party. In addition, the court may order that all labels, signs, packaging, and advertisements in the possession of the defendant that bear the registered mark or a colorable imitation thereof be delivered up and destroyed.

Therefore, on behalf of our client, we hereby demand that you immediately cease any uses of the name "Brown Stone Community" or any other imitation or version of our client's registered marks in connection with any present or projected condominium development. Our client will require destruction of any printed advertising or promotion materials bearing the infringing name, including brochures and signage. In addition, your corporation must agree to cease giving out any news stories or causing any advertisements to be published or promulgating any materials connected with the offering of your condominiums that contain any reference to those condominiums as the "Brown Stone Community" development.

Due to the serious nature of your infringing conduct, we require your response to our demands not later than ten days after your receipt of this letter. If you agree to our terms, we will forward an appropriate settlement agreement for execution by an officer of your corporation. If we do not hear from you within ten days or if you refuse to comply with our demands, we are authorized by our client Brownstone Management Corporation to commence an action in federal court on its behalf seeking an injunction, damages, your profits, our costs and attorney's fees, and all other relief allowed by law, without further notice to you.

Although we are hopeful that we can obtain satisfaction for our client without litigation, this letter is written without prejudice to our client's rights and remedies, all of which are expressly reserved.

Sincerely,
Romano and Tortellini, Attorneys

Signature (handwritten or script typeface)
Hubert Tortellini
HT/tb

attachments: registration certificates 1,985,065 and 1,985,094

Appendix B
Directory of State
Trademark Offices

Most, but not all, state trademark offices are a division of the office of the secretary of state. Most state trademark offices will mail forms to you to fill out and return. In addition, many states now offer downloadable trademark registration forms online; others offer forms that can be filled out online and then printed. Usually, however, the filled-out forms must be returned to the state trademark agency for filing, as they require a signature and a filing fee. You can access most state trademark offices and their forms through that state's secretary of state's office. A site that offers links to all fifty states is that for the National Association of Secretary of States (NASS); the page with links is located at *www.nass.org/sos/sosflags.html*. On each secretary of state's Web site, look for a "Business Services" or "Corporations" button. Sometimes information on trademark searches and filings is hard to locate and not all the Web sites for the offices of secretaries of state offer the ability to search the site. Refer to the list below to make sure you can use the NASS Web site link to access the information you need.

Alabama
Office of the Secretary of State
Lands and Trademarks Division
P.O. Box 5616
Montgomery, AL 36103-5616
(334) 242-5325

Alaska
State of Alaska
Division of Banking, Securities,
  and Corporations
Corporations Section
P.O. Box 110808
Juneau, AK 99811-0808
(907) 465-2530

Arizona
Secretary of State
Business Services, Seventh Floor
1700 Washington Street
Phoenix, AZ 85007
(602) 542-6187

Arkansas
Secretary of State
State Building Authority Building
Business and Commercial
  Services Division, Suite 310
501 Woodlane Avenue
Little Rock, AR 72201
(501) 682-3409

California
Secretary of State
Trademarks/Service Marks
P.O. Box 944225
Sacramento, CA 94244-2250
(916) 653-4984

Colorado
Secretary of State
Business Division, Suite 200
1560 Broadway
Denver, CO 80202-5169
(303) 894-2200

Connecticut
Secretary of State
Commercial Recording
  Division
30 Trinity Street
Hartford, CT 06106
(860) 509-6003

Delaware
Department of State
Division of Corporations
P.O. Box 898
Dover, DE 19903
(302) 739-3073

Florida
Department of State
Registration Section
Division of Corporations
P.O. Box 6327
Tallahassee, FL 32314
(850) 245-6051

Georgia
Office of Secretary of State
Corporations Division
315 West Tower
2 Martin Luther King Jr. Drive
Atlanta, GA 30334-1530
(404) 656-2861

Hawaii
Department of Commerce and
   Consumer Affairs
Business Registration Division
P. O. Box 40
Honolulu, HI 96810
(808) 586-2744

Idaho
Secretary of State
Trademark Division, Room 203
700 W. Jefferson Street
P.O. Box 83720
Boise, ID 83720-0080
(208) 332-2810

Illinois
Secretary of State
Department of Business Services
Howlett Building, Third Floor
Springfield, IL 62756
(217) 524-0400

Indiana
Secretary of State
Trademarks Division, Room E111
302 W. Washington Street
Indianapolis, IN 46204
(317) 232-6540

Iowa
Secretary of State
Business Services Division
Lucas Building, First Floor
Des Moines, IA 50319
(515) 281-5204

Kansas
Secretary of State
Corporations Division
Memorial Hall, First Floor
120 S.W. Tenth Avenue
Topeka, KS 66612-1594
(785) 296-4564

Kentucky
Office of the Secretary
   of State
Trademark Division
P.O. Box 718
Frankfort, KY 40602-0718
(502) 564-2848, ext. 442

Louisiana
Secretary of State
Corporations Section
P.O. Box 94125
Baton Rouge, LA 70804-9125
(225) 925-4704

Maine
Bureau of Corporations,
   Elections, and Commissions
101 State House Station
Augusta, ME 04333-0101
(207) 624-7740

Maryland
Secretary of State
Trademark Division
State House
Annapolis, MD 21401
(410) 974-5531

Massachusetts
Secretary of the Commonwealth
Corporations Division,
　　Room 337
State House
Boston, MA 02133
(617) 727-7030

Michigan
Department of Labor and
　　Economic Growth
Bureau of Commercial
　　Services
Corporation Division
7150 Harris Drive
P.O. Box 30054
Lansing, MI 48909
(517) 241-6470

Minnesota
Office of the Secretary
　　of State
Business Services Division
180 State Office Building
100 Rev. Dr. Martin Luther
　　King Jr. Boulevard
Saint Paul, MN 55155-1299
(651) 296-2803

Mississippi
Secretary of State
Business Services
　　(Corporations)
P.O. Box 136
Jackson, MS 39205-0136
(601) 359-1333

Missouri
Office of the Secretary of State
Commissions Division
P.O. Box 784
Jefferson City, MO 65102
(573) 751-4756

Montana
Secretary of State
P.O. Box 202801
Helena, MT 59620-2801
(406) 444-3665

Nebraska
Secretary of State
Corporations Division
State Capitol, Room 1301,
P.O. Box 94608
Lincoln, NE 68509-4608
(402) 471-4079

Nevada
Office of the Secretary
　　of State
Commercial Recordings Division
Secretary of State Annex Office
202 N. Carson Street
Carson City, NV 89701-4201
(775) 684-5708

New Hampshire
Corporation Division
Department of State
107 North Main Street
Concord, NH 03301-4989
(603) 271-3244

New Jersey
Division of Revenue
Business Services
Trademarks/Service Marks Unit
(Commercial Recording)
P.O. Box 453
Trenton, NJ 08625
(609) 292-9292

New Mexico
Secretary of State
325 Don Gaspar Avenue,
    Suite 301
Santa Fe, NM 87503
(505) 827-3600 or
    (800) 477-3632

New York
Department of State
Bureau of State Records
41 State Street
Albany, NY 12231-0001
(518) 473-2492

North Carolina
Trademarks Section
Department of the Secretary
    of State
P.O. Box 29622
Raleigh, NC 27626-0622
(919) 807-2162

North Dakota
Secretary of State
Business Division
Department 108
600 E. Boulevard Ave.

Bismark, ND 58505-0500
(701) 328-4284 or
    (800) 352-0867 (ext. 8-4284)

Ohio
Secretary of State
Corporations Department
P.O. Box 1329
Columbus, OH 43216
(614) 466-3910 or (877)
    767-3453

Oklahoma
Secretary of State
Trademark Services
2300 N. Lincoln Boulevard,
    Room 101
Oklahoma, OK 73105-4897
(405) 521-3912

Oregon
Secretary of State
Corporation Division
Public Services Building,
    Suite 151
255 Capitol Street N.E.
Salem, OR 97310-1327
(503) 986-2200

Pennsylvania
Department of State
Corporation Bureau
P.O. Box 8722
Harrisburg, PA 17105-8722
(717) 787-1057

Rhode Island
Secretary of State
Corporations Division
Trademark Section
100 North Main Street
Providence, RI 02903-1335
(401) 222-1487

South Carolina
Secretary of State
P.O. Box 11350
Columbia, SC 29211
(803) 734-1728

South Dakota
Secretary of State
State Capitol Building
500 East Capitol Avenue
Pierre, SD 57501
(605) 773-3539

Tennessee
Department of State
Division of Business Services
Trademarks Unit
William R. Snodgrass Tower,
    Sixth Floor
312 Eighth Avenue North
Nashville, TN 37243
(615) 741-0531

Texas
Secretary of State
Corporations Section
P.O. Box 13697
Austin, TX 78711-3697
(512) 475-2755

Utah
Department of Commerce
Division of Corporations and
    Commercial Code
P.O. Box 146705
Salt Lake City, UT 84114-6705
(801) 530-4849

Vermont
Secretary of State
81 River Street
Drawer 09
Montpelier, VT 05609
(802) 828-2386

Virginia
State Corporation Commission
Division of Securities
P.O. Box 1197
Richmond, VA 23218
(804) 371-9967

Washington
Office of the Secretary
    of State
Corporations Division
P.O. Box 40234
Olympia, WA 98504-0234
(360) 753-7115

West Virginia
Secretary of State
Business Organizations Division
Building 1, Suite 157K
1900 Kanawha Boulevard East.
Charleston, WV 25305-0770
(304) 558-8000

Wisconsin
Secretary of State
Trademark Records
P.O. Box 7848
Madison, WI 53707-7848
(608) 266-5653

Wyoming
Secretary of State
The Capitol Building
200 W. 24th Street, Room 110
Cheyenne, WY 82002-0020
(307) 777-7311

Appendix C
Basic Facts about Trademarks from the U.S. Patent and Trademark Office

TRADEMARK, COPYRIGHT OR PATENT?

What is a trademark or service mark?
A trademark is a word, phrase, symbol or design, or a combination of words, phrases, symbols or designs, that identifies and distinguishes the source of the goods of one party from those of others.

A service mark is the same as a trademark, except that it identifies and distinguishes the source of a service rather than a product. Throughout this booklet, the terms "trademark" and "mark" refer to both trademarks and service marks.

Do Trademarks, Copyrights and Patents protect the same things?
No. Trademarks, copyrights and patents all differ. A copyright protects an original artistic or literary work; a patent protects an invention. For copyright information, go to **http://lcweb.loc.gov/copyright/**. For patent information, go to **http://www.uspto.gov/main/patents.htm**.

SHOULD I REGISTER MY MARK?

Is registration of my mark required?
No. You can establish rights in a mark based on legitimate use of the mark. However, owning a federal trademark registration on the Principal Register provides several advantages, e.g., constructive notice to the public of the registrant's claim of ownership of the mark; a legal presumption of the registrant's ownership of the mark and the registrant's exclusive right to use the mark nationwide on or in connection with the goods and/or services listed in the registration; the ability to bring an action concerning the mark in federal court; the use of the U.S. registration as a basis to obtain registration in foreign countries; and the ability to file the U.S. registration with the U.S. Customs Service to prevent importation of infringing foreign goods.

When can I use the trademark symbols TM, SM and ®?
Any time you claim rights in a mark, you may use the "TM" (trademark) or "SM" (service mark) designation to alert the public to your claim, regardless of whether you have filed an application with the USPTO. However, you may use the federal registration symbol "®" only after the USPTO actually registers a mark, and not while an application is pending. Also, you may use the registration symbol with the mark only on or in connection with the goods and/or services listed in the federal trademark registration.

WHAT DOES THE USPTO DO?

The United States Patent and Trademark Office (USPTO) reviews trademark applications for federal registration and determines whether an applicant meets the requirements for federal registration. We do not decide whether you have the right to use a mark (which differs from the right to register). Even without a registration, you may still use any mark adopted to identify the source of your goods and/or services.

Once a registration issues, it is up to the owner of a mark to enforce its rights in the mark based on ownership of a federal registration.

USPTO employees will gladly answer questions about the application process. However, USPTO employees cannot:

- conduct trademark searches for the public;
- comment on the validity of registered marks;
- answer questions on whether a particular mark or type of mark is eligible for trademark registration; or
- offer legal advice or opinions about common law trademark rights, state registrations, or trademark infringement claims.

HOW DO I FILE A TRADEMARK APPLICATION?

194

Is there a form for filing my application?
Yes. Using the Trademark Electronic Application System (TEAS) available at **http://www.uspto.gov/teas/index.html**, you can file your application directly over the Internet. Features of electronic filing include:

- On-line Help. Hyper-links provide help sections for each of the application fields.
- Validation Function. Helps avoid the possible omission of important information.
- Immediate Reply. The USPTO immediately issues an initial filing receipt via e-mail containing the assigned application serial number and a summary of the submission.
- 24 Hour Availability. TEAS is available 24 hours a day, 7 days a week (except 11 p.m. Saturday to 6 a.m. Sunday), so receipt of a filing date is possible up until midnight EST.

If you do not have Internet access, you can access TEAS at any **Patent and Trademark Depository Library (PTDL)** throughout the United States. Many public libraries also provide Internet access.

Are there other ways to file besides the Internet?
Yes. While we greatly prefer that you file electronically using TEAS, you may either mail or hand deliver a paper application to the USPTO. You can call the USPTO's automated telephone line, at (703) 308-9000 or

(800) 786-9199 to obtain a printed form. You may NOT submit an application by facsimile. Our mailing address to file a new application is:

Commissioner for Trademarks
2900 Crystal Drive
Arlington, VA 22202-3514

Must I hire an attorney?

No. However, if you prepare and submit your own application, you must comply with all requirements of the trademark statute and rules. If you choose to appoint an attorney to represent your interests before the USPTO, we will correspond only with your attorney. The USPTO cannot help you select an attorney.

What must the application include?

- **NAME OF THE APPLICANT**
- **NAME AND ADDRESS FOR CORRESPONDENCE**
- **DEPICTION OF THE MARK ("THE DRAWING")**
- **GOODS AND/OR SERVICES**
- **APPLICATION FILING FEE**
- **BASIS FOR FILING**
- **SPECIMEN**
- **SIGNATURE**

An application must include the following elements before the USPTO will accept it:

- the name of the applicant;
- a name and address for correspondence;
- a clear drawing of the mark;
- a listing of the goods or services; and
- the filing fee for at least one class of goods or services.

If your application does not meet these requirements, the USPTO will return the application papers and refund any fees submitted.

If you file a paper application, and it meets the minimum filing requirements, the USPTO will assign a serial number and send a filing receipt. You should review this receipt for accuracy, and notify the USPTO of any errors, following the directions on the receipt.

An electronically filed application must include the same information to receive a filing date. However, at the time of filing, an e-mail summary, including a serial number, is sent. No paper filing receipt is generated. If through later review the USPTO determines that the application did not include the required information, we will cancel the serial number and filing date, return the application, and refund the filing fee.

If you transmit your application over the Internet, the filing date is the date the transmission reaches the USPTO server. Otherwise, the filing date of an application is the date the USPTO receives the application.

NOTE: Receiving a filing date does not mean that you have satisfied ALL registration requirements. To obtain a registration, you must comply with all application requirements, and overcome any refusal(s) issued by the examining attorney during examination.

Although only the minimum filing requirements must appear in your initial application to receive a filing date, submitting all available information requested in the application form will help reduce delays in processing your application. See below for more information about these requirements.

Name of the Applicant

The application must be filed in the name of the owner of the mark. The owner of the mark is the person or entity who controls the nature and quality of the goods identified by the mark and/or the services rendered in connection with the mark. The owner may be an individual, corporation, partnership, or other type of legal entity.

Do I have to be a U.S. citizen to apply?

No. However, if you do not reside in the United States, you must appoint a "domestic representative" as part of the application process (see below).

Name and Address for Correspondence

The name and address for correspondence is the address where the USPTO will send communications concerning the application. It may be that of the applicant or the applicant's legal representative. Also, an applicant residing outside the United States may list a domestic representative, that is, the name and address of any person residing in the U.S. "upon whom notices or process may be served for proceedings affecting the mark."

You must keep your mailing address up-to-date with the USPTO. This can be done through TEAS at **http://eteas.uspto.gov/V2.0/ca200/ WIZARD.htm**. If you send a notice of change of address on paper, please include at the top of the request a "heading" listing the applicant's name, mark, and the application serial number. Mail the change of address to:

Commissioner for Trademarks
2900 Crystal Drive
Arlington, VA 22202-3514

Depiction of the Mark ("The Drawing")

Every application must include a clear drawing of the mark you want to register. We use the drawing to file the mark in the USPTO search records and to print the mark in the Official Gazette and on the registration certificate. TEAS (Trademark Electronic Application System) generates a proper drawing for you, based on the information you entered. See **http://www.uspto.gov/web/offices/tac/notices/examguide1-03.htm#IC** for more information about electronically-submitted drawings. If you are preparing the drawing page yourself, use white, non-shiny paper that is $8\frac{1}{2}$ inches wide by 11 inches long (21.59 cm by 27.94 cm). The mark can be no larger than 3.5 inches high by 3.5 inches wide (8 cm by 8 cm). The drawing page should include a "heading" with the following elements:

- applicant's name;
- correspondence address;
- listing of goods and/or services; and
- dates of use (if already using the mark in commerce); or, wording "Intent to Use."

The representation of the mark must then appear below the heading, in the middle of the page, in the proper format for either a "typed" drawing or a "stylized or special form" drawing. Once filed, you cannot make a material change to your mark.

What is a "standard character" drawing (formerly known as a "typed" drawing)?

You may submit a standard character drawing if:

- All letters and words in the mark are depicted in Latin characters;
- All numerals in the mark are depicted in Roman or Arabic numerals;
- The mark includes only common punctuation or diacritical marks; and
- The mark does not include a design element. 37 C.F.R. §2.52(a).

You must also submit the following statement:

The mark is presented in standard character format without claim to any particular font style, size or color.

You may depict the mark in any font style; may use bold or italicized letters; and may use both uppercase and lowercase letters, all uppercase letters or all lowercase letters. See **http://www. uspto.gov/web/offices/tac/notices/examguide1-03.htm** for further information.

The Office has created a standard character set that lists letters, numerals, punctuation marks, and diacritical marks that may be used in a standard character drawing, available on the Office's Web site at **http://www.uspto.gov/teas/StandardCharacterSet.html**. If the applicant wants to register characters that are not in the set, then the applicant must file a special form drawing.

NOTE: Actual size would be $8^{1}/_{2}''$ × $11''$ (21.6 cm × 27.9 cm).

Applicant's Name: A-OK Software Development Group
Correspondence Address: 100 Main Street, Any Town, MO 12345
Goods and Services: Computer services, namely on-line magazine in the field of business management
Date of First Use: January 15, 1995
Date of First Use in Commerce: May 15, 1995
Standard Character Claim: The mark is presented in standard character format without claim to any particular font style, size or color.
The Mark:

THEORYTEC

What is a "Stylized or Special Form" drawing?

If the particular style of lettering is important or the mark includes a design or logo, you must select the "stylized or special form" drawing format. The drawing page should show a black and white image of the mark, no larger than 3.5 inches by 3.5 inches (8 cm by 8 cm). The drawing in special form must be a substantially exact representation of the mark as it appears on the specimen or on the foreign registration, as appropriate.

The following is an example of a proper special form drawing: NOTE: Actual size would be $8^1/2'' \times 11''$ (21.6 cm $\times$ 27.9 cm), with an image no larger than 3.5 inches by 3.5 inches (8 cm by 8 cm).

Applicant's Name: Pinstripes, Inc.
Applicant's Address: 100 Main Street, Any Town,
MO 12345
Goods and Services: Clothing, namely baseball caps and
t-shirts
Date of First Use: Intent-to-Use Application
Date of First Use in Commerce: Intent-to-Use Application
The Mark:

PINSTRIPES

What if I want to show color on the drawing?
If you want to register a mark in color, you must submit a color drawing. 37 C.F.R. §2.52(b)(1). You must also submit: (1) a color claim naming the colors that are a feature of the mark; and (2) a separate statement describing where the color(s) appear on the mark. See **http://www.uspto.gov/web/offices/tac/notices/examguide1-03.htm#IB1** for further information.

Goods and/or Services
You must list the specific goods/services for which registration is sought, regardless of the basis for the application. For information on "basis," see BASIS FOR FILING.

- If based on use in commerce, you must already be using the mark in commerce on or in connection with all the goods and/or services listed.
- If based on intent to use, on a foreign application or registration, or on a request for extension of protection of an international registration to the United States pursuant to section 66(a) of the Trademark Act, you must have a bona fide intention to use the mark in commerce on or in connection with all the listed goods and/or services.

When specifying the goods and/or services, use clear, concise terms, i.e., common commercial names and language that the general public easily understands. If you fail to list any recognizable goods or services, we will return your application and refund your fee.

Please note that the terms in the classification listing of goods and services in the "International Schedule of Classes of Goods and Services" are generally too broad and should not be used alone as an identification. Also, an international class number alone is never an acceptable listing. For a listing of acceptable wording for goods and services, see the USPTO's Acceptable Identification of Goods and Services Manual, at http://www.uspto.gov/web/offices/tac/doc/gsmanual/index.html.

Can I change the goods and/or services after filing my application?

You can clarify or limit the goods and/or services. However, you may not expand or broaden the identification of goods and/or services after filing the application.

Application Filing Fee

For current fees for trademark applications and amendments, please see the current **USPTO Fee Schedule**. Fee increases, when necessary, usually take effect on October 1 of any given year. Please call 1-800-PT0-9199 for up-to-date fee information.

For a listing of classes, see **International Schedule of Classes of Goods and Services**.

The filing fee must be paid in United States currency. The USPTO accepts payment by credit card, check or money order, or through an existing USPTO deposit account. Personal, business and certified checks are accepted and should be made payable to "Director of the USPTO." A form for authorizing charges to a credit card can be accessed through all TEAS forms. If you are filing on paper, you can download the form for authorizing credit card charges from the USPTO Web site at **http://www.uspto.gov/web/forms/2038.pdf**. NOTE: If the application meets the minimum filing requirements and is given a filing date, the application filing fee cannot be refunded.

Basis for Filing

The application should include your "basis" for filing. Most U.S. applicants base their application on their current use of the mark in commerce, or their intent to use their mark in commerce in the future.

What is "use in commerce"?

For the purpose of obtaining federal registration, "commerce" means all commerce that the U.S. Congress may lawfully regulate; for example, interstate commerce or commerce between the U.S. and another country. "Use in commerce" must be a bona fide use of the mark in the ordinary course of trade, and not use simply made to reserve rights in the mark. Generally, acceptable use is as follows:

For goods: the mark must appear on the goods, the container for the goods, or displays associated with the goods, and the goods must be sold or transported in commerce.

For services: the mark must be used or displayed in the sale or advertising of the services, and the services must be rendered in commerce.

If you have already started using the mark in commerce, you may file based on that use. A "use" based application must include a sworn statement (usually in the form of a declaration) that the mark is in use in commerce, listing the date of first use of the mark anywhere and the date of first use of the mark in commerce. A properly worded declaration is included in the USPTO standard application form. The applicant or a person authorized to sign on behalf of the applicant must sign the statement. The application should include a specimen showing use of the mark in commerce.

What is "intent to use"?

If you have not yet used the mark, but plan to do so in the future, you may file based on a good faith or bona fide intention to use the mark in commerce. You do not have to use the mark before you file your application.

An "intent to use" application must include a sworn statement (usually in the form of a declaration) that you have a bona fide intention to use the mark in commerce. A properly worded declaration is included in the USPTO standard application form. The applicant or a person authorized to sign on behalf of the applicant must sign the statement.

NOTE: If you file based on intent to use, you must begin actual use of the mark in commerce before the USPTO will register the mark; that is, after filing an application based on "intent to use," you must later file another form ("Allegation of Use") to establish that use has begun. See "Additional Requirements for 'Intent to Use' Applications" for more information.

Is there any other possible filing basis?

Yes. Although not as common, you may base your application on international agreements. Under certain international agreements, if you qualify, you may file in the U.S. based on a foreign application or on a registration in your country of origin. See **TMEP Chapter 1000.**

Also, section 66(a) of the Trademark Act permits the holder of an international registration to file a request for extension of protection of the international registration to the United States under the Madrid Protocol. See **http://www.uspto.gov/web/trademarks/madrid/madridguide.htm** for further information about the Madrid Protocol.

202

Specimen

What is "a specimen" of use?

A specimen is an actual example of how you are using the mark in commerce on or in connection with the identified goods and/or services. This is not the same as the drawing of the mark, which merely represents what you are claiming as the **mark.**

What is a proper specimen for use of a mark on goods (products)?

Normally, a specimen for a mark used on goods shows the mark on the actual goods or packaging for the goods. You may submit a tag or label for the goods; a container for the goods; a display associated with the goods; or a photograph of the goods that shows use of the mark on the goods. Do not submit the actual product.

Invoices, announcements, order forms, bills of lading, leaflets, brochures, publicity releases, letterhead and business cards generally are NOT acceptable specimens for goods.

What is a proper specimen for use of a mark with services?

A specimen for a mark used in connection with services must show the mark used in the sale or advertising for the services. You may submit a sign; a brochure about the services; an advertisement for the services; a business card or stationery showing the mark in connection with the services; or a photograph showing the mark as used in rendering or advertising the services. There must be some reference to the type of services rendered on the specimen, i.e., not just a display of the mark itself. For example, if the mark sought to be registered is "XYZ,"a business card that only shows the mark "XYZ"; would not be acceptable. A business card that states "XYZ REAL ESTATE" would be acceptable.

How do I file the specimen?
If filing electronically, you must attach an image of your specimen in .jpg format. In order to show the context in which the mark is used, the image should include as much of the label or advertisement as possible.

If filing a paper application, the specimen submitted with the application must be flat and no larger than 8½ by 11 inches. If you submit a larger specimen, the USPTO will create a facsimile of the specimen, insert it in the application file wrapper, and destroy the original submission. However, specimens consisting of videotapes, audiotapes, CDs or computer diskettes are acceptable for marks, such as sound marks, that cannot be used any other way.

When do I file the specimen?
For an application based on "use": If you are using the mark in commerce and you file based on that use, you should submit one specimen for each class of goods/services listed in the original application.

For an application based on "intent to use": You must submit one specimen for each class of goods/services when filing the "Allegation of Use." See section "**Additional Requirements for 'Intent to Use' Applications**". For an application based solely on a foreign application or registration: No specimen is required.

Signature

Who can sign the application?
A person who is properly authorized to sign a verification on behalf of the applicant is:
- a person with legal authority to bind the applicant; or
- a person with firsthand knowledge of the facts and actual or implied authority to act on behalf of the applicant; or

- an attorney as defined in 37 C.F.R. §10.1© who has an actual written or verbal power of attorney or an implied power of attorney from the applicant.

How do I sign a TEAS application?

In a TEAS application, you do not apply a conventional signature. Instead, you enter a "symbol" that you have adopted as a signature. The USPTO will accept any combination of letters, numbers, spaces and/or punctuation marks placed between two forward slash ("/") symbols. Examples of acceptable signatures for TEAS applications include /john doe/, /drl/, and /544-4925/.

What happens after I file my application?

LEGAL AND PROCEDURAL REVIEW OF APPLICATION

After the USPTO determines that you have met the **minimum filing requirements,** the application is forwarded to an examining attorney. This may take a number of months. The examining attorney reviews the application to determine whether it complies with all applicable rules and statutes and includes all required fees. Federal registration of trademarks is governed by the Trademark Act of 1946, 15 U.S.C. §1051 et seq., and the Trademark Rules of Practice, 37 C.F.R. Part 2.

A complete examination includes a search for conflicting marks, and an examination of the written application, the drawing, and any specimen.

If the examining attorney decides that a mark should not be registered, the examining attorney will issue a letter (Office action) explaining any substantive reasons for refusal, and any technical or procedural deficiencies in the application. If only minor corrections are required, the examining attorney may contact the applicant by telephone or e-mail (if the applicant has authorized communication by e-mail). If the examining attorney sends an Office action, the applicant's response to the Office action must be received in the Office within six months of the mailing date of the Office action, or the application will be declared abandoned.

If the applicant's response does not overcome all objections, the examining attorney will issue a final refusal. To attempt to overcome a final refusal, the applicant may, for an additional fee, appeal to the Trademark Trial and Appeal Board, an administrative tribunal within the USPTO.

Does the examining attorney search for conflicting marks?

Yes. After an application is filed, the assigned examining attorney will search the USPTO records to determine if a conflict, i.e., a likelihood of confusion, exists between the mark in the application and another mark that is registered or pending in the USPTO. The USPTO will not provide any preliminary search for conflicting marks before an applicant files an application. The principal factors considered by the examining attorney in determining whether there would be a likelihood of confusion are:

- the similarity of the marks; and
- the commercial relationship between the goods and/or services listed in the application.

To find a conflict, the marks do not have to be identical, and the goods and/or services do not have to be the same. It may be enough that the marks are similar and the goods and/or services related. 205

If a conflict exists between your mark and a registered mark, the examining attorney will refuse registration on the ground of likelihood of confusion. If a conflict exists between your mark and a mark in a pending application that was filed before your application, the examining attorney will notify you of the potential conflict. If the earlier-filed application registers, the Examining Attorney will refuse registration of your mark on the ground of likelihood of confusion.

Can I search for conflicting marks before filing?

Yes. You should search the USPTO records before filing your application to determine if any party is already claiming rights in a particular mark. You may conduct a search online at **http://tess2.uspto.gov/bin/gate.exe? f = login&p_lang = english&p_d = trmk,** or by visiting the USPTO Trademark Public Search Library at 2900 Crystal Drive, 2nd Floor, Arlington, Virginia. The library is open between 8:00 a.m. – 5:00 p.m., Monday through Friday. Both on-line searching and use of the Public Search Library are free.

Additionally, registered and pending trademarks may be searched at a Patent and Trademark Depository Library (PTDL). PTDLs are located throughout the U.S. See **PTDL** for a listing of their locations, or **http://www.uspto.gov/web/offices/ac/ido/ptdl/index.html.** Private trademark search firms will conduct a search for a fee. A listing of search firms can be found in the Yellow Pages of local phone directories or through an Internet search. The USPTO cannot assist you in selecting a search firm.

You can check the status of any pending application or registration through the Trademark Application and Registration Retrieval (TARR) database, available on-line at **http://tarr.uspto.gov**. If you do not have access to the Internet, you can call the Trademark Assistance Center at 1-800-786-9199 (or (703) 308–9000 if you live in Northern Virginia) to request a status check.

Are there other reasons the examining attorney might refuse my mark?
Yes. In addition to likelihood of confusion (discussed above), an examining attorney will refuse registration if the mark is:

- primarily merely descriptive or deceptively misdescriptive of the goods/services;
- primarily geographically descriptive or primarily geographically deceptively; misdescriptive of the goods/services;
- primarily merely a surname; or
- ornamental.

This is not a complete list of all possible grounds of refusal. See Chapter 1200 of the Trademark Manual of Examining Procedure (TMEP), available at **http://www.uspto.gov/web/offices/tac/tmep/**, for a complete discussion of the grounds for refusal of registration of a mark.

Publication for Opposition

If the examining attorney raises no objections to registration, or if the applicant overcomes all objections, the examining attorney will approve the mark for publication in the Official Gazette, a weekly publication of the USPTO.

The USPTO will send a NOTICE OF PUBLICATION to the applicant stating the date of publication. Any party who believes it may be damaged by registration of the mark has thirty (30) days from the publication date to file either an opposition to registration or a request to extend the time to oppose. An opposition is similar to a proceeding in a federal court, but is held before the Trademark Trial and Appeal Board, a USPTO administrative tribunal. If no opposition is filed or if an opposition is unsuccessful, the application enters the next stage of the registration process. A Certificate of Registration will issue for applications based on use, or a Notice of Allowance will issue for intent-to-use applications.

Certificate of Registration or Notice of Allowance

If the mark is published based upon the actual use of the mark in commerce, on a foreign registration under section 44 of the Trademark Act, or on an extension of protection of an international registration to the United States pursuant to section 66(a) of the Trademark Act, and no party files an opposition or request to extend the time to oppose, the USPTO will normally register the mark and issue a registration certificate about twelve (12) weeks after the date the mark was published.

If the mark is published based upon the applicant's bona fide intention to use the mark in commerce, the USPTO will issue a NOTICE OF ALLOWANCE about twelve (12) weeks after the date the mark was published, if no party files either an opposition or request to extend the time to oppose. The applicant then has six (6) months from the date of the NOTICE OF ALLOWANCE to either: use the mark in commerce and submit a STATEMENT OF USE; or request a six-month EXTENSION OF TIME TO FILE A STATEMENT OF USE. Both forms are available at **http://www.uspto.gov/teas/eTEASforms.htm**. See **Additional Requirements for 'Intent to Use' Applications**. If the STATEMENT OF USE is filed and approved, the USPTO will issue the registration certificate.

207

ADDITIONAL REQUIREMENTS FOR "INTENT TO USE" APPLICATIONS

Before the USPTO will register a mark that is based upon a bona fide intention to use the mark in commerce, the owner must:
- use the mark in commerce; and
- file an Allegation of Use.

What is an Allegation of Use?

An Allegation of Use is a sworn statement signed by the applicant or a person authorized to sign on behalf of the applicant (see **signature**) attesting to use of the mark in commerce. With the Allegation of Use, the owner must submit:
- a filing fee of $100 per class of goods/services; and
- one specimen showing use of the mark in commerce for each class of goods/services.

A form for filing the allegation of use is available at **http://www.uspto.gov/teas/eTEASforms.htm**.

When do I file an Allegation of Use?
You may file the Allegation of Use only

- on or before the day the examining attorney approves the mark for publication in the Official Gazette (an Allegation of Use filed before the mark is approved for publication is called an Amendment to Allege Use); or
- on or after the day the USPTO issues the Notice of Allowance (an Allegation of Use filed after the Notice of Allowance is issued is called a Statement of Use).

The Amendment to Allege Use and the Statement of Use include the same information, and differ only as to the time when it is filed. If you file an Allegation of Use between the period after the mark is approved for publication but before the Notice of Allowance is issued, the USPTO will return it.

Is there a deadline for filing the Statement of Use after the Notice of Allowance issues?
Yes. Once the USPTO issues the Notice of Allowance, you have six (6) months to file the Statement of Use. The six-month period runs from the date the USPTO issues the Notice of Allowance, not the date you receive it. If you have not used the mark in commerce, you must file a Request for an Extension of Time to File a Statement of Use (Extension Request) before the end of the six-month period, or the application will be declared "abandoned."

What is a Request for an Extension of Time to file a Statement of Use?
An Extension Request is a sworn statement signed by the owner or a person authorized to sign on behalf of the owner (see **signature**), stating that the applicant still has a bona fide intention to use the mark in commerce, and needs additional time to use the mark in commerce. A filing fee of $150 per class of goods/services must accompany the Extension Request. The form for filing the Extension Request is available at http://www.uspto.gov/teas/eTEASforms.htm.

The Extension Request, if granted, gives the owner an additional six (6) months to either:

- use the mark in commerce and file a Statement of Use; or
- file another Extension Request.

You may continue to file Extension Requests every six (6) months. However, you must use the mark and file a Statement of Use within three (3) years of the date the Notice of Allowance issues. The USPTO will not register a mark if, after thirty-six (36) months of the mailing date of the Notice of Allowance, no Statement of Use has been filed.

MAINTAINING A FEDERAL TRADEMARK REGISTRATION

Rights in a federally-registered trademark can last indefinitely if the owner continues to use the mark on or in connection with the goods and/or services in the registration and files all necessary documentation in the USPTO at the appropriate times. In general, the owner of a registration must periodically file:

209

- Affidavits of Continued Use or Excusable Nonuse under 15 U.S.C. §1058; and
- Applications for Renewal under 15 U.S.C. §1059.

Forms for filing these documents are available at **http://www.uspto. gov/teas/**. For further information on maintaining a federal trademark registration, please contact the Post Registration Division at (703) 308-9500.

USPTO CONTACTS FOR MORE INFORMATION

Below is a listing of various USPTO divisions' telephone and facsimile numbers. For general information about federal trademark registrations, or inquiries pertaining to a specific trademark application or registration, visit the USPTO web site, at **http://www.uspto.gov**.

Division	Phone	Fax
Assignment Division	(703) 308-9723	(703) 308-7124
For recording assignments		
Certification Division	(703) 308-9726	(703) 308-7048
For certified copies of registrations		

Copy Sales Department   (703) 305-8716   (703) 308-8759
For copies of files and registrations

Government Printing Office   (202) 512-1800   (202) 512-2250
For copies of the Official Gazette and other USPTO publications

Intent to Use/Divisional Unit   (703) 308-9550   (703) 308-7196
For filing Statements of Use, Extension Requests and Requests to Divide Applications

Office of the Commissioner   (703) 308-8900   (703) 308-7220
for Trademarks
For filing petitions to the Commissioner

Post Registration Division   (703) 308-9500   (703) 308-7178
For filing post registration documents

Publication and Issue Division   (703) 308-9401   (703) 305-4100
For original certificate of registration

Trademark Assistance Center   (703) 308-9000   (703) 308-7016
For general trademark information and printed application forms

Trademark Trial and   (703) 308-9300   (703) 308-9333
Appeal Board
For filing notices of opposition and petitions to cancel registrations

OTHER TRADEMARK RESOURCES

International Schedule of Classes of Goods and Services

Goods

1.	Chemicals used in industry, science and photography, as well as in agriculture, horticulture and forestry; unprocessed artificial resins; unprocessed plastics; manures; fire extinguishing compositions; tempering and soldering preparations; chemical substances for preserving foodstuffs; tanning substances; adhesives used in industry.

2.	Paints, varnishes, lacquers; preservatives against rust and against deterioration of wood; colorants; mordants; raw natural resins; metals in foil and powder form for painters, decorators, printers and artists.
3.	Bleaching preparations and other substances for laundry use; cleaning, polishing, scouring and abrasive preparations; soaps; perfumery, essential oils, cosmetics, hair lotions; dentifrices.
4.	Industrial oils and greases; lubricants; dust absorbing, wetting and binding compositions; fuels (including motor spirit) and illuminants; candles, wicks.
5.	Pharmaceutical, veterinary, and sanitary preparations; dietetic substances adapted for medical use, food for babies; plasters, materials for dressings; material for stopping teeth, dental wax; disinfectants; preparations for destroying vermin; fungicides, herbicides.
6.	Common metals and their alloys; metal building materials; transportable buildings of metal; materials of metal for railway tracks; nonelectric cables and wires of common metal; iron-mongery, small items of metal hardware; pipes and tubes of metal; safes; goods of common metal not included in other classes; ores.
7.	Machines and machine tools; motors and engines (except for land vehicles); machine coupling and transmission components (except for land vehicles); agricultural implements other than hand-operated; incubators for eggs.
8.	Hand tools and implements (hand-operated); cutlery; side arms; razors.
9.	Scientific, nautical, surveying, electric, photographic, cinemato-graphic, optical, weighing, measuring, signalling, checking (supervision), life-saving and teaching apparatus and instruments; apparatus for recording, transmission or reproduction of sound or images; magnetic data carriers, recording discs; automatic vending machines and mechanisms for coin operated apparatus; cash registers, calculating machines, data processing equipment and computers; fire extinguishing apparatus.

10.	Surgical, medical, dental, and veterinary apparatus and instruments, artificial limbs, eyes, and teeth; orthopedic articles; suture materials.
11.	Apparatus for lighting, heating, steam generating, cooking, refrigerating, drying, ventilating, water supply, and sanitary purposes.
12.	Vehicles; apparatus for locomotion by land, air, or water.
13.	Firearms; ammunition and projectiles; explosives; fireworks.
14.	Precious metals and their alloys and goods in precious metals or coated therewith, not included in other classes; jewelry, precious stones; horological and chronometric instruments.
15.	Musical instruments.
16.	Paper, cardboard and goods made from these materials, not included in other classes; printed matter; bookbinding material; photographs; stationery; adhesives for stationery or household purposes; artists' materials; paint brushes; typewriters and office requisites (except furniture); instructional and teaching material (except apparatus); plastic materials for packaging (not included in other classes); playing cards; printers' type; printing blocks.
17.	Rubber, gutta-percha, gum, asbestos, mica and goods made from these materials and not included in other classes; plastics in extruded form for use in manufacture; packing, stopping and insulating materials; flexible pipes, not of metal.
18.	Leather and imitations of leather, and goods made of these materials and not included in other classes; animal skins, hides; trunks and travelling bags; umbrellas, parasols and walking sticks; whips, harness and saddlery.
19.	Building materials (non-metallic); nonmetallic rigid pipes for building; asphalt, pitch and bitumen; nonmetallic transportable buildings; monuments, not of metal.
20.	Furniture, mirrors, picture frames; goods (not included in other classes) of wood, cork, reed, cane, wicker, horn, bone, ivory, whalebone, shell, amber, mother-of-pearl, meerschaum and substitutes for all these materials, or of plastics.

21.	Household or kitchen utensils and containers (not of precious metal or coated therewith); combs and sponges; brushes (except paint brushes); brush-making materials; articles for cleaning purposes; steel-wool; unworked or semi-worked glass (except glass used in building); glassware, porcelain and earthenware not included in other classes.
22.	Ropes, string, nets, tents, awnings, tarpaulins, sails, sacks and bags (not included in other classes); padding and stuffing materials (except of rubber or plastics); raw fibrous textile materials.
23.	Yarns and threads, for textile use.
24.	Textiles and textile goods, not included in other classes; beds and table covers.
25.	Clothing, footwear, headgear.
26.	Lace and embroidery, ribbons and braid; buttons, hooks and eyes, pins and needles; artificial flowers.
27.	Carpets, rugs, mats and matting, linoleum and other materials for covering existing floors; wall hangings (non-textile).
28.	Games and playthings; gymnastic and sporting articles not included in other classes; decorations for Christmas trees.
29.	Meat, fish, poultry and game; meat extracts; preserved, dried and cooked fruits and vegetables; jellies, jams, fruit sauces; eggs, milk and milk products; edible oils and fats.
30.	Coffee, tea, cocoa, sugar, rice, tapioca, sago, artificial coffee; flour and preparations made from cereals, bread, pastry and confectionery, ices; honey, treacle; yeast, baking powder; salt, mustard; vinegar, sauces (condiments); spices; ice.
31.	Agricultural, horticultural and forestry products and grains not included in other classes; live animals; fresh fruits and vegetables; seeds, natural plants and flowers; foodstuffs for animals; malt.
32.	Beers; mineral and aerated waters and other nonalcoholic drinks; fruit drinks and fruit juices; syrups and other preparations for making beverages.
33.	Alcoholic beverages (except beers).
34.	Tobacco; smokers' articles; matches.

Services

35.	Advertising; business management; business administration; office functions.
36.	Insurance; financial affairs; monetary affairs; real estate affairs.
37.	Building construction; repair; installation services.
38.	Telecommunications.
39.	Transport; packaging and storage of goods; travel arrangement
40.	Treatment of materials.
41.	Education; providing of training; entertainment; sporting and cultural activities.
42.	Scientific and technological services and research and design relating thereto; industrial analysis and research services; design and development of computer hardware and software; legal services.
43.	Services for providing food and drink; temporary accommodations.
44.	Medical services; veterinary services; hygienic and beauty care for human beings or animals; agriculture, horticulture and forestry services.
45.	Personal and social services rendered by others to meet the needs of individuals; security services for the protection of property and individuals.

The following more detailed list of the international classes is taken from the FAQs section of the Trademark Office Web site.

Goods

Class 1 (Chemicals)

Chemicals used in industry, science and photography, as well as in agriculture, horticulture and forestry; unprocessed artificial resins, unprocessed plastics; manures; fire extinguishing compositions; tempering and soldering preparations; chemical substances for preserving foodstuffs; tanning substances; adhesives used in industry.

Explanatory Note

This class includes mainly chemical products used in industry, science and agriculture, including those which go to the making of products belonging to other classes. Includes, in particular:

- compost;
- salt for preserving other than for foodstuffs.

Does not include, in particular:

- raw natural resins (Cl. 02);
- chemical products for use in medical science (CL 05);
- fungicides, herbicides and preparations for destroying vermin (CL 05);
- adhesives for stationery or household purposes (CL 16);
- salt for preserving foodstuffs (CL 30);
- straw mulch (CL 31).

Class 2 (Paints)

Paints, varnishes, lacquers; preservatives against rust and against deterioration of wood; colorants; mordants; raw natural resins; metals in foil and powder form for painters, decorators, printers and artists.

Explanatory Note

This class includes mainly paints, colorants and preparations used for the protection against corrosion. Includes, in particular:

- paints, varnishes and lacquers for industry, handicrafts and arts;
- dyestuffs for clothing;
- colorants for foodstuffs and beverages.

Does not include, in particular:

- unprocessed artificial resins (CL 01);
- laundry bluing (CL 03);
- cosmetic dyes (CL 03);
- mordants for seed (CL 05);
- paint boxes (articles for use in school) (CL 16);
- insulating paints and varnishes (CL 17).

Class 3 (Cosmetics and cleaning preparations)

Bleaching preparations and other substances for laundry use; cleaning, polishing, scouring and abrasive preparations; soaps; perfumery, essential oils, cosmetics, hair lotions; dentifrices.

Explanatory Note
This class includes mainly cleaning preparations and toilet preparations. Includes, in particular:
- deodorants for personal use;
- sanitary preparations being toiletries.

Does not include, in particular:
- chemical chimney cleaners (CL 01);
- degreasing preparations for use in manufacturing processes (CL 01);
- deodorants other than for personal use (CL 05);
- sharpening stones and grindstones (hand tools) (CL 08).

Class 4 (Lubricants and fuels)

Industrial oils and greases; lubricants; dust absorbing, wetting and binding compositions; fuels (including motor spirit) and illuminants; candles, wicks.

Explanatory Note
This class includes mainly industrial oils and greases, fuels and illuminants.

Does not include, in particular:
- certain special industrial oils and greases (consult the Alphabetical List of Goods).

Class 5 (Pharmaceuticals)

Pharmaceutical, veterinary and sanitary preparations; dietetic substances adapted for medical use, food for babies; plasters, materials for dressings; material for stopping teeth, dental wax; disinfectants; preparations for destroying vermin; fungicides, herbicides.

Explanatory Note
This class includes mainly pharmaceuticals and other preparations for medical purposes. Includes, in particular:
- sanitary preparations for medical purposes and for personal hygiene;
- deodorants other than for personal use;
- cigarettes without tobacco, for medical purposes.

Does not include, in particular:

- sanitary preparations being toiletries (CL 03);
- deodorants for personal use (CL 03);
- supportive bandages (CL 10).

Class 6 (Metal goods)

Common metals and their alloys; metal building materials; transportable buildings of metal; materials of metal for railway tracks; non-electric cables and wires of common metal; iron mongery, small items of metal hardware; pipes and tubes of metal; safes; goods of common metal not included in other classes; ores.

Explanatory Note

This class includes mainly unwrought and partly wrought common metals as well as simple products made of them. Does not include, in particular:

- bauxite (CL 01);
- mercury, antimony, alkaline and alkaline-earth metals (CL 01);
- metals in foil and powder form for painters, decorators, printers and artists (CL 02).

Class 7 (Machinery)

Machines and machine tools; motors and engines (except for land vehicles); machine coupling and transmission components (except for land vehicles); agricultural implements other than hand-operated; incubators for eggs.

Explanatory Note

This class includes mainly machines, machine tools, motors and engines. Includes, in particular:

- parts of motors and engines (of all kinds);
- electric cleaning machines and apparatus.

Does not include, in particular:

- certain special machines and machine tools (consult the Alphabetical List of Goods);
- hand tools and implements, hand operated (CL 08);
- motors and engines for land vehicles (CL 12).

Class 8 (Hand tools)

Hand tools and implements (hand operated); cutlery; side arms; razors.
Explanatory Note
This class includes mainly hand operated implements used as tools in
the respective professions. Includes, in particular:
- cutlery of precious metals;
- electric razors and clippers (hand instruments).

Does not include, in particular:
- certain special instruments (consult the Alphabetical List of Goods);
- machine tools and implements driven by a motor (CL 07);
- surgical cutlery (CL 10);
- paperknives (CL 16);
- fencing weapons (CL 28).

Class 9 (Electrical and scientific apparatus)

Scientific, nautical, surveying, electric, photographic, cinematographic,
optical, weighing, measuring, signaling, checking (supervision), lifesaving
and teaching apparatus and instruments; apparatus for recording, transmission or reproduction of sound or images; magnetic data carriers,
recording discs; automatic vending machines and mechanisms for coin
operated apparatus; cash registers, calculating machines, data processing
equipment and computers; fire-extinguishing apparatus.
Explanatory Note
Includes, in particular:
- apparatus and instruments for scientific research in laboratories;
- apparatus and instruments for controlling ships, such as apparatus and instruments, for measuring and for transmitting orders;
- the following electrical apparatus and instruments:
  - certain electrothermic tools and apparatus, such as electric
    soldering irons, electric flat irons which, if they were not elec-
    tric, would belong to Class 8;
  - apparatus and devices which, if not electrical, would be listed
    in various classes, i.e., electrically heated clothing, cigar-
    lighters for automobiles;
- protractors; punched card office machines; amusement apparatus
  adapted for use with television receivers only.

Does not include, in particular:
- the following electrical apparatus and instruments:
  - electromechanical apparatus for the kitchen (grinders and mixers for foodstuffs, fruit-presses, electrical coffee mills, etc.), and certain other apparatus and instruments driven by an electrical motor, all coming under Class 7;
  - electric razors and clippers (hand instruments) (CL 08); electric toothbrushes and combs (CL 21);
  - electrical apparatus for space heating or for the heating of liquids, for cooking, ventilating, etc. (CL 11);
- clocks and watches and other chronometric instruments (CL 14);
- control clocks (CL 14).

Class 10 (Medical apparatus)

Surgical, medical, dental and veterinary apparatus and instruments, artificial limbs, eyes and teeth; orthopedic articles; suture materials.

Explanatory Note

This class includes mainly medical apparatus, instruments and articles.

Includes, in particular:
- special furniture for medical use;
- hygienic rubber articles (consult the Alphabetical List of Goods);
- supportive bandages.

Class 11 (Enviromental control apparatus)

Apparatus for lighting, heating, steam generating, cooking, refrigerating, drying, ventilating, water supply and sanitary purposes.

Explanatory Note

Includes, in particular:
- air conditioning apparatus;
- bedwarmers, hot water bottles, warming pans, electric or non-electric;
- electrically heated cushions (pads) and blankets, not for medical purposes;
- electric kettles;
- electric cooking utensils.

Does not include, in particular:
- steam producing apparatus (parts of machines) (CL 07);
- electrically heated clothing (CL 09).

Class 12 (Vehicles)

Vehicles; apparatus for locomotion by land, air or water.

Explanatory Note

Includes, in particular:
- motors and engines for land vehicles;
- couplings and transmission components for land vehicles;
- air cushion vehicles.

Does not include, in particular:
- certain parts of vehicles (consult the Alphabetical List of Goods);
- railway material of metal (CL 06);
- motors, engines, couplings and transmission components other than for land vehicles (CL 07);
- parts of motors and engines (of all kinds) (CL 07).

Class 13 (Firearms)

Firearms; ammunition and projectiles; explosives; fireworks.

Explanatory Note

This class includes mainly firearms and pyrotechnical products. Does not include, in particular:
- matches (CL 34).

Class 14 (Jewelry)

Precious metals and their alloys and goods in precious metals or coated therewith, not included in other classes; jewelry, precious stones; horological and chronometric instruments.

Explanatory Note

This class includes mainly precious metals, goods in precious metals and, in general, jewelry, clocks and watches. Includes, in particular:
- jewelry (i.e. imitation jewelry and jewelry of precious metal and stones);
- cuff links, tie pins.

Does not include, in particular:
- certain goods in precious metals (classified according to their function or purpose), for example:
- metals in foil and powder form for painters, decorators, printers and artists (CL 02);
- amalgam of gold for dentists (CL 05);
- cutlery (CL 08);
- electric contacts (CL 09);
- pen nibs of gold (CL 16);
- objects of art not in precious metals (classified according to the material of which they consist).

Class 15 (Musical Instruments)

Musical instruments.

Explanatory Note   221

Includes, in particular:
- mechanical pianos and their accessories;
- musical boxes;
- electrical and electronic musical instruments.

Does not include, in particular:
- apparatus for the recording, transmission, amplification and reproduction of sound (CL 09).

Class 16 (Paper goods and printed matter)

Paper, cardboard and goods made from these materials, not included in other classes; printed matter; bookbinding material; photographs; stationery; adhesives for stationery or household purposes; artists' materials; paint brushes; typewriters and office requisites (except furniture); instructional and teaching material (except apparatus); plastic materials for packaging (not included in other classes); playing cards; printers' type; printing blocks.

Explanatory Note

This class includes mainly paper, goods made from that material and office requisites. Includes, in particular:
- paper knives;
- duplicators;
- plastic sheets, sacks and bags for wrapping and packaging.

Does not include, in particular:
- certain goods made of paper and cardboard (consult the Alphabetical List of Goods);
- colors (CL 02);
- hand tools for artists (for example: spatulas, sculptors' chisels) (CL 08).

Class 17 (Rubber goods)

Rubber, gutta-percha, gum, asbestos, mica and goods made from these materials and not included in other classes; plastics in extruded form for use in manufacture; packing, stopping and insulating materials; flexible pipes, not of metal.

Explanatory Note

This class includes mainly electrical, thermal and acoustic insulating materials and plastics, being for use in manufacture in the form of sheets, blocks and rods.

Includes, in particular:
- rubber material for recapping tires;
- padding and stuffing materials of rubber or plastics;
- floating anti-pollution barriers.

Class 18 (Leather goods)

Leather and imitations of leather, and goods made of these materials and not included in other classes; animal skins, hides; trunks and traveling bags; umbrellas, parasols and walking sticks; whips, harness and saddlery.

Explanatory Note

This class includes mainly leather, leather imitations, travel goods not included in other classes and saddlery. Does not include, in particular:
- clothing, footwear, headgear (consult the Alphabetical List of Goods).

Class 19 (Nonmetallic building materials)

Building materials (nonmetallic); nonmetallic rigid pipes for building; asphalt, pitch and bitumen; nonmetallic transportable buildings; monuments, not of metal.

Explanatory Note

This class includes mainly nonmetallic building materials. Includes, in particular:

- semi-worked woods (for example: beams, planks, panels);
- veneers;
- building glass (for example: floor slabs, glass tiles);
- glass granules for marking out roads;
- letter boxes of masonry.

Does not include, in particular:

- cement preservatives and cement-waterproofing preparations (CL 01);
- fireproofing preparations (CL 01).

Class 20 (Furniture and articles not otherwise classified)

Furniture, mirrors, picture frames; goods (not included in other classes) of wood, cork, reed, cane, wicker, horn, bone, ivory, whalebone, shell, amber, mother-of-pearl, meerschaum and substitutes for all these materials, or of plastics.

Explanatory Note

This class includes mainly furniture and its parts and plastic goods, not included in other classes. Includes, in particular:

- metal furniture and furniture for camping;
- bedding (for example: mattresses, spring mattresses, pillows);
- looking glasses and furnishing or toilet mirrors;
- registration number plates not of metal;
- letter boxes not of metal or masonry.

Does not include, in particular:

- certain special types of mirrors, classified according to their function or purpose (consult the Alphabetical List of Goods);
- special furniture for laboratories (CL 09);
- special furniture for medical use (CL 10);
- bedding linen (CL 24);
- eiderdowns (CL 24).

Class 21 (Housewares and glass)

Household or kitchen utensils and containers (not of precious metal or coated therewith); combs and sponges; brushes (except paint brushes); brush-making materials; articles for cleaning purposes; steel wool; un-worked or semi-worked glass (except glass used in building); glassware, porcelain and earthenware not included in other classes.

Explanatory Note

This class includes mainly small, hand-operated, utensils and apparatus for household and kitchen use as well as toilet utensils, glassware and articles in porcelain. Includes, in particular:

- utensils and containers for household and kitchen use, for example:
- kitchen utensils, pails, and pans of iron, aluminum, plastics and other materials, small hand-operated apparatus for mincing, grinding, pressing, etc.;
- candle extinguishers, not of precious metal;
- electric combs;
- electric toothbrushes;
- dish stands and decanter stands.

Does not include, in particular:

- certain goods made of glass, porcelain and earthenware (consult the Alphabetical List of Goods);
- cleaning preparations, soaps, etc. (Cl. 03);
- small apparatus for mincing, grinding, pressing, etc., driven by electricity (Cl. 07);
- razors and shaving apparatus, clippers (hand instruments), metal implements and utensils for manicure and pedicure (Cl. 08);
- cooking utensils, electric (Cl. 11);
- toilet mirrors (Cl. 20).

Class 22 (Cordage and fibers)

Ropes, string, nets, tents, awnings, tarpaulins, sails, sacks and bags (not included in other classes); padding and stuffing materials (except of rubber or plastics); raw fibrous textile materials.

Explanatory Note

This class includes mainly rope and sail manufacture products, padding and stuffing materials and raw fibrous textile materials. Includes, in particular:

- cords and twines in natural or artificial textile fibres, paper or plastics.

Does not include, in particular:

- certain nets, sacs and bags (consult the Alphabetical List of Goods);
- strings for musical instruments (Cl. 15).

Class 23 (Yarns and threads)

Yarns and threads, for textile use.

Class 24 (Fabrics)

Textiles and textile goods, not included in other classes; bed and table covers.

Explanatory Note

This class includes mainly textiles (piece goods) and textile covers for household use. Includes, in particular:

- bedding linen of paper.

Does not include, in particular:

- certain special textiles (consult the Alphabetical List of Goods);
- electrically heated blankets (Cl. 10);
- table linen of paper (Cl. 16);
- horse blankets (Cl. 18).

Class 25 (Clothing)

Clothing, footwear, headgear.

Explanatory Note

Does not include, in particular:

- certain clothing and footwear for special use (consult the Alphabetical List of Goods).

Class 26 (Fancy goods)

Lace and embroidery, ribbons and braid; buttons, hooks and eyes, pins and needles; artificial flowers.

Explanatory Note

This class includes mainly dressmakers' articles. Includes, in particular:

- slide fasteners.

Does not include, in particular:

- certain special types of hooks (consult the Alphabetical List of Goods);

225

- certain special types of needles (consult the Alphabetical List of Goods);
- yarns and threads for textile use (Cl. 23).

Class 27 (Floor coverings)
Carpets, rugs, mats and matting, linoleum and other materials for covering existing floors; wall hangings (non-textile).

Explanatory Note
This class includes mainly products intended to be added as furnishings to previously constructed floors and walls.

Class 28 (Toys and sporting goods)
Games and playthings; gymnastic and sporting articles not included in other classes; decorations for Christmas trees.

Explanatory Note
Includes, in particular:
- fishing tackle;
- equipment for various sports and games.

Does not include, in particular:
- Christmas tree candles (Cl. 04);
- diving equipment (Cl. 09);
- amusement apparatus adapted for use with television receivers only (Cl. 09);
- electrical lamps (garlands) for Christmas trees (Cl. 11);
- playing cards (Cl. 16);
- fishing nets (Cl. 22);
- clothing for gymnastics and sports (Cl. 25);
- confectionery and chocolate decorations for Christmas trees (Cl. 30).

Class 29 (Meats and processed foods)
Meat, fish, poultry and game; meat extracts; preserved, dried and cooked fruits and vegetables; jellies, jams, fruit sauces; eggs, milk and milk products; edible oils and fats.

Explanatory Note
This class includes mainly foodstuffs of animal origin as well as vegetables and other horticultural comestible products which are prepared for consumption or conservation. Includes, in particular:
- milk beverages (milk predominating).

226

Does not include, in particular:
- certain foodstuffs of plant origin (consult the Alphabetical List of Goods);
- baby food (Cl. 05);
- dietetic substances adapted for medical use (Cl. 05);
- salad dressings (Cl. 30);
- fertilized eggs for hatching (Cl. 31);
- foodstuffs for animals (Cl. 31);
- living animals (Cl. 31).

Class 30 (Staple foods)

Coffee, tea, cocoa, sugar, rice, tapioca, sago, artificial coffee; flour and preparations made from cereals, bread, pastry and confectionery, ices; honey, treacle; yeast, baking-powder; salt, mustard; vinegar, sauces (condiments); spices; ice.

Explanatory Note

This class includes mainly foodstuffs of plant origin prepared for consumption or conservation as well as auxiliaries intended for the improvement of the flavour of food. Includes, in particular:
- beverages with coffee, cocoa or chocolate base;
- cereals prepared for human consumption (for example: oat flakes and those made of other cereals).

Does not include, in particular:
- certain foodstuffs of plant origin (consult the Alphabetical List of Goods);
- salt for preserving other than for foodstuffs (Cl. 01);
- medicinal teas and dietetic substances adapted for medical use (Cl. 05);
- baby food (Cl. 05);
- raw cereals (Cl. 31);
- foodstuffs for animals (Cl. 31).

Class 31 (Natural agricultural products)

Agricultural, horticultural and forestry products and grains not included in other classes; living animals; fresh fruits and vegetables; seeds, natural plants and flowers; foodstuffs for animals, malt.

Explanatory Note

This class includes mainly land products not having been subjected to any form of preparation for consumption, living animals and plants as well as foodstuffs for animals. Includes, in particular:

- raw woods;
- raw cereals;
- fertilized eggs for hatching;
- mollusca and crustacea (live).

Does not include, in particular:

- cultures of micro-organisms and leeches for medical purposes (Cl. 05);
- semi-worked woods (Cl. 19);
- artificial fishing bait (Cl. 28);
- rice (Cl. 30);
- tobacco (Cl. 34).

Class 32 (Light beverages)

Beers; mineral and aerated waters and other nonalcoholic drinks; fruit drinks and fruit juices; syrups and other preparations for making beverages.

Explanatory Note

This class includes mainly nonalcoholic beverages, as well as beer. Includes, in particular:

- de-alcoholized drinks.

Does not include, in particular:

- beverages for medical purposes (Cl. 05);
- milk beverages (milk predominating) (Cl. 29);
- beverages with coffee, cocoa or chocolate base (Cl. 30).

Class 33 (Wine and spirits)

Alcoholic beverages (except beers).

Explanatory Note

Does not include, in particular:

- medicinal drinks (Cl. 05);
- de-alcoholized drinks (Cl. 32).

Class 34 (Smokers' articles)

Tobacco; smokers' articles; matches.

Explanatory Note

Includes, in particular:

- tobacco substitutes (not for medical purposes).

Does not include, in particular:

- cigarettes without tobacco, for medical purposes (Cl. 05);
- certain smokers' articles in precious metal (Cl. 14) (consult the Alphabetical List of Goods).

Services
Class 35 (Advertising and business)

Advertising; business management; business administration; office functions.

Explanatory Note

This class includes mainly services rendered by persons or organizations principally with the object of:

1. help in the working or management of a commercial undertaking, or
2. help in the management of the business affairs or commercial functions of an industrial or commercial enterprise, as well as services rendered by advertising establishments primarily undertaking communications to the public, declarations or announcements by all means of diffusion and concerning all kinds of goods or services.

Includes, in particular:

- services consisting of the registration, transcription, composition, compilation, or systematization of written communications and registrations, and also the exploitation or compilation of mathematical or statistical data;
- services of advertising agencies and services such as the distribution of prospectuses, directly or through the post, or the distribution of samples. This class may refer to advertising in connection with other services, such as those concerning bank loans or advertising by radio; the bringing together, for the benefit of others, of a variety of goods (excluding the transport thereof), enabling customers to conveniently view and purchase those goods.

Does not include, in particular:

- activity of an enterprise the primary function of which is the sale of goods, i.e., of a so-called commercial enterprise;
- services such as evaluations and reports of engineers which do not directly refer to the working or management of affairs in a commercial or industrial enterprise (consult the Alphabetical List of Services);
- professional consultations and the drawing up of plans not connected with the conduct of business (Cl. 42).

Class 36 (Insurance and financial)

Insurance; financial affairs; monetary affairs; real estate affairs.

Explanatory Note

This class includes mainly services rendered in financial and monetary affairs and services rendered in relation to insurance contracts of all kinds. Includes, in particular:

- services relating to financial or monetary affairs comprise the following:
  - services of all the banking establishments, or institutions connected with them such as exchange brokers or clearing services;
  - services of credit institutions other than banks such as cooperative credit associations, individual financial companies, lenders, etc.;
  - services of "investment trusts," of holding companies;
  - services of brokers dealing in shares and property;
  - services connected with monetary affairs vouched for by trustees;
  - services rendered in connection with the issue of travelers'checks and letters of credit;
  - services of realty administrators of buildings, i.e., services of letting or valuation, or financing;
  - services dealing with insurance such as services rendered by agents or brokers engaged in insurance, services rendered to insured, and insurance underwriting services.

Class 37 (Building construction and repair)

Building construction; repair; installation services.

Explanatory Note

This class includes mainly services rendered by contractors or subcontractors in the construction or making of permanent buildings, as well as services rendered by persons or organizations engaged in the restoration of objects to their original condition or in their preservation without altering their physical or chemical properties. Includes, in particular:

- services relating to the construction of buildings, roads, bridges, dams or transmission lines and services of undertakings specializing in the field of construction such as those of painters, plumbers, heating installers or roofers;
- services auxiliary to construction services like inspections of construction plans;
- services of shipbuilding;
- services consisting of hiring of tools or building materials;
- repair services, i.e., services which undertake to put any object into good condition after wear, damage, deterioration or partial destruction (restoration of an existing building or another object that has become imperfect and is to be restored to its original condition);
- various repair services such as those in the fields of electricity, furniture, instruments, tools, etc.;
- services of maintenance for preserving an object in its original condition without changing any of its properties (for the difference between this class and Class 40 see the Explanatory Note of Class 40).

Does not include, in particular:

- services consisting of storage of goods such as clothes or vehicles (Cl. 39);
- services connected with dyeing of cloth or clothes (Cl. 40).

Class 38 (Telecommunications)

Explanatory Note

This class includes mainly services allowing at least one person to communicate with another by a sensory means. Such services include those which:

1. allow a person to talk to another,
2. transmit messages from one person to another, and
3. place a person in oral or visual communication with another (radio and television).

Includes, in particular:

- services which consist essentially of the diffusion of radio or television programs.

Does not include, in particular:
- radio advertising services (Cl. 35).

Class 39 (Transportation and storage)

Transport; packaging and storage of goods; travel arrangement.

Explanatory Note

This class includes mainly services rendered in transporting people or goods from one place to another (by rail, road, water, air or pipeline) and services necessarily connected with such transport, as well as services relating to the storing of goods in a warehouse or other building for their preservation or guarding. Includes, in particular:
- services rendered by companies exploiting stations, bridges, railroad ferries, etc., used by the transporter;
- services connected with the hiring of transport vehicles;
- services connected with maritime tugs, unloading, the functioning of ports and docks and the salvaging of wrecked ships and their cargoes;
- services connected with the functioning of airports;
- services connected with the packaging and parceling of goods before dispatch;
- services consisting of information about journeys or the transport of goods by brokers and tourist agencies, information relating to tariffs, timetables and methods of transport;
- services relating to the inspection of vehicles or goods before transport.

Does not include, in particular:
- services relating to advertising transport undertakings such as the distribution of prospectuses or advertising on the radio (Cl. 35);
- services relating to the issuing of travelers' checks or letters of credit by brokers or travel agents (Cl. 36);
- services relating to insurance (commercial, fire or life) during the transport of persons or goods (Cl. 36);
- services rendered by the maintenance and repair of vehicles, nor the maintenance or repair of objects connected with the transport of persons or goods (Cl. 37);
- services relating to reservation of rooms in a hotel by travel agents or brokers (Cl. 42).

Class 40 (Treatment of materials)

Treatment of materials.

Explanatory Note

This class includes mainly services not included in other classes, rendered by the mechanical or chemical processing or transformation of objects or inorganic or organic substances.

For the purposes of classification, the mark is considered a service mark only in cases where processing or transformation is effected for the account of another person. A mark is considered a trade mark in all cases where the substance or object is marketed by the person who processed or transformed it. Includes, in particular:

- services relating to transformation of an object or substance and any process involving a change in its essential properties (for example, dyeing a garment); consequently, a maintenance service, although usually in Class 37, is included in Class 40 if it entails such a change (for example, the chroming of motor vehicle bumpers);
- services of material treatment which may be present during the production of any substance or object other than a building; for example, services which involve cutting, shaping, polishing by abrasion or metal coating.

Does not include, in particular:

- repair services (Cl. 37).

Class 41 (Education and entertainment)

Education; providing of training; entertainment; sporting and cultural activities.

Explanatory Note

This class contains mainly services rendered by persons or institutions in the development of the mental faculties of persons or animals, as well as services intended to entertain or to engage the attention. Includes, in particular:

- services consisting of all forms of education of persons or training of animals;
- services having the basic aim of the entertainment, amusement or
- recreation of people.

Class 42 (Computer, scientific & legal)

Scientific and technological services and research and design relating thereto:

- industrial analysis and research services; design and development of computer hardware and software;
- legal services.

Explanatory Note

Class 42 includes mainly services provided by persons, individually or collectively, in relation to the theoretical and practical aspects of complex fields of activities; such services are provided by members of professions such as chemists, physicists, engineers, computer specialists, lawyers, etc. Includes, in particular:

- the services of engineers who undertake evaluations, estimates, research and reports in the scientific and technological fields
- scientific research services for medical purposes

Does not include, in particular:

- business research and evaluations (Cl. 35);
- word processing and computer file management services (Cl. 35);
- financial and fiscal evaluations (Cl. 36);
- mining and oil extraction (Cl. 37);
- computer (hardware) installation and repair services (Cl. 37);
- services provided by the members of professions such as medical doctors, veterinary surgeons, psychoanalysts (Cl. 44);
- medical treatment services (Cl. 44);
- garden design (Cl. 44).

Class 43 (Hotels and Restaurants)

Services for providing food and drink; temporary accommodations.

Explanatory Note

Class 43 includes mainly services provided by persons or establishments whose aim is to prepare food and drink for consumption and services provided to obtain bed and board in hotels, boarding houses or other establishments providing temporary accommodations. Includes, in particular:

- reservation services for travellers' accommodations, particularly through travel agencies or brokers;
- boarding for animals.

Does not include, in particular:

- rental services for real estate such as houses, flats, etc., for permanent use (Cl. 36);
- arranging travel by tourist agencies (Cl. 39);
- preservation services for food and drink (Cl. 40);
- discotheque services (Cl. 41);
- boarding schools (Cl. 41);
- rest and convalescent homes (Cl. 44).

Class 44 (Medical, beauty & agricultural)

Medical services; veterinary services; hygienic and beauty care for human beings or animals; agriculture, horticulture and forestry services.

Explanatory Note

Class 44 includes mainly medical care, hygienic and beauty care given by persons or establishments to human beings and animals; it also includes services relating to the fields of agriculture, horticulture and forestry. Includes, in particular:

- medical analysis services relating to the treatment of persons (such as x-ray examinations and taking of blood samples);
- artificial insemination services;
- pharmacy advice;
- animal breeding;
- services relating to the growing of plants such as gardening;
- services relating to floral art such as floral compositions as well as garden design.

Does not include, in particular:

- vermin extermination (other than for agriculture, horticulture and forestry) (Cl. 37);
- installation and repair services for irrigation systems (Cl. 37);
- ambulance transport (Cl. 39);
- animal slaughtering services and taxidermy (Cl. 40);
- timber felling and processing (Cl. 40);
- animal training services (Cl. 41);
- health clubs for physical exercise (Cl. 41);
- scientific research services for medical purposes (Cl. 42);
- boarding for animals (Cl. 43);
- retirement homes (Cl. 43).

Class 45 (Personal)

Personal and social services rendered by others to meet the needs of individuals; security services for the protection of property and individuals.

Explanatory Note

Includes, in particular:

- investigation and surveillance services relating to the safety of persons and entities;
- services provided to individuals in relation with social events, such as social escort services, matrimonial agencies, funeral services.

Does not include, in particular:

- professional services giving direct aid in the operations or functions of a commercial undertaking (Cl. 35);
- services relating to financial or monetary affairs and services dealing with insurance (Cl. 36);
- escorting of travellers (Cl. 39);
- security transport (Cl. 39);
- services consisting of all forms of education of persons (Cl. 41);
- performances of singers and dancers (Cl. 41);
- legal services (Cl. 42);
- services provided by others to give medical, hygienic or beauty care for human beings or animals (cl. 44);
- certain rental services (consult the Alphabetical List of Services and General Remark (b) relating to the classification of services).

237

Glossary

actual confusion—when proven in court, actual confusion is prima facie evidence that trademark infringement has occurred. Any event that demonstrates that consumers are confusing one product or service with another is proof of actual confusion; consumers' asking for one product by a name similar to that of the product they actually want or mail misdirected to a company that has a name similar to that of another company that offers similar services are examples of such events. Actual confusion proves that confusion between two marks is no longer merely a likelihood, which is the usual standard for proving trademark infringement, but has become a continuing reality. This is usually sufficient to convince any judge in a trademark infringement lawsuit that the plaintiff's rights are being infringed.

actual damages—the profits a trademark infringer made by the infringement and the money the plaintiff lost because of the infringement. A court deciding a trademark infringement case may award either actual damages or statutory damages.

case law—law that originates in the decisions of courts as opposed to written laws passed by state legislatures or the U.S. Congress, which are called "statutes."

cease and desist letter—a letter written by the lawyer for the plaintiff in a lawsuit telling the defendant to immediately cease certain specified actions that infringe the plaintiff's trademark and thereafter desist from any further such actions. These letters are usually the first indication that a defendant has that his or her actions may have violated the plaintiff's rights. Depending on the merits of the plaintiff's claims of infringement, a defendant will decide to comply with the plaintiff's demands and try to settle the infringement dispute out of court or to fight the plaintiff's assertions of infringement in court.

constructive notice—the presumption that because a trademark registration is reflected in the records of the Trademark Office, which are public, everyone knows of the claim of trademark ownership that the registration evidences, regardless of whether any examination of those records is actually made.

contingency fee—a lawyer's fee taken from an award of damages to the plaintiff. Trademark infringement suits are sometimes filed by lawyers who agree to work for a contingency fee; that is, the lawyer agrees that the fee for his or her work is to be taken from and is contingent upon an award by the court in favor of the plaintiff. If the plaintiff loses, the lawyer is not paid a fee. Usually a plaintiff is still responsible for bearing the costs of the suit, such as his or her lawyer's travel expenses, the costs of court reporters for depositions, and the fees of expert witnesses. Lawyers never agree to work on a contingency fee basis for defendants, who have no expectation of any awards.

copyright—the set of exclusive rights that are granted, initially to the creators of works eligible for copyright protection, by the various copyright statutes that exist in most countries.

In the United States, copyright protection begins when a work is first "fixed" in a tangible form and endures, in most cases, until seventy years after the death of the creator.

generic trademark—a product or service name that is merely the generic name for the class of products or services it is being used to market. Such marks do not function as trademarks until they have gained enough fame to escape the anonymity inherent in them. That is, a generic mark does not point to one particular source for the product it names and, therefore, does not function as a true trademark. The reverse situation also occurs. That is, when a name for a product comes, through public usage, to indicate a whole class of products rather than one particular product, it is said to have lost its trademark status and to have become generic.

injunction—a court order that directs the enjoined party to do something or, more typically, to cease doing something and to refrain from doing it in future. Plaintiffs in trademark infringement suits typically seek injunctions to stop defendants from continuing to infringe the plaintiff's copyrights. The scope of an injunction and whether a litigant's motion for one is granted is at the discretion of the judge who hears the suit. A temporary injunction is usually granted at the same time a suit is filed and endures only ten days. A preliminary injunction is granted by a judge after hearing arguments for and against the injunction from both the plaintiff and the defendant and usually lasts until the end of the lawsuit, when it may ripen into a permanent injunction by means of a paragraph to that effect in the judge's order rendering his or her decision.

intent-to-use application—since November of 1989, marketers may file what is called an "intent-to-use" application to register a trademark with the U.S. Patent and Trademark Office, as opposed to a "use-based" application, which was formerly the only sort of registration application that was allowed. Application for registration may be made before actual use of a new trademark, so long as the trademark owner has a "bona fide intent" to begin to use the mark in interstate commerce within six months of the date the registration application is filed. The period of time for beginning use of the mark may be extended, in six-month increments and upon making the proper filings, to a total period of thirty-six months. Registration may then be granted after use of the mark is made in interstate commerce. This system allows a company to claim ownership of a mark by filing an intent-to-use application to register it; when a second company conducts a trademark search to ascertain the availability of the mark, the first company's application will appear in the search report and warn the second company away from the mark. Further, intent-to-use applications confer one other important benefit not formerly

available: when a registration is eventually granted to an intent-to-use applicant, the date the applicant filed the registration application is deemed to be the date the applicant's rights in the mark commenced. This has the effect of "backdating" the applicant's rights to a date prior to the date of actual use of the mark, which was formerly the date ownership rights commenced.

likelihood of confusion—the test courts apply in determining infringing similarity between trademarks. If consumers are likely to confuse the new mark with the older, established trademark because of the similarity of the marks, gauged by comparing the appearance, sound, and meaning of the two marks, likelihood of confusion is said to exist.

overall commercial impression—an important, usually determinative, factor in any evaluation of possible trademark infringement. The term refers to the whole impression created by a trademark on the consumer who encounters it in the marketplace. In a proper analysis, the two marks said to be in conflict are not dissected and their minor dissimilarities tallied and totaled; rather, the total effect the marks have on consumers who encounter them in the environments where they are sold is judged.

patent—the rights granted by the federal government to the originator of a physical invention or industrial or technical process (a "utility patent") or an ornamental design for an "article of manufacture" (a "design patent)." Utility patents last seventeen years; design patents last fourteen years. A patent holder earns the exclusive right to make, use, and sell the invention for which the patent was granted. Any unauthorized manufacture, use, or sale of the patented invention within this country during the term of the patent is infringement.

secondary meaning—when a trademark has become widely known through advertising and the popularity of the product or service it names, it is said to have acquired "secondary meaning." Secondary meaning is necessary for an otherwise generic or unregistrable mark to be entitled to registration on the Principal Register and to enjoy the full benefits of federal trademark registration.

service mark—The Lanham Act, which is the federal statute governing unfair competition and trademarks, defines a service mark as "a mark used in the sale or advertising of services to identify the services of one person and distinguish them from the services of others." A word or symbol qualifies as a service mark when it is actually used in commerce to identify the services of one particular provider of services and when it functions to identify and distinguish those services form those of others. In this country, service mark ownership accrues by virtue of use of a service mark rather

than by registration, although registration significantly enhances the rights of service mark owners. Roughly speaking, service mark owners acquire ownership of their marks commensurate with the duration and scope of their use of them. Service marks are often considered a variety of trademark and referred to as trademarks, or, simply, as "marks."

statutory damages—a range of money damages the trademark statute allows courts to award a plaintiff in a trademark infringement suit instead of the money lost by the plaintiff as a result of an infringer's actions plus the actual amount by which the infringer profited from the use of the plaintiff's work. Because actual damages can be very difficult, time-consuming, expensive, or impossible to prove during infringement lawsuits, and because infringers often do not profit from their infringements, awards of statutory damages are often desirable.

trade dress—the packaging and labeling of a product, including the nonfunctional aspects of the shape and design of the product itself and its container. The combination of these elements create the whole visual image of the product encountered by consumers and can become a sort of indication of the origin of the product in the same way that trademarks do. Trade dress infringement, that is, the imitation of a product's packaging and container, is a variety of unfair competition; if a defendant's trade dress is likely to cause consumers to confuse the plaintiff's product with that of the defendant, the plaintiff's trade dress has been infringed.

trademark—a word, phrase, sound, or symbol that represents in the marketplace the commercial reputation of a product or service. The Lanham Act, which is the U.S. federal statute governing unfair competition and trademarks, defines a trademark as "any word, name, symbol or device or any combination thereof adopted and used by a manufacturer or merchant to identify his goods and distinguish them from those manufactured or sold by others." A word or symbol qualifies as a trademark when it is actually used in commerce to identify the goods of a particular manufacturer or merchant and when it functions to identify and distinguish those goods from those of others. In this country, trademark ownership accrues by virtue of use of a trademark rather than by registration, although trademark registration significantly enhances the rights of trademark owners. Roughly speaking, trademark owners acquire rights in their marks commensurate with the duration and scope of their use of them.

trademark abandonment—the cessation of use of a trademark by its owner, with intent to permanently cease any such use of the mark. Trademark abandonment makes a mark available for use by another marketer; however, it is dangerous to assume that a mark has been abandoned merely because it has fallen into disuse. A trademark owner may cease use of a mark for a time without abandoning it.

Trademark Dilution Act of 1995—a federal law that formalizes and makes a part of the federal trademark statute a principle of trademark law that was formerly available as a ground for suit in only about half the states. The act allows the owners of an existing "famous" trademark to ask the court to enjoin the use of the same mark by another company— even if there is no likelihood of confusion between the marks—on the ground that the defendant's use of the mark, even for noncompeting goods or services, "dilutes" the distinctive quality of the famous mark. "Dilution" is defined in the act as "the lessening of the capacity of a famous mark to identify and distinguish goods or services, regardless of the presence or absence of 1) competition between the owner of the famous mark and other parties, or 2) likelihood of confusion, mistake, or deception."

trademark directory—a trademark directory lists trademarks that are registered and therefore already in use by someone else. Marks are listed alphabetically, according to the category of product or service they name or designate. A trademark directory is most useful in the case of marks that consist solely of words. A trademark directory only short-circuits further pursuit of

242

unavailable marks; it cannot finally clear a mark for use. For this, a full trademark search is necessary.

trademark infringement—the use of a trademark without permission of the trademark owner or the use of a trademark that is confusingly similar to a trademark owned by someone else. Trademark infringement is judged by the "sight, sound, and meaning test." That is, the new mark is compared to the established trademark for similarities of appearance, sound, and meaning. If the two marks are so similar that the average consumer is likely to confuse the products or services the marks name, or to believe that they are somehow related, the new name infringes the older mark. Intent is immaterial in evaluating most trademark infringement cases. In other words, use of a trademark that is confusingly similar to an established trademark will create problems whether or not it was an intentional effort to trade on the good commercial reputation of the established mark.

trademark licensing—when a trademark owner allows another marketer of goods or services to use the trademark owner's mark, under terms and conditions specified in a written agreement and for specified products or services within a specified territory, in return for specified royalty payments.

trademark registration—the registration of a claim to ownership of a trademark, made in Washington, DC in the U.S. Patent and Trademark Office, a division of the Department of Commerce. Trademark registration enhances the rights an owner gains by virtue of the use of a trademark but does not of itself create those rights. Among other advantages, a federal registrant is presumed to have rights in the registered mark superior to anyone else except prior users of the mark and is entitled to use the ® symbol (or another prescribed form of federal trademark notice) that signifies federal trademark registration. While it is possible to register a trademark both with the state governments in the states where it is used *and* in the (federal) U.S. Patent and Trademark Office if it is used in interstate or international commerce, federal registration rather than state registration is generally sought by trademark owners who can qualify for it because it confers much greater benefits than state trademark registration. The sort of federal trademark registration that bestows the full benefits of federal registration is registration on the Principal Register. However, if a mark is unable to qualify for the Principal Register, a Supplemental Register registration is also useful; most marks on the Supplemental Register are descriptive, surname, or geographic marks that do not yet function as trademarks in the eyes of the Trademark Office. Marks registered on the Supplemental Register are entitled to use the ® symbol and gain some benefits of federal registration, such as access to federal courts, and are presumed, after a period of five years, to have gained enough fame to qualify for an upgrade (upon request by the registrant) to the Principal Register. Trademark registration is difficult and usually requires the services of a lawyer experienced in trademark law, unlike copyright registration, which is usually readily granted after a registration process that is simple enough that copyright owners can usually accomplish it themselves.

trademark search—a survey of data on existing trademarks performed by a trademark search service in order to clear a proposed trademark for use or, alternately, eliminate it from consideration because it is determined to infringe an established mark. Most marks are cleared for use by "full" trademark searches, which are searches of United States federal and state trademark registrations as well as of data regarding valid but unregistered marks. The results of trademark searches are reported in trademark search reports and are interpreted in trademark search opinion letters.

unfair competition—generally speaking, unfair competition is commercial competition by means that are overly aggressive or less than honest, although several forms of unfair competition can result from otherwise innocent blunders. By declaring certain actions "unfair" in commerce, the courts seek to promote both free competition *and* fair competition. Among the types of trademark-related commercial conduct that have been held to constitute unfair competition are: trademark infringement; trademark dilution; use of confusingly similar business names; use of confusingly similar literary titles; the unauthorized use of a distinctive literary or performing style; copying a product's trade dress and configuration; and infringement of the right of publicity. Not every action that has been or could be labeled unfair competition is codified, that is, enumerated and written down, in a statute. Judges may add to the list of "unfair" business tactics as new situations are presented that seem to them to entail overreaching by a marketer.

unregistrable trademarks—names (or design marks) for products or services that, because of certain inherent characteristics, are deemed by the U.S. trademark statute to be unworthy of registration. The ten statutory grounds for denial by the U.S. Patent and Trademark Office of an application to register a name or design as a trademark are: the mark is confusingly similar to a trademark that is already federally registered; the word or, more usually, symbol for which registration is sought does not function as a trademark, that is, does not act in the marketplace to identify the source of the goods or services to which it is applied; the mark is "immoral, deceptive, or scandalous"; the mark disparages or falsely suggests a connection with persons, institutions, beliefs, or national symbols, or brings them into contempt or disrepute; the mark consists of or simulates the flag or coat of arms or other insignia of the United States of or a state or municipality or a foreign nation; the mark is the name, portrait, or signature of a particular living individual who has not given his or her consent for use of the mark or is the name, signature, or portrait of deceased president of the United States during the life of his or her surviving spouse, unless that spouse has given consent to use of the mark; the mark is "merely descriptive" of the goods or services it names; the mark

is "deceptively misdescriptive" of the goods or services it names; the mark is "primarily geographically descriptive or deceptively misdescriptive" of the goods or services it names; and the mark is primarily a surname.

use-based application—an application to register a trademark in the U.S. Patent and Trademark Office based on current use of the mark in interstate or international commerce. Use-based applications were once the only sort of registration application available; since a change in the law that allows registration applications based on "bona fide intent" to use the marks that are the subject of such applications, this is no longer the case.

245

Index

U

Books from Allworth Press

Allworth Press is an imprint of Allworth Communications, Inc. Selected titles are listed below.

The Copyright Guide: A Friendly Handbook to Protecting and Profiting from Copyrights, Third Edition
by Lee Wilson (paperback, 6 × 9, 256 pages, $19.95)

The Advertising Law Guide: A Friendly Desktop Reference for Advertising Professionals
by Lee Wilson (paperback, 6 × 9, 272 pages, $19.95)

The Patent Guide: A Friendly Guide to Protecting and Profiting from Patents
by Carl W. Battle (paperback, 6 × 9, 224 pages, $18.95)

The Law (in Plain English)® for Small Businesses, Third Edition
by Leonard DuBoff (paperback, 6 × 9, 256 pages, $19.95)

Turn Your Idea or Invention into Millions
by Don Kracke (paperback, 6 × 9, 224 pages, $18.95)

Citizen Brand: 10 Commandments for Transforming Brands in a Consumer Democracy
by Marc Gobé (hardcover, $5^1/_2$ × $8^1/_2$, 288 pages, 46 b&w illus., $24.95)

Emotional Branding: The New Paradigm for Connecting Brands to People
by Marc Gobé (hardcover, $6^1/_4$ × $9^1/_4$, 352 pages, 134 b&w illus., $24.95)

The Entrepreneurial Age: Awakening the Spirit of Enterprise in People, Companies and Countries
by Larry C. Farrell (hardcover, $6^1/_4$ × $9^1/_4$, 352 pages, 17 figures, $24.95)

Dead Ahead: The Web Dilemma and the New Rules of Business
by Laurie Windham with Jon Samsel (hardcover, $6^1/_4$ × $9^1/_4$, 256 pages, 14 b&w figures, $24.95)

NetSlaves® 2.0: Tales of "Surviving" the Great Tech Gold Rush
by Bill Lessard and Steve Baldwin (paperback, 6 × 9, 224 pages, $19.95)

Please write to request our free catalog. To order by credit card, call 1-800-491-2808 or send a check or money order to Allworth Press, 10 East 23rd Street, Suite 510, New York, NY 10010. Include $5 for shipping and handling for the first book ordered and $1 for each additional book. Ten dollars plus $1 for each additional book if ordering from Canada. New York State residents must add sales tax.

To see our complete catalog on the World Wide Web, or to order online, you can find us at ***www.allworth.com***.